40

A WATERFALL LOVER'S GUIDE TO THE PACIFIC NORTHWEST

Where to Find Hundreds of Spectacular Waterfalls in Washington, Oregon, and Idaho

Third Edition
Gregory Alan Plumb

THE
MOUNTAINEERS

This book is dedicated to Tina, Amber, and Savanah

Published by
The Mountaineers
1001 SW Klickitat Way, Suite 201
Seattle, WA 98134

© 1983, 1989, 1998 by Gregory Alan Plumb

First edition 1983, Second edition 1989, Third edition 1998

Published simultaneously in Great Britain by Cordee, 3a DeMontfort Street, Leicester, England, LE1 7HD

Manufactured in the United States of America

Edited by Cynthia Newman Bohn
Maps by the author
Photographs by the author unless otherwise noted.
Cover design by Kristy L. Welch
Book design and layout by Ani Rucki

Cover photograph: *Triple Falls at the Oneonta Gorge in Oregon*

Library of Congress Cataloging-in-Publication Data
Plumb, Gregory Alan, 1956–
    A waterfall lover's guide to the Pacific Northwest : where to find
    hundreds of spectacular waterfalls in Washington, Oregon, and Idaho
    / Gregory Alan Plumb. — 3rd ed.
        p.   cm.
    Includes bibliographical references and index.
    ISBN 0-89886-593-X
        1. Hiking—Northwest, Pacific—Guidebooks.   2. Waterfalls—
    Northwest, Pacific.   3. Northwest, Pacific—Guidebooks.   I. Title.
    GV199.42.N69P58   1998
    917.9504'43—dc21   98-36763
                                                                             CIP

CONTENTS

The North Cascades

The Olympics and Vicinity

Mount Rainier Region

Gifford Pinchot Country

The Inland Empire

The Columbia Gorge

The South Cascades

The Columbia Plateau

The Idaho Panhandle

PREFACE

Water, in its many forms, provides some of the earth's most beautiful landscapes. Rivers, lakes, and coasts all offer images of scenic beauty, but undoubtedly waterfalls are the most impressive of hydrologic features. People have always been drawn to falls as places of wonder, relaxation, and inspiration.

As a youth, my first experience of this sparkling water formation was the popular Tahquamenon Falls in Michigan's Upper Peninsula. The shimmering waters of this block-type waterfall naturally tint to a burnt orange during its descent. Our family so enjoyed this waterfall that we began including stops at other falls in our itinerary on vacations "up north." However, we had difficulty finding waterfalls other than those marked by "point of interest" symbols on the state highway map. Even these were not always easy to find.

As an adult, my interest in waterfalls peaked while I was living in northern Idaho in the late 1970s. The Pacific Northwest was a new region to be explored, and on many trips I discovered waterfalls. After visiting a few, I wanted to see more. Unfortunately, I discovered that no text had been written on the subject. At that point an idea was kindled. The first version of this recreational guidebook was the result.

Several years have passed since the publication of the original edition, *Waterfalls of the Pacific Northwest,* and its successor, *A Waterfall Lover's Guide to the Pacific Northwest.* In this revision, additional information such as magnitude rating, watershed size, elevation, and trail difficulty has been added. Full accounts of several "new" cataracts have also been included. A revised index provides an alphabetical listing of the 529 falls described in this book. An appendix has also been added, listing 724 additional falls arranged by geographic region.

Whether you are a novice or an old waterfall buff, I hope you enjoy using this third edition of the guidebook on your explorations.

ACKNOWLEDGMENTS

No endeavor of this type can be accomplished without the direct and indirect contributions of others. I am indebted to my wife, Robin, for her understanding and support, as it takes a substantial commitment away from other activities to revise a guidebook. Robin was of great assistance on some of our long-distance trips to the Northwest and helped in spirit during my solo journeys away from home.

The manuscript and maps were prepared at the offices of the Geographic Information System Division, City of Johnson City, Tennessee. The city was reimbursed for use of their facilities. The maps were designed electronically using Arc/Info computer mapping software, a product of Environmental Systems Research Institute. The geographic base was derived from TIGER/Line files, which are products of the U.S. Bureau of the Census and state-level Digital Line Graphs obtained from the U.S. Geological Survey.

The most enjoyable part of continually updating this book is, of course, seeking out the falls of the Pacific Northwest! The personnel at Park Service and Forest Service ranger stations were very helpful in providing road and travel information. I also thank the following individuals for their assistance with this edition: Ralph Baggett and the Jerry Hyatt family, Vancouver, Washington; Margaret Calger, Marietta, Georgia; Joe Poracsky, Portland, Oregon; Amber England and Yiqiang Wu, Johnson City, Tennessee; Jacci Lackey, Henryetta, Oklahoma; the Andy Norton family, Seattle; and Miriam Kelly, Woodland, Washington.

An inventory of waterfalls was compiled by reviewing every 7½-minute topographic map produced by the U.S. Geological Survey for waterfall symbols. U.S. Forest Service maps provided a secondary reference. Maps were first examined during the early 1980s at the University of Idaho library, with more recent map publications reviewed over the years at the libraries of East Tennessee State University and the University of Oklahoma. Additional falls were found in the hiking and travel guides listed in the bibliography in the back of the book. A few cataracts were encountered during field travels, mainly from tips by the local populace, and I fortuitously stumbled upon a few.

Lastly, I am grateful to God for placing these magnificent features in the universe and creating us to experience them.

INTRODUCTION

Welcome to the waterfalls of the Pacific Northwest! This book has been written as a field guide to lead you to falls of all shapes and sizes. Whether you want an afternoon trip or an extensive vacation, a short walk or a backpacking trek, this guidebook will tell you where to find the waterfalls. Extraordinary adventures await you!

But first, a warning. The grandeur of waterfalls is accompanied by an element of risk. Accidents can occur at even the most developed locations, particularly when youngsters are left unsupervised or people act unwisely and unduly place themselves in dangerous situations. Worldwide, many persons are injured each year and several die near waterfalls. Such tragedies are almost always due to irresponsible behavior. Think safety first! Here are some basic guidelines:

- use common sense
- closely supervise your children
- do not take children on long, difficult, or uncertain journeys
- do not stray from observation points or trails in steep areas
- never try to climb up or down a waterfall
- stay away from sloping, bare (non-vegetated) surfaces
- know your physical capabilities and do not exceed them
- turn back whenever you feel insecure about the route ahead
- remember the first guideline

When hiking, do not forget to carry sufficient water and food. Bringing along the rest of the Ten Essentials—a map, compass, first-aid kit, flashlight, knife, matches in a waterproof container, fire starter, sunglasses, and extra clothes—is also a good idea, especially as the journey's distance increases. Bushwhackers should wear long pants to aid in protection against scrapes, poison ivy, ticks, and snakes. Refer to other books dedicated to hiking or backpacking for further information on preparation.

You also have ethical responsibilities. Maintain respect for the land, its ownership, and other visitors. Do not litter and if you encounter a bit of trash, please consider packing it out. Some falls may be located on private property, so be considerate as to when you visit. Heed all "No Trespassing" signs, as landowners may decide not to allow access, even though it may have been previously granted.

Regional Format

This guidebook is organized into fourteen geographic regions. Use the map on page 16, the table of contents, and the index to help you navigate through the book. The regional chapters are further segmented into smaller areas containing waterfalls in relative proximity to one another.

Waterfall Entries

Waterfalls with a scenic rating of two or more stars are described in complete entries consisting of the following elements:

Name: The name of the falls is considered to be official if it occurs in the federal government's Geographic Names Information System listing or is used by a federal, state, or local agency. A designation of (u) following the name of the falls indicates an unofficial name.

Rating: Each waterfall included in this book was assigned a rating from one to five stars (one-star falls are given only a brief listing, generally in the "Others" category at the end of the chapter subsections). This provides a quick initial impression of the scenic value of each entry.

☆   Uninspiring. Probably not interesting except to waterfall collectors.

☆☆   Modest. Nice background for a picnic.

☆☆☆   Good. Scenic feature worth a trip.

☆☆☆☆   Very good. Outstanding scenic feature.

☆☆☆☆☆   Exceptional. An awe-inspiring sight.

Waterfall Forms: The form listed is the one most representative of the falls. It is not uncommon for falls to possess elements of more than one form.

 Plunge. Descends vertically from the stream, losing contact with the bedrock surface.

 Horsetail. Descends vertically or nearly so, maintaining substantial contact with the bedrock surface.

 Fan. Similar to the horsetail form, except for the breadth of the spray, which increases toward the bottom of the falls.

 Punchbowl. Descends from a narrow stream into a pool below.

 Block. Descends as a wide band from a broad stream.

 Tiered. Descends as a distinct series of several falls, with at least two tiers visible from a single vantage point.

 Segmented. Descends in multiple threads as the stream diverges, with at least two threads visible from a single vantage point.

 Cascades. Descends as a series of steps along a dipping bedrock surface.

Waterfall Magnitude: The one-to-five-star scenic ratings described earlier were assigned in part based on waterfall magnitude. This numeric measure is calculated using four waterfall elements: height, width, discharge, and verticality. Greater importance is placed upon height versus width, with the final value modified by the latter two variables.

The ten greatest falls in magnitude known to occur within the Pacific Northwest are:

1	Shoshone Falls, Idaho	120
2	Comet Falls, Washington	106
3	Fairy Falls, Washington	101
4	Snoqualmie Falls, Washington	100
5	Clear Creek Falls, Washington	99
6	Watson Falls, Oregon	99
7	Falls Creek Falls, Washington	99
8	Sahalie Falls, Oregon	99
9	Salt Creek Falls, Oregon	98
10	Spray Falls, Washington	98

Each increase by a value of ten corresponds to a waterfall that is twice as impressive. For example, Shoshone Falls in its full fury has four times the magnitude of Snoqualmie Falls. (A magnitude of 120 is twice that of 110, which is two times the magnitude of 100; therefore, a 120 magnitude is quadruple that of 100.) By way of comparison, the magnitudes of two of the most awesome waterfalls in the world, Niagara Falls, New York/Ontario, and Yosemite Falls, California, are 130 and 123, respectively. So the best of the Pacific Northwest waterfalls rank favorably.

The magnitude values were calculated based upon the discharge conditions when field-truthed. If stream flow was other than moderate, the following codes are included:

(t)   trickle
(l)   low flow
(h)   heavy flow

Watershed Size, Precipitation, Elevation, and Seasonality: It is typical for many of the streams and rivers of Washington, Oregon, and Idaho to vary in their water flow from one time period to the next. This, of course, can have a significant impact on viewing waterfalls, since one would wish to visit them when a sufficient amount of water is flowing over their escarpments.

The volume of water present (the stream discharge) at a falls location is primarily determined by two factors: the size of the watershed and its long-term and short-term precipitation history. A watershed is defined as the entire area from which runoff can flow to a given location. Other factors being equal, the larger the watershed, the longer the periods of adequate discharge.

Included with each falls description is watershed information with the following recommendations:

(vsm)=very small	less than 1 sq. mile	visit during wet periods
(sm)=small	1–4 sq. miles	visit during or soon after wet periods
(med)=medium	4–16 sq. miles	visit anytime except during or soon after droughts
(lg)=large	greater than 16 sq. miles	visit anytime except during long droughts

The preceding guidelines apply to most watersheds within the Northwest that average at least twenty inches of precipitation per year. In drier areas, the drainage basins must be substantially larger in order to sustain even modest flows.

If the letter (d) follows the watershed category, it means a dam exists upstream from the falls. The letter (g) indicates the waterfall is fed in part by glacial meltwaters. In both cases, this has the impact of reducing the variability of discharge, thus lengthening the time periods in which their beauty can be enjoyed.

If a question mark (?) is included, the size of the watershed is a rough estimate. This occurs where most or all of the water volume at the falls is fed by springs or other sources of uncertain discharge.

Seasons can be both a blessing and a curse to the waterfall visitor. As a general guideline, cataracts at lower elevations are best visited from autumn through spring. Visits to waterfalls at higher elevations are usually limited to summer, due to snowpack during the rest of the year. For more specific information, you should check with local officials about discharge and accessibility conditions before planning a trip.

Accessibility:

located next to a road accessible by a passenger vehicle; or within a short, quick, and easy walk from such a road

located next to a road accessible by a high-clearance (4WD) vehicle; or within a short, easy walk from such a road

reaching the falls requires between a ten-minute and a three-hour walk along an established path or primitive road (i.e., a day hike)

access requires a substantial hike such that overnight or multiple-night camping is recommended

🚶 access requires bushwhacking, that is, no developed trail leads to the falls. A strong pair of hiking boots is suggested. Not recommended for young children; may be risky for skittish adults or those with physical limitations.

🛶 access by canoe, boat, or raft

Difficulty: Trails and bushwhacks are rated Easy ①, Fairly Easy ②, Moderate ③, Fairly Hard ④, and Hard ⑤. These ratings were determined primarily by considering trail length and overall steepness, as well as the condition of the trail surface and whether streams can be crossed via footbridges or must be forded by hopping rocks and/or wading. Unsigned or minimally signed trails are rated more difficult than those with clear signage.

Keep in mind these ratings are relative and will vary according to the abilities of each individual. If you are not sure of your physical condition, start with easier walks, then progress to more strenuous hikes. If you are in poor health, it would be wise to consult your doctor before embarking on trails that are more than fairly easy.

Topographic Maps: The U.S. Geological Survey (USGS) has published a series of large-scale topographic maps of the entire United States. Each 1:24,000 scale map (1 map inch = 2000 feet on the ground) encompasses an area bounded within 7½ minutes of longitude and 7½ minutes of latitude, which corresponds to a little over 49 square miles at the northern extreme of the Pacific Northwest, increasing to nearly 55½ square miles at the southern end.

Accompanying each waterfall listed in this book is the name of the USGS 7½ minute map on which it can be found. Since these maps are periodically revised, the version (i.e., year published) used by the author is also reported. If a cataract is not labeled on the map, the annotation (nl) also appears. If it is not shown at all on the map, the annotation (ns) appears.

Most university libraries and libraries in major cities throughout the United States have a complete collection of these maps and can also provide instructions for purchasing them through the USGS.

A Note About Safety

Safety is an important concern in all outdoor activities. No guidebook can alert you to every hazard or anticipate the limitations of every reader. Therefore, the descriptions of roads, trails, routes, and natural features in this book are not representations that a particular place or excursion will be safe for your party. When you visit any of the waterfalls described in this book, you assume responsibility for your own safety. Under normal conditions, such excursions require the usual attention to traffic, road and trail conditions, weather, terrain, the capabilities of your party, and other factors. Keeping informed on current conditions and exercising common sense are the keys to a safe, enjoyable outing.

The Mountaineers

Region Map

Black dots show the distribution of 1,319 falls throughout the Pacific Northwest.

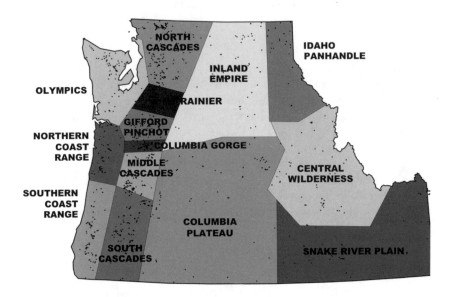

Key to map symbols

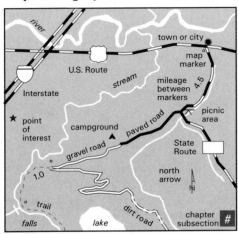

THE NORTH CASCADES

The Cascade Range extends from British Columbia through Washington and Oregon to northern California. A progression of spectacular volcanic peaks marks the range from north to south, with Mount Baker, Mount Rainier, and Mount Adams in Washington; Mount Hood, Three Sisters, and Mount McLoughlin in Oregon; and Mount Shasta in California. Since the Cascades encompass a large part of the Pacific Northwest and contain many waterfalls, the range has been divided into six chapters in this book.

The North Cascades extend from Interstate 90 to the Canadian border, dividing the Puget Sound area of Washington from the dry, eastern part of the state. This region features three large national forests, three wilderness areas, two national recreation areas, and North Cascades National Park. Of the 198 falls identified within the region, 62 are listed in this chapter.

Aside from two volcanoes, Mount Baker and Glacier Peak, most of the mountains of the North Cascades are older than those of the range's counterparts to the south. The North Cascades are a rugged and complex arrangement of various non-volcanic materials, including large masses of granite. Other rock forms found in the area include gneiss and schists. These rock types vary from 50 million to 500 million years in age, but their arrangement in today's mountainous terrain is due to uplifting over the past 10 million years.

Intensive glaciation accounts for the region's pronounced relief. Four major periods of glacial activity occurred between 10,000 and 2 million years ago. The heads of glaciers eroded into the mountains, sharpening their peaks, and extended to lower elevations, deepening and widening valleys.

The abundance of waterfalls in the North Cascades is largely due to the glacial scouring of the range's bedrock surfaces. Many descents plum-

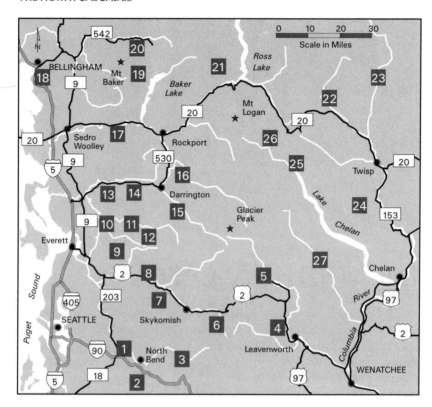

met into glacial troughs, or valleys. *Wallace Falls* and *Rainbow Falls* (the one near Lake Chelan) are stunning examples. Others skip and bounce off rock walls into the troughs, for instance, *Bridal Veil Falls, Gate Creek Falls,* and *Preston Falls*.

Sometimes cataracts are associated with a rounded depression previously carved by the upper portion of a glacier. Water may pour into this cirque from ridge tops, or tumble from its outlet into a trough. The *Falls of Horseshoe Basin* and *Twin Falls* (at Twin Falls Lake) are examples.

Glaciers may erode unevenly when carving out their U-shaped troughs. The streams that presently occupy such valley floors are called misfit streams, and falls occur wherever there are sharp drops. Such descents are generally less dramatic than the types previously mentioned. Representative falls of this form include *Sunset Falls* and *Teepee Falls*.

I. Snoqualmie

One should not be surprised, particularly in developed areas, to see hydroelectric facilities in association with waterfalls. A great amount of force is required to turn turbines for generating kilowatts of electricity.

Because water can serve as that force, and its power is maximized where it is free-falling, falls sites can be desirable sources of energy. Water lines may be built into or beside the vertical escarpment and stream flow diverted to them. The scenic quality of the cataracts need not be lost, however, if enough water is allowed to continue its natural course. Such is the case, thankfully, for the following entry.

Snoqualmie Falls ✫✫✫✫✫

Form: plunge   *Magnitude:* 100 (h)   *Watershed:* lg (d)
Elevation: 390 feet   *USGS Map:* Snoqualmie (1982)

This 268-foot plunge is one of Washington's most visited attractions. Puget Sound Power and Light Company preserves the integrity of the falls while diverting enough of the Snoqualmie River to provide power for 16,000 homes. This spectacle is located next to S.R. 202, 1 mile northwest of Snoqualmie and 4 miles southeast of Fall City. Look for signs and parking areas. There are several vantages of the cataract at the gorge rim adjacent to the lodge. Snoqualmie Falls River Trail, a steep 0.5-mile hike, offers views from the base of the falls.

Snoqualmie Falls

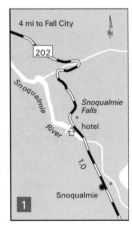

2. North Bend

While the Snoqualmie River is best known for its namesake falls, additional descents occur several miles upstream from the main attraction. The construction of I-90 made these falls fairly difficult to reach. But recently a new trail system has been built that has re-opened this area and made accessible the following falls.

Twin Falls ★★★★ ③

Form: fan   *Magnitude:* 59   *Watershed:* lg (d)
Elevation: 1020 feet   *USGS Map:* Chester Morse Lake (1989)

An exhilarating experience is to be gained from cliff-side viewing decks adjacent to this 135- to 150-foot plummet. Also known as *Upper Snoqualmie Falls*, this waterfall as well as the next two entries, is located within Twin Falls State Park, which is a day-use area.

Depart I-90 at Edgewick Road (Exit 34) and follow 468th Avenue SE for 0.7 mile. Turn left (east) at SE 159th Street and drive another 0.5 mile to the parking area at the end of the street. From the signed trailhead, hike 0.8 mile to the first, moderately distant, vantage of the cataract. Continue another 0.5 mile up the hillside, bearing left at the signed "Old Growth Fir Tree." Eventually you will reach an unsigned spur, to the right, consisting of a set of wooden stairs. Proceed down the steps, ending at the observation decks and the falls.

Middle Twin Falls (u) ★★ ③

Form: tiered   *Magnitude:* 41   *Watershed:* lg (d)
Elevation: 1080 feet   *USGS Map:* Chester Morse Lake (1989 ns)

This pair of 10- to 15-foot punchbowls is located on the Snoqualmie River just upstream from Twin Falls (previously described). From the spur junction for Twin Falls, continue along the main trail for a moderately easy 0.1 mile to a wooden footbridge spanning the gorge. Looking upstream provides an excellent view of this entry.

Upper Twin Falls (u) ★★ ④

Form: tiered   *Magnitude:* 47   *Watershed:* lg (d)
Elevation: 1090 feet   *USGS Map:* Chester Morse Lake (1989 ns)

The Snoqualmie River plunges 20 to 30 feet before fanning out another 25 to 35 feet into a natural pool. From the footbridge below Middle Twin Falls (described previously), hike another 0.1 mile up the steep trail to an open vista of this falls.

Weeks Falls ★★

Form: cascade   *Magnitude:* 37   *Watershed:* lg (d)
Elevation: 1260 feet   *USGS Map:* Chester Morse Lake (1989 ns)

This series of cascades descends 30 to 40 feet along the South Fork Snoqualmie River. It can be reached by hiking several additional miles

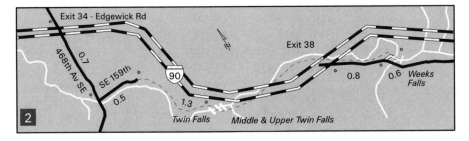

beyond Twin Falls State Park (described previously), but the easiest access is by vehicle.

Depart I-90 at the Forest Fire Training Center (Exit 38) and drive east for 0.8 mile to the obscurely signed entrance to Ollalie State Park. Continue 0.4 mile to an overlook of the falls. More cascades can be found by driving past the park entrance for 0.6 mile to a small hydroelectric facility. When leaving this area, eastbounders must first go west on I-90, then use Exit 34 as a U-turn.

3. Snoqualmie Pass

This area's main campground and one of its waterfalls have the unfavorable distinction of lying between the lanes of I-90! Actually it is not as bad as it sounds, but the soft buzzing of the passing traffic does detract from the natural setting. Leave I-90 at Snoqualmie Pass Recreation Area (Exit 47 or 52) and follow Denny Creek Road #5800 for 2 to 3 miles to Road #5830, located 0.25 mile northeast of Denny Creek Camp. All of the following falls are located within North Bend Ranger District, Mount Baker–Snoqualmie National Forest.

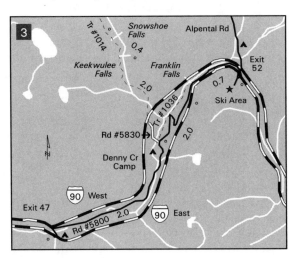

Keekwulee Falls ★★   ④

Form: tiered   *Magnitude:* 34 (l)   *Watershed:* sm
Elevation: 3330 feet   *USGS Map:* Snoqualmie Pass (1989)

Water plunges 60 to 70 feet before tumbling another 15 feet along Denny Creek. *Keekwulee* is a Chinook word meaning "falling down." From

Denny Creek Camp, take Road #5830 for 0.25 mile to its end at the trailhead to Denny Creek Trail #1014. The trail goes underneath the interstate and crosses Denny Creek twice, the second time at 1.5 miles. The trail ascends fairly steeply 0.5 mile farther to a full view of the cataract.

Franklin Falls ☆☆☆
Form: plunge   *Magnitude:* 59   *Watershed:* med
Elevation: 2800 feet   *USGS Map:* Snoqualmie Pass (1989)
The South Fork Snoqualmie River plummets 70 feet into a small pool. Drive about 2 miles northeast of Denny Creek Camp to the historic Snoqualmie Pass Wagon Road. This route, now a footpath, leads to the falls in less than 300 yards. Alternatively, one may take a moderately easy hike of about 1.5 miles along Franklin Falls Trail #1036 from Denny Creek Camp on Road #5830 (described previously).

Others: *Snowshoe Falls* ☆ USGS Snoqualmie Pass (1989). This 125- to 175-foot cataract along Denny Creek would deserve a higher scenic rating except the heavily timbered and dangerously steep slopes limit the viewpoints to obscured trailside glimpses. After reaching Keekwulee Falls (described previously), begin a steep 0.4-mile hike along Trail #1014. Both of these falls were named in 1916 by The Mountaineers.

4. Leavenworth
Downtown Leavenworth is a place of Old World character, where seasonal activities such as the Mai Fest, Autumn Leaf Festival, and Christmas Lighting can be enjoyed. The traditional storefronts and the surrounding alpine setting are reminiscent of the German province of Bavaria.

Drury Falls ☆☆
Form: horsetail   *Magnitude:* 51   *Watershed:* sm
Elevation: 4120 feet   *USGS Map:* Winton (1989)
Fall Creek, located within Leavenworth Ranger District, Wenatchee National Forest, drops over 100 feet from the cliffs of Tumwater Canyon into the Wenatchee River. Only a moderately distant cross-river view of the cataract is possible. Drive 6 miles north of Leavenworth, or 1 mile south of Swiftwater Picnic Area, along U.S. 2 to an unsigned turnout.

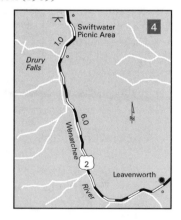

5. Lake Wenatchee

Lake Wenatchee is a popular vacation area for family camping, with several campsites on the eastern shore. Drive 14 miles northwest of Leavenworth along U.S. 2 to S.R. 207, then 10 miles north to the ranger station for Lake Wenatchee Ranger District, Wenatchee National Forest. All the area's falls are located upstream from Lake Wenatchee.

White River Falls ★★★   ② ⋏

Form: punchbowl   *Magnitude:* 53 (h)   *Watershed:* lg
Elevation: 2200 feet   *USGS Map:* Mount David (1989)

This forceful 60- to 100-foot cataract along the White River is situated next to a camp, but the best views require a modest hike. Drive to the end of White River Road #293 and park. Follow Panther Creek Trail #1602 across the White River, then go downstream. In 1 mile, a spur trail to the left leads to good views of the falls. At White River Falls Campground, adults can also climb on chunks of bedrock for obstructed overviews of the descent. Be careful! This is definitely not a place for fooling around.

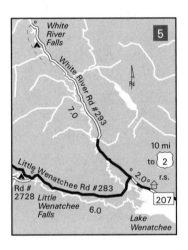

Others: *Little Wenatchee Falls* (u) ★ USGS Mount Howard (1989 ns). The Little Wenatchee River tumbles 20 to 30 feet over a series of rock steps. Turn off S.R. 207 onto Little Wenatchee River Road #283. In 6 miles Road #283 meets with Rainy Creek Road #2728. Park at the junction and backtrack about 150 feet to a primitive trail. The cascade is a short easy walk away.

6. Stevens Pass

Many waterfalls beckon from the roadside as you travel westward along U.S. 2 from the 4,061-foot elevation of Stevens Pass.

Alpine Falls ★★   ③, ⋏ or 🚗

Form: segmented   *Magnitude:* 17 (l)   *Watershed:* lg
Elevation: 1450 feet   *USGS Map:* Scenic (1982)

The South Fork Skykomish River tumbles 30 to 50 feet downward. Situated on land owned by the state of Washington. Drive along U.S. 2 about 8.5 miles east of Skykomish or 1.5 miles west of Deception Falls (described later). Park at the unsigned turnout just past the bridge crossing the Tye River.

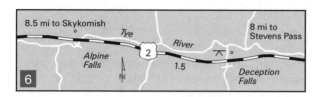

A very short trail leads to the top of this entry. Determined bushwhackers can find better views by hiking down the slope to the river from the far end of the parking turnout.

Others: *Deception Falls* ☆ USGS Scenic (1982). Deception Creek cascades steeply for 30 to 60 feet. Take U.S. 2 to Deception Falls Picnic Area, located 8 miles west of Stevens Pass and 10 miles east of Skykomish. The waterfall is located across the highway from the parking area.

7. Index

Although the following trio of falls are located near U.S. 2 and labeled as points of interest on many state highway maps, most persons never see them because there are no signs.

Canyon Falls ☆☆☆☆   ②, 🚶 or 🥾
Form: punchbowl   *Magnitude:* 52 (h)   *Watershed:* lg
Elevation: 680 feet   *USGS Map:* Index (1989)

The geology of this 20- to 30-foot waterfall is interesting. Granite, which is common in the North Cascades, slowly dissolves when it comes into contact with water. As a stream flows over granitic outcrops, the rock is decomposed grain by grain. The water hollows and smooths the surface, often creating unusual shapes. Here the South Fork Skykomish River has physically eroded and widened a fracture in the granite to form the falls, dramatically illustrating how running water can modify a landscape both chemically and physically.

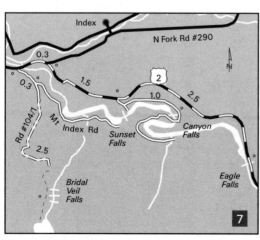

Turn south off U.S. 2 between mile markers 36 and 37, about 1.5 miles east of Index, onto a private road. Proceed along the road for 0.2 mile and park next to a gate. Bear left and walk down the road for 1 mile. Close-up views are possible, but be careful. Stay away from the slippery, moss-covered boulders and bare rocks that slope toward the river.

Sunset Falls ☆☆☆

Form: cascade   *Magnitude:* 37 (h)   *Watershed:* lg
Elevation: 620 feet   *USGS Map:* Index (1989)

The South Fork Skykomish River slides 60 to 100 feet in impressive fashion. Follow the directions to Canyon Falls (described previously), but take the right fork at the beginning of the walk. The descent is less than 0.25 mile away. For views from the other side of the river, drive along Mount Index Road (see Bridal Veil Falls entry below).

Bridal Veil Falls ☆☆
③ 大

Form: tiered   *Magnitude:* 44 (l)   *Watershed:* sm
Elevation: 1800 feet   *USGS Map:* Index (1989)

Water pours off Mount Index in four parts, each descending 100 to 200 feet along Bridal Veil Creek. The falls is also visible from the main highway, appearing as silvery white threads. Located within Skykomish Ranger District, Mount Baker–Snoqualmie National Forest.

Sunset Falls

Leave U.S. 2 at Mount Index Road, 0.3 mile past the turn for the hamlet of Index and immediately south of the bridge over the South Fork Skykomish River. After another 0.3 mile, turn right (south) on Road #104/1. Only high-clearance vehicles can follow the entire 1.5-mile length of the road. Most automobiles should park after 1 mile. A hiking trail begins at the road's end and ascends moderately to the first of the cataracts in 1 more mile.

Others: *Eagle Falls* ☆ USGS Index (1989). Noisy frothing water tumbles 25 to 40 feet along the South Fork Skykomish River. From Skykomish proceed west along U.S. 2 for about 9 miles and find the parking turnout closest to mile marker 39. A path immediately east of the marker quickly leads to the descent.

8. Gold Bar

Wallace Falls State Park opened in 1977 to showcase and preserve one of the tallest single-drop cataracts in the Northwest.

Wallace Falls ☆☆☆☆☆   ③ 🚶

Form: horsetail   *Magnitude:* 88   *Watershed:* med
Elevation: 1300 feet   *USGS Map:* Gold Bar (1989)

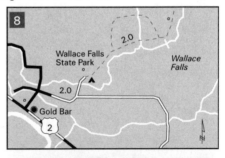

The Wallace River curtains 260 feet in great splendor into a small natural pool, surrounded by bedrock and coniferous forest. Depart U.S. 2 at Gold Bar and follow the signs to the state park. Start hiking along Woody Trail, named after Frank Woody, a former state senator and lifelong outdoorsman. The way soon diverges, the right fork ascending moderately, while the left goes up at a gentler rate. The trails converge after 1 mile on the steeper path or 2 miles on the gradual path. A short distance farther is a picnic area and a first view of the falls; another favorite viewpoint is 0.5 mile beyond. The trail continues on to an upper falls and a vista of the Skykomish Valley.

Wallace Falls

9. Lake Roesiger

Reach cottage-lined Lake Roesiger by driving 13 miles north from Monroe on Woods Creek Road. Alternatively, drive about 8 miles south from Granite Falls on Lake Roesiger Road.

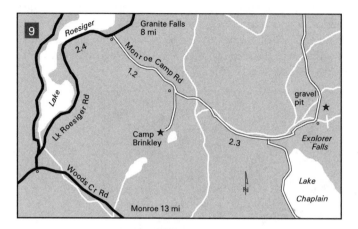

Explorer Falls ★ USGS Lake Chaplain (1989 ns). An unnamed tributary of Woods Creek drops 50 to 70 feet from a cliff. Being secluded, the falls are perfect for taking an invigorating soapless shower, if you dare. From Lake Roesiger Road, turn east on gravel Monroe Camp Road. After 3.5 miles, park at a gravel pit on the right side of the road. Hike upstream a few hundred feet to an open view of the waterfall.

10. Granite Falls

The community of Granite Falls is named after these cascades, located north of town on the Mountain Loop Highway, which is an extension of S.R. 92.

Granite Falls ★★

Form: cascade   *Magnitude:* 27   *Watershed:* lg
Elevation: 300 feet   *USGS Map:* Granite Falls (1989)
        Water froths along the South Fork Stillaguamish River in a series of descents totaling 30 to 40 feet. A 580-foot fishway connects the upper and lower levels of the river via a 240-foot tunnel, allowing salmon to bypass the cascades and proceed upstream to spawn. Drive 1.4 miles north of town on the Mountain Loop Highway. Just before a bridge crossing the river, find a parking area and a short trail that leads to the falls.

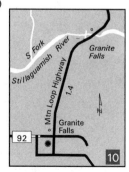

11. Robe Valley

Waterfalls abound in this area, where creeks flow from Mount Pilchuck into the South Fork Stillaguamish River. They all occur either on state land or within Darrington Ranger District, Mount Baker–Snoqualmie National Forest. Follow the Mountain Loop Highway 10 miles northeast from Granite Falls to the Verlot Ranger Station and townsite. After the main road crosses the South Fork Stillaguamish, about 1 mile east of the ranger station, make two successive right turns, first on Pilchuck State Park Road #42, then onto gravel Monte Cristo Grade Road #4201.

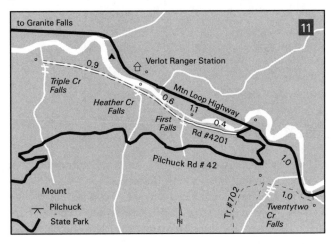

Triple Creek Falls (u) ☆☆   ② 🏃

Form: fan   *Magnitude:* 32   *Watershed:* vsm
Elevation: 980 feet   *USGS Map:* Verlot (1989 ns)

Upstream from this pretty 15- to 25-foot drop along Triple Creek is a 40-foot upper falls that can be reached by climbing (no trail) a few hundred feet. Drive along Road #4201 (described previously) to its end. Walk along a well-worn path for a few hundred yards to the base of the waterfall.

Twentytwo Creek Falls (u) ☆☆   ④ 🏃

Form: tiered   *Magnitude:* 34   *Watershed:* sm
Elevation: 1400 feet   *USGS Map:* Verlot (1989 ns)

This series of three small falls is accessible from trails within Lake Twentytwo Research Natural Area. Drive along Mountain Loop Highway 2 miles past the Verlot Ranger Station to Twentytwo Creek Trailhead #702. The lowest falls is encountered after 0.5 mile of easy walking and 0.5 mile of moderately strenuous hiking. A short distance farther, follow short spur trails to view the two other falls.

Others: *First Falls* (u) ☆ USGS Verlot (1989 ns). This 30- to 40-foot cataract drops along an unnamed creek. I gave it this name because it is the first falls encountered along the way to Triple Creek Falls (described earlier). Drive along Road #4201 for 0.4 mile beyond its junction with Pilchuck Road.

Heather Creek Falls (u) ✭ USGS Verlot (1989 ns). Water tumbles 60 to 100 feet along Heather Creek. Drive along Road #4201 for 0.6 mile past First Falls to a small pond. Walk along its far (west) bank to a series of cascades.

12. Twin Falls Lake

Spend the day hiking to an inspiring set of falls within which Wilson Creek pauses at minuscule Twin Falls Lake. Drive 4.7 miles east of the Verlot Ranger Station along the Mountain Loop Highway and turn right onto Ashland Lakes Road #4020. In another 2.3 miles turn right (west) at the junction with Road #4021. Drive to the next fork, in 1.5 miles, and turn left onto narrow Road #402/1016. After another 0.2 mile reach the signed trailhead.

Twin Falls ✭✭✭✭   ⑤ 🚶

Form: plunge   *Magnitude:* 81 (h)   *Watershed:* sm
Elevation: 2300 feet   *USGS Map:* Mallardy Ridge (1989)

Wilson Creek pounds 125 feet into Twin Falls Lake, then tumbles another 400 feet from the lake's outlet as *Lower Twin Falls* (u) ✭ USGS Mallardy Ridge (1989 nl). Unfortunately, the only safe views of the lower falls are moderately distant and mostly obscured by the surrounding vegetation. An interpretive sign at the lake provides a geologic history of the area.

From the trailhead, begin a demanding, but rewarding journey along a path built by the state's Department of Natural Resources. The way begins in unassuming fashion, following an old dirt road for the first mile. When you reach a footpath signed for Ashland Lakes turn left. The way steepens a bit and after another mile, a spur goes left to Beaver Plant Lake. For the most direct way to the destination stay to the right at this and all subsequent junctions. The trail becomes more difficult as wood planks, circular cedar cross-cuts, and granite blocks are provided to negotiate the marshy terrain over the next mile past Upper and Lower Ashland Lakes. The route then steepens considerably along its last 1.5 miles to the falls.

13. Arlington

Ryan Falls ☆ USGS Stimson Hill (1985 ns).
Water slides 50 to 75 feet down a hillside along an
unnamed creek located on private property, with
views restricted to the highway. Best viewed during late autumn, the falls is located just west of
mile marker 28 on S.R. 530 almost 7 miles northeast of Arlington, about 1.1 miles west of the
highway's crossing of the North Fork Stillaguamish
River.

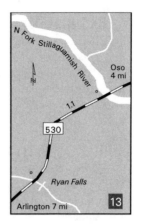

14. Boulder River

The following entry occurs within Boulder River Wilderness, a part of
Darrington Ranger District, Mount Baker–Snoqualmie National Forest. Access the area by taking S.R. 530 to French Creek Road #2010, located 8 miles
west of Darrington, or 8 miles east of Oso. Proceed south on Road #2010 for
4.5 miles, where the gravel road takes a sharp bend. Park at the trailhead at
the apex of the bend.

Feature Show Falls ☆☆　　　　　　　　　　　　　② 🚶

Form: horsetail　*Magnitude:* 23 (l)　*Watershed:* vsm
Elevation: 1100 feet　*USGS Map:* Meadow Mtn (1989 nl)

An unnamed creek
curtains 80 feet over a cliff into
Boulder River. This entry was
erroneously identified as *Boulder Falls,* USGS Meadow Mtn
(1989), in previous editions of
this book. The latter cataract
occurs a short distance downstream along Boulder Creek,
but it cannot be seen from the
trail and there is no developed
access. Walk along the trail for
1 mile to a cross-river vista of
Feature Show Falls.

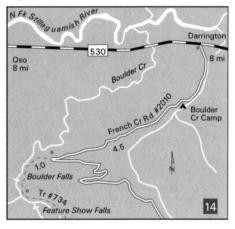

15. Sauk River

Both cataracts described below are located within Darrington Ranger
District, Mount Baker–Snoqualmie National Forest.

North Fork Falls ☆☆☆☆ ②

Form: punchbowl   *Magnitude:* 57 (h)
Watershed: lg
Elevation: 1480 feet   *USGS Map:* Sloan
Peak (1982)

Water thunders 60 to 80 feet along
the North Fork Sauk River. From Darrington,
take Sauk River Road #20 south for 15.6 miles
to North Fork Road #49. Turn left and drive
1.2 miles to the sign for Trail #660. Hike 0.3
mile to an overlook above the falls.

Others: Asbestos Creek Falls ☆ USGS Helena
Ridge (1989 ns). Asbestos Creek splashes 35 to
45 feet steeply downward from the
mountainside. Take Sauk River Road #20 south
from Darrington for 2.4 miles. Turn right onto
Clear Creek Road #2060 and proceed another
2.5 miles to an unsigned turnout where Asbestos Creek flows beneath the gravel road.
Scramble a few hundred feet up the drainage
to a view of this entry.

16. Suiattle River

The following trio of falls increase in
stature as one progresses up the drainage basin of the Suiattle River. Reach Suiattle River
Road #26 via S.R. 530 by driving 6.5 miles
north of Darrington or 12 miles south of
Rockport. Look for the turn 0.2 mile east of
the highway's crossing of the Sauk River.

Teepee Falls ☆☆

Form: cascade   *Magnitude:* 34
Watershed: med
Elevation: 1000 feet   *USGS Map:* Prairie
Mtn (1982)

Peer straight down from a bridge
spanning the chasm of Big Creek into this series of 50- to 60-foot cascading waters. Proceed
along Road #26 for 6.7 miles to reach this entry.

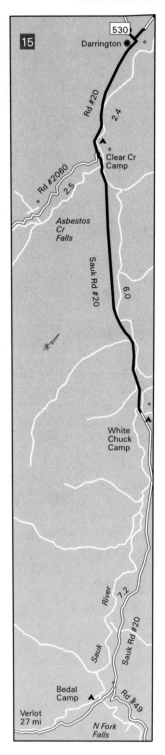

Gibson Falls ★★★

Form: fan   *Magnitude:* 44   *Watershed:* sm
Elevation: 1600 feet   *USGS Map:* Huckleberry Mtn (1982)

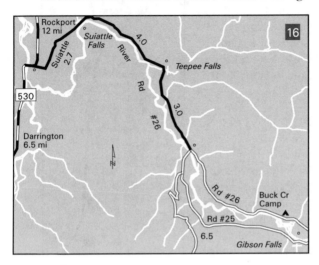

A narrow veil of water glistens 25 to 35 feet in a dimly lit recess of an unnamed stream. Located within Darrington Ranger District, Mount Baker–Snoqualmie National Forest. Continue 3 miles past Teepee Falls (described previously) along Road #26 and turn right onto Road #25. Go 6.5 miles along this gravel route to an unsigned turnout. (Watch for a dip in the culvert over signed Circle Creek: the turnout is 0.1 mile past this point.) Follow the creek upstream for 200 feet to the base of the falls.

Others: *Suiattle Falls* (u) ★ USGS Darrington (1982 nl). This double cascade along an unnamed creek drops a total of 70 to 100 feet from Suiattle Mountain on undeveloped state land. Drive 2.7 miles along Suiattle River Road to an unsigned turnout on the right side of the road, past a culvert for the small creek. Walk to the drainage and scramble upstream 100 feet to a vantage of the cataract.

17. Sauk Valley

Teenagers and nimble adults will enjoy this waterfall. Depart S.R. 20 on Sauk Valley Road, located 1 mile west of Concrete. Proceed south, then

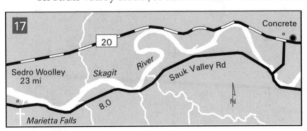

after crossing the Skagit River, bear right (west). Look for a creek crossing 8 miles from the state highway. Park at the unsigned area immediately west of the bridge.

Marietta Falls ★★★

Form: tiered   *Magnitude:* 53   *Watershed:* med
Elevation: 400 feet   *USGS Map:* Hamilton (1989)

O'Toole Creek, also called Marietta Creek, tumbles a total of 100 to 125 feet with a plunge at the end of its final descent. Probably on private property. The trail begins as a well-worn 0.3-mile path. It will require fording the creek once or twice and climbing over a small rock outcrop near the base of the falls.

18. Bellingham

The following entry provides a natural refuge from the urbanization of the Bellingham area.

Whatcom Falls ★★★

Form: tiered   *Magnitude:* 58   *Watershed:* lg
Elevation: 300 feet   *USGS Map:* Bellingham North (1994 ns)

One tier of the falls on Whatcom Creek pours 10 to 15 feet before the main display tumbles 25 to 30 feet over water-sculpted sandstone. *Lower Whatcom Falls* (u) ★ USGS Bellingham North (1994 ns) can be found 500 feet down the trail along the creek, which is the outlet for Lake Whatcom.

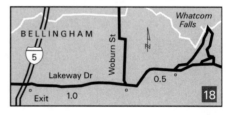

Depart I-5 at the Lakeway Exit. Drive 1.5 miles east along Lakeway Drive, then turn left onto Silver Beach Road at the sign marked for Whatcom Falls Park. Continue 1 more mile to the parking area, which is 50 feet from the descent.

19. Mount Baker

Mount Baker is one of the dominant features of the North Cascades. This glacier-covered volcano rises thousands of feet above the surrounding mountains. Meltwaters from its northeast-facing glaciers feed the waterfalls described in the following two subsections.

Rainbow Falls ★★★

Form: plunge   *Magnitude:* 70   *Watershed:* med (g)
Elevation: 1700 feet   *USGS Map:* Shuksan Arm (1989)

Rainbow Creek pours 150 feet into a gorge. Most of the cataract is visible from a moderately distant overlook across the canyon; the bottom

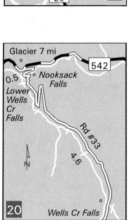

portion is hidden by vegetation and the canyon escarpment. The waterfall occurs within Mount Baker Wilderness, in Mount Baker Ranger District, Mount Baker–Snoqualmie National Forest.

At Concrete, turn north off the North Cascades Highway (S.R. 20), onto Baker Lake Road #11. (Eastbounders can take a shortcut to Road #11 by using the signed turnoff 6 miles west of Concrete.) After 16 or 18.5 miles, depending upon the route taken, turn left on Road #1130. There are views of Mount Baker and Mount Shuksan before the turn. Follow Road #1130 for 4.4 miles to the signed parking lot for the falls. The viewpoint is only a few steps away.

20. Nooksack River

As you near Washington's boundary with British Columbia you can explore some wild and woolly cataracts.

Nooksack Falls ☆☆☆☆

Form: segmented   *Magnitude:* 97 (h)   *Watershed:* lg (g)
Elevation: 2600 feet   *USGS Map:* Bearpaw Mtn (1989)

This 170-foot waterfall explodes over a sheer escarpment along the Nooksack River. The landowner, Puget Sound Power and Light, has constructed an observation platform, but only partial views are possible. Looking to the right of the main falls, you will also see *Lower Wells Creek Falls* (u) ☆☆ USGS Bearpaw Mtn (1989 ns), descending 80 to 100 feet into the river.

Drive 34 miles east of Bellingham along S.R. 542 to the hamlet of Glacier and continue 7 miles east to Wells Creek Road #33. Turn right and drive 0.5 mile. Do not cross the bridge over the river or you will miss the cataracts.

Wells Creek Falls (u) ☆☆   ③,

Form: plunge   *Magnitude:* 97 (h)   *Watershed:* med (g)
Elevation: 2600 feet   *USGS Map:* Mount Baker (1989 nl)

The roadside view of this beautiful 80- to 100-foot plunge, located within Mount Baker Ranger District, Mount Baker–Snoqualmie National Forest, is somewhat distant and obscured. From Nooksack Falls (described previously) continue 4.6 miles farther on Wells Creek Road #33 to an unsigned turnout, with a view of Mount Baker along the way. Better vantages of the falls require walking and scrambling along the creek, so plan on getting wet.

21. Ross Lake National Recreation Area
North Cascades National Park is bisected by Ross Lake National Recreation Area and its three reservoirs: Gorge Lake, Diablo Lake, and Ross Lake. Reach this rugged portion of Washington via the North Cascades Highway (S.R. 20), which is normally open only from June through October.

Ladder Creek Falls ★★★★
Form: tiered   *Magnitude:* 58   *Watershed:* med (g)
Elevation: 1410 feet   *USGS Map:* Diablo Dam (1963)
    This series of falls is unique because Seattle City Light illuminates them at night with colored lights. The major set of four descents totals 80 to 120 feet. Take S.R. 20 to the eastern side of Newhalem and park near the Gorge Powerhouse. Walk across the footbridge spanning the Skagit River and follow the trail through a landscaped rock garden, which contains many miniature cataracts.

Gorge Creek Falls ★★★
Form: tiered   *Magnitude:* 66   *Watershed:* sm
Elevation: 1660 feet   *USGS Map:* Diablo Dam (1963 ns)
    Gorge Creek streams down 120 to 150 feet in three sections. Two smaller falls can also be seen adjacent to the featured attraction. From the Gorge Powerhouse (described previously) take S.R. 20 east 2.6 miles to a parking area on the near (west) side of Gorge Creek Bridge. There are moderately distant views from the bridge walkway.

Ketchum Creek Falls ★★
Form: horsetail   *Magnitude:* 24 (l)   *Watershed:* vsm
Elevation: 2280 feet   *USGS Map:* Diablo Dam (1963 ns)
    This cataract descends 80 to 100 feet along Ketchum Creek. Drive 1 mile east from Gorge Creek Falls (described previously). Park at the unsigned turnout on the far (east) side of the creek.

John Pierce Falls ★★★
Form: horsetail   *Magnitude:* 49   *Watershed:* sm
Elevation: 2200 feet   *USGS Map:* Ross Dam (1963)
    Water slides 40 to 50 feet toward Diablo Lake. Although the drainage extends 400 to 450 feet farther down, it is usually dry, its runoff absorbed by the rocky substrate. Also called *Pierce Falls* and *Horsetail Falls*.

Drive east on S.R. 20 for 3.5 miles from Colonial Creek Camp, or west for 0.5 mile past the junction for Ross Dam, to an unsigned turnout on the northeast side of the highway.

Skymo Creek Falls ★★

Form: horsetail   *Magnitude:* 41
Watershed: med
Elevation: 1700 feet   *USGS Map:* Pumpkin Mtn (1969 ns)

Skymo Creek rushes 40 to 60 feet into Ross Lake about halfway up the reservoir. To reach Ross Dam and Ross Lake Resort, take a tugboat from Diablo Lake or hike 1 mile from the North Cascades Highway as shown on the map. Rent a boat at the resort. Unfortunately, there are reportedly no launching facilities for private craft. The falls are on the west shore of the lake across from aptly named Tenmile Island.

22. Methow Valley

The town of Mazama represents the eastern outpost for travel along the North Cascades Highway (S.R. 20). For westbound travelers, it has the last facilities for 75 miles. The pair of falls located in this area are both within

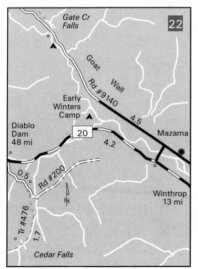

Okanogan National Forest, as are the entries under the Chewuch River and Foggy Dew Creek subsections of this chapter.

Cedar Falls ★★★   ③ 🚶

Form: tiered   *Magnitude:* 39   *Watershed:* med
Elevation: 3670 feet   *USGS Map:* Mazama (1991)

Cedar Creek has cut deeply into granite bedrock to form this series of 20- to 30-foot cataracts. Drive 4.2 miles west of Mazama along S.R. 20 and turn left (south) on Sandy Butte–Cedar Creek Road #200. Follow this gravel route for 0.5 mile and park near the marked Cedar Creek Trail #476, leading to the right. The trail ascends moderately for 1.7 miles before reaching the falls.

Others: *Gate Creek Falls* (u) ⋆ USGS McLeod Mtn (1991 nl). This 100-foot drop skips down a portion of the Goat Wall, a glaciated cliff rising 2,000 feet above the floor of the Methow Valley. The falls are not very impressive, but the valley view is nice. Recommended only for those who like climbing rocks. Drive to an informal campsite located along West Fork Methow Road #9140, 4.5 miles north of S.R. 20. Find the creek on the far side of the camp and climb a rigorous 0.3 mile upstream along a steep talus (rocky) slope.

23. Chewuch River

Falls Creek Falls ⋆⋆⋆
Form: horsetail   *Magnitude:* 57   *Watershed:* lg
Elevation: 2490 feet   *USGS Map:* Doe Mtn (1991)
      Falls Creek pours over faulted (fractured) bedrock in a refreshing 35- to 50-foot drop. Just west of the frontier-style town of Winthrop turn north off S.R. 20 onto Chewuch Road #51. Drive 11.5 miles to Falls Creek Campground. An access trail along the south side of the creek leads quickly to the descent.

Chewuch Falls ⋆⋆ ④ 𝕏
Form: tiered   *Magnitude:* 35   *Watershed:* lg
Elevation: 4000 feet   *USGS Map:* Coleman Peak (1969)
      The Chewuch River descends 30 feet over granite benches. On some maps the falls and its surrounding features are spelled phonetically as *Chewack Falls.* Follow Chewuch River Road, labeled #5160 along its northern portion, to its end a short distance past Thirtymile Campground and park. Hike 2.8 miles along Thirtymile Trail #510 to this entry.

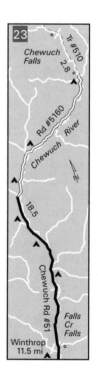

24. Foggy Dew Creek

Foggy Dew Falls ⋆⋆ ③ 𝕏
Form: horsetail   *Magnitude:* 30   *Watershed:* med
Elevation: 4410 feet   *USGS Map:* Martin Peak (1969)
      Foggy Dew Creek accelerates 100 feet through a narrow chute. Take S.R. 153 to Gold Creek Road #4340, about halfway between the towns of Twisp and Pateros, and turn west. Go 5 miles and turn left (south) on

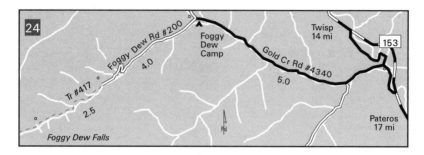

Foggy Dew Road #200. The trailhead is 4 miles farther, at the end of the road. A 2.5-mile hike along Foggy Dew Trail #417 brings you to the falls.

25. Lake Chelan

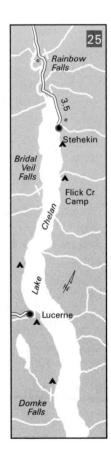

Lake Chelan is a classic example of a large paternoster lake. (A paternoster lake is one of a series of small lakes occupying depressions in a glacial valley—so-called after the chain's resemblance to the rosary beads used when reciting a *paternoster,* a k a The Lord's Prayer.) When glaciers carved out the Chelan Valley 10,000 to 12,000 years ago, they left behind an accumulation of rock debris known as a terminal moraine. The moraine acts as a natural dam for meltwater entering the valley from the adjacent snow-laden mountains. The lake is 51 miles long and attains a depth of over 1,500 feet. It is one of the largest alpine lakes in the contiguous United States.

Rainbow Falls ★★★★★

Form: tiered   *Magnitude:* 92   *Watershed:* med
Elevation: 1530 feet   *USGS Map:* Stehekin (1987)
Accessible by shuttle bus

Rainbow Creek makes a spectacular plunge—some 470 feet with a main plunge of 312 feet. Situated within Lake Chelan National Recreation Area. Board Lake Chelan Boat Company's *Lady of the Lake,* or pilot your own craft from Chelan to the secluded village of Stehekin. Once in Stehekin, bus service is available to shuttle visitors 3.5 miles to the falls.

Domke Falls ✯✯

Form: fan   *Magnitude:* 33   *Watershed:* med
Elevation: 1340 feet   *USGS Map:* Lucerne (1988)

Water rushes 30 to 50 feet into Lake Chelan from Domke Creek. The falls and the creek are named for the first settler in the vicinity. Located within Glacier Peak Wilderness, a part of Chelan Ranger District, Wenatchee National Forest. The tour boat *Lady of the Lake* (described previously) passes near the falls, located on the west side of the lake, on the return trip from Lucerne to Chelan.

Domke Falls

Others: *Bridal Veil Falls* ★ USGS Stehekin (1987). This 50- to 75-foot waterfall, located within Lake Chelan National Recreation Area, is distantly visible to the west from the tour boat on the return trip from Stehekin to Lucerne. It earns a higher rating if you have a private boat to approach it more closely.

26. North Cascades National Park

While the majority of national parks within the continental United States have developed routes for motorized travel, North Cascades National Park remains overwhelmingly wilderness in character. The remote Stehekin River Road, one of only two gravel roads entering the park, allows access to five falls in the park's southeast sector. Take the Lake Chelan Boat Company's *Lady of the Lake* from Chelan to Stehekin and the River Road. A shuttle service transports hikers and backpackers to various campsites and trailheads along the road.

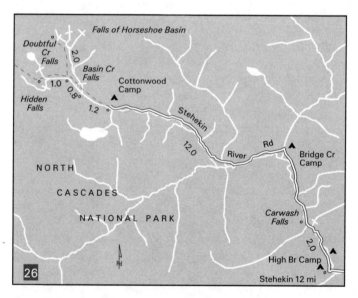

Carwash Falls ★★
Form: horsetail   *Magnitude:* 24 (l)   *Watershed:* sm
Elevation: 1880 feet   *USGS Map:* McGregor Mtn (1987 ns)
Accessible by shuttle bus

McGregor Creek descends 40 to 60 feet before splashing next to Stehekin River Road. If the tour bus gets wet 2 miles past High Bridge, you have obviously not missed this aptly named waterfall.

Basin Creek Falls (u) ★★ ③

Form: plunge   *Magnitude:* 82   *Watershed:* sm (g)
Elevation: 3430 feet   *USGS Map:* Cascade Pass (1963 ns)

This 125- to 175-foot drop from Basin Creek would deserve a higher scenic rating, except only a distant view is possible. Take the shuttle bus to its farthest destination at Cottonwood Camp. Hike 1.2 miles west from the camp to the best vantage of the cataract 50 yards downstream from the Basin Creek swinging bridge.

Falls of Horseshoe Basin (u) ★★★★ ⑤

Form: segmented   *Magnitude:* 63   *Watershed:* vsm (g)
Elevation: 6070 feet   *USGS Map:* Cascade Pass (1963 ns)

An entire series of waterfalls pours off the surrounding mountain ridges into Horseshoe Basin. Nineteen falls can be seen in a single view! The basin is a good example of a cirque, a bowl-shaped depression eroded by the upper portion of a former alpine glacier.

From Basin Creek Falls (described previously), continue hiking for 0.8 mile to a fork in the trail. Bear right and follow switchbacks steeply upward, meeting Basin Creek in 0.5 mile. The basin and falls are 1.5 miles farther, a total of 4 miles from the trailhead. Hope that there is a breeze to keep the black flies from biting you.

Falls of Horseshoe Basin

Doubtful Creek Falls (u) ★★

Form: tiered   *Magnitude:* 40   *Watershed:* vsm
Elevation: 4470 feet   *USGS Map:* Cascade Pass (1963 ns)

The outlet of Doubtful Lake pours down a mountainside in a series of 20- to 50-foot cataracts. Hike 1 mile beyond the fork leading to Horseshoe Basin (described previously), continuing along the left fork to the crossing of Doubtful Creek. The upper tier of the waterfall is directly above the ford, the other tier below.

Hidden Falls (u) ★★★

Form: cascade   *Magnitude:* 61   *Watershed:* sm (g)
Elevation: 4630 feet   *USGS Map:* Cascade Pass (1963 ns)

Water cascades steeply 260 to 300 feet from the meltwaters of Yawning Glacier. Hike to Doubtful Creek (described previously) and look across the valley at the falls; Pelton Peak provides a backdrop. It is 3 miles back to the trailhead.

27. Entiat Valley

Apple orchards are common along the fertile plain of the lower Entiat Valley. Farther upstream the valley becomes less gentle and the orchards give way to coniferous forest. The upper valley has three scenic, though not overwhelming, waterfalls. They are all a part of Entiat Ranger District, Wenatchee National Forest.

Preston Falls ★★

Form: horsetail   *Magnitude:* 22 (l)   *Watershed:* med
Elevation: 2040 feet   *USGS Map:* Brief (1987)

Preston Creek slides 75 to 100 feet down the mountainside. Turn west off U.S. 97 onto Entiat River Road #371 less than 1 mile south of Entiat. Reach Ardenvoir in 8.5 miles and the falls 13.5 miles farther, approximately 1.2 miles past Entiat Valley Ski Area.

Silver Falls ★★★

Form: block   *Magnitude:* 47 (l)   *Watershed:* med
Elevation: 2960 feet   *USGS Map:* Silver Falls (1987)

Silver Creek pours 100 to 140 feet from a cliff. The best shows are provided during wet conditions. From Preston Falls (described previously), continue 9 miles along Road #371, which becomes Wenatchee National Forest Road #51. There is a good, but moderately distant roadside view of the cataract from Silver Falls Service Station. For closer

Silver Falls

vantages, ascend Silver Falls National Recreation Trail for 0.5 mile to the base of the falls. The trail is dedicated to J. Kenneth and Opal F. Blair, stewards of public lands in the 1950s and 1960s.

Entiat Falls ★★

Form: block   *Magnitude:* 69 (h)   *Watershed:* lg
Elevation: 2780 feet   *USGS Map:* Silver Falls (1987)

The Entiat River breaks over a rock ledge and thunders 30 feet onto boulders below. *Entiat* is an Indian word meaning "rapid water." Continue 3 miles past Silver Falls (described previously) to Entiat Falls viewpoint.

THE OLYMPICS AND VICINITY

The Olympic Peninsula is dominated by the mountains that rise 6,000 to 8,000 feet above its coastal margins. This abrupt relief causes moist air masses moving into the area to produce some of the highest annual precipitation in the continental United States. Normal figures reach 140 inches of rain on the Pacific

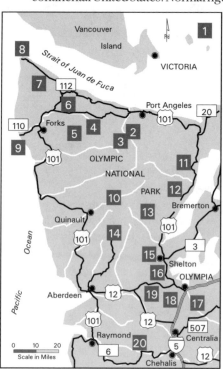

Coast and 40 feet of snow in the high mountains. Most precipitation occurs from November to April.

Many small glaciers lie on the northern flanks of the highest mountains. Meltwater from the glaciers as well as from snowfields feeds the region's rivers and streams during the drier summer season. As a result, the larger watersheds throughout the Olympics drain liberally year-round. An abundance of water flowing over a mountainous landscape dissected by glaciation has created most of the 85 waterfalls that have been recognized throughout the peninsula. This chapter provides information for 33 of these falls.

The Olympic Mountains are quite youthful geologically. The range was formed when two of the earth's large *crustal plates* collided and the contact zone was forced upward. The collision of these plates began about 70 million years ago and has continued to the present so the mountain-building process is ongoing. During the four Ice Age episodes that occurred between 2 million and 10,000 years ago, alpine glaciers stretched to lower elevations than they do today and carved large U-shaped valleys. Major rivers presently rush along the base of these glacial troughs, sometimes descending over rocks that erode at unequal rates. More common are the falls created when tributary streams pour over the steep sides of glacial troughs on their way to the valley floors.

Gigantic continental glaciers played an important role in shaping Puget Sound and the Strait of Juan de Fuca. About 10,000 years ago the Laurentide Ice Sheet covered almost all of Canada and the northern tier of the eastern United States. A lobe of this massive glacial system extended into western Washington and gouged out large expanses of the Puget Lowland. As the glacier retreated, ocean water inundated the land area that had been eroded below sea level. Puget Sound and its surrounding bodies of water are the result of this inrush. Vashon, Bainbridge, Whidbey, and Camano Islands to the east and the San Juan Islands to the north represent remnants of the preglacial landscape that were not eroded away by the Puget Lobe of the ice sheet.

Coastal waterfalls are also distributed around the Olympic Peninsula. Along the northwestern portion of the coast, small streams tumble over marine cliffs carved by the wave action of the sea. Although most of these falls are visible only from watercraft, a few are accessible by trail.

1. Orcas Island

The San Juan Islands are one of the most beautiful archipelagos in the world. Orcas Island, the largest of the chain's 172 islands, has four miniature waterfalls. Board a Washington State ferry at Anacortes. After an enjoyable hour and a half churning across Puget Sound, get off at Orcas Landing. Follow Horseshoe Highway north for 12.8 miles, passing the hamlets of Westsound,

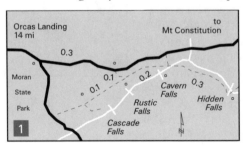

Crow Valley, and Eastsound before arriving at Moran State Park. Drive 1.2 miles within the park to a fork in the road. Bear left and continue 0.3 mile farther and park at a turnout for the marked trailhead of the aptly named Cascade Creek Trail.

Cascade Falls ★★

Form: fan   *Magnitude:* 38   *Watershed:* sm
Elevation: 620 feet   *USGS Map:* Mount Constitution (1994)

This is the largest of the four waterfalls on Orcas Island, spraying downward 40 to 50 feet. Although it is named after the creek, it is actually fan-shaped in form. Follow a short spur trail from the road to the small canyon of Cascade Creek, and walk downstream to the falls in 0.2 mile.

Others: *Rustic Falls* ✫ USGS Mount Constitution (1994). This small 5- to 10-foot cataract is the first of the falls seen from the main access point for Cascade Creek Trail. Follow the short spur trail from the road into the small canyon. Cascade Creek and Rustic Falls are in 0.1 mile.

    Cavern Falls ✫ USGS Mount Constitution (1994). Water steeply tumbles 20 to 40 feet into a recess in the canyon. Walk upstream from Rustic Falls for a short 0.2 mile. This entry will be seen to the right of the trail.

    Hidden Falls ✫ USGS Mount Constitution (1994). This 15- to 20-foot drop is "hidden" only if you are not observant. Continue walking upstream past Cavern Falls along Cascade Creek Trail. Cross the creek twice. The second crossing is above the top of the falls, 0.6 mile from the trailhead.

2. Elwha Valley

Olympic National Park is best known for its lush rain-forest valleys and snow-topped mountains, but its soothing cataracts also deserve attention. The waterfalls of seven of this chapter's sections are located within the park.

Madison Creek Falls (u) ✫✫

Form: horsetail   *Magnitude:* 47
Watershed: sm
Elevation: 540 feet   *USGS Map:* Elwha
(1985 ns)

    This unpublicized 40- to 50-foot descent is just off one of the main roads into the park. Take U.S. 101 west from Port Angeles for 8 miles and turn left onto Olympic Hot Springs Road. Drive 2 miles to the park boundary and stop at an unsigned turnout on the left side of the road. A short walk into a wooded tract brings this entry into view.

Wolf Creek Falls (u) ✫✫✫   ③ 🚶

Form: horsetail   *Magnitude:* 41   *Watershed:* sm
Elevation: 850 feet   *USGS Map:* Hurricane Hill (1976 nl)

    This is actually a double-tiered falls, but only the 30- to 40-foot lower section is clearly visible. The 50- to 70-foot upper portion is hidden by the shape of the gorge. Drive 2 miles beyond the park boundary on Olympic Hot Springs Road (described previously); just past the ranger station turn left onto a gravel road. After another 4 miles, park along the turnout at the marked trailhead for Lake Mills. Follow the steep trail to its end in 0.4 mile. Walk around

Wolf Creek Falls

the ridge to the right to Wolf Creek. The base of the cataract is easily reached by heading upstream less than 100 feet.

3. Mount Carrie

The trail system for the following falls is reached by staying on paved Olympic Hot Springs Road (described previously) to its end. The north shore of Lake Mills is 2 miles past the ranger station, with Boulder Creek Campground and Trailhead 5.5 miles farther.

Lower Boulder Creek Falls ★★   ③

Form: horsetail   *Magnitude:* 48   *Watershed:* sm
Elevation: 2650 feet   *USGS Map:* Mount Carrie (1950 nl)

Water froths 25 to 35 feet downward into the upper reaches of Boulder Creek Gorge. Just beyond the campsites of Boulder Creek Campground, begin hiking along Boulder Creek Trail. Bear left at the fork in 0.6 mile, hiking along South Fork Boulder Creek. The way ascends moderately over the next 0.6 mile before intersecting with a short spur path that soon leads to the falls.

Upper Boulder Creek Falls ★★   ③

Form: tiered   *Magnitude:* 56   *Watershed:* sm
Elevation: 3030 feet   *USGS Map:* Mount Carrie (1950 nl)

Boulder Creek tumbles 15 to 25 feet before taking a 75- to 100-foot plunge. A full view of the upper portion can be had at the end of the

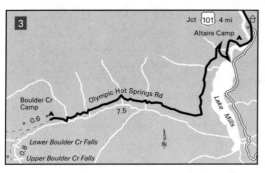

trail, but only the top of the main display is safely visible. Take the Boulder Creek Trail 0.2 mile beyond Lower Boulder Creek Falls (described previously) to a second marked spur trail. This short path quickly leads to a viewpoint between the descents.

4. Lake Crescent

Lake Crescent is in the northwestern corner of Olympic National Park's inland section as is one of the most scenic falls of the region. Drive along

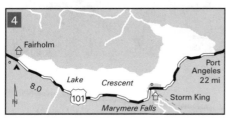

U.S. 101, either 22 miles west from Port Angeles or 8 miles east from Fairholm, to Storm King Visitor Center and Ranger Station. The following entry is a short hike away.

Marymere Falls ★★★★   ②

Form: tiered   *Magnitude:* 62   *Watershed:* sm
Elevation: 1030 feet   *USGS Map:* Lake Crescent (1985)

Falls Creek plunges and horsetails 90 feet over a rock wall. At Storm King Visitor Center, embark upon Falls Nature Trail, which leads to the cataract in 0.8 mile. Take a self-guided tour or accompany a scheduled group.

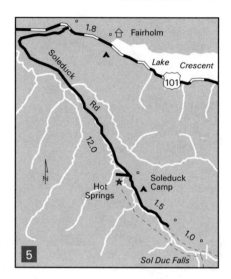

5. Soleduck

For years, many of the names in this valley have been given as *Soleduck,* an English variant of the Native American phrase *Sol Duc,* meaning "magic waters." The Geographic Names Information System, a database maintained by the U.S. Geological Survey, now uses the original spelling for the names of natural features but has retained the variant for cultural places.

Sol Duc Falls ☆☆☆   ③ 🏃

Form: segmented   *Magnitude:* 58   *Watershed:* med
Elevation: 2190 feet   *USGS Map:* Bogachiel Peak (1950)

The waters of the Sol Duc River rush 40 to 60 feet downward at a right angle. Also spelled *Soleduck Falls* (u). Drive west from Fairholm for 1.8 miles on U.S. 101 to Soleduck Road, which leads to Sol Duc Hot Springs in 12 miles. The road ends at Soleduck Trailhead 1.5 miles farther. Hike 1 mile beyond the trailhead, then turn right (south) at the first junction. The falls can be seen from the footbridge crossing the river.

6. Beaver Creek

The entries in this and the next section are located outside Olympic National Park, but were accessible to the public when last surveyed.

Beaver Falls ☆☆☆   ③ 🏃

Form: segmented   *Magnitude:* 34 (l)
Watershed: med
Elevation: 600 feet   *USGS Map:* Lake Pleasant (1984)

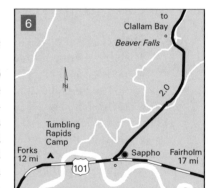

Beaver Creek tumbles 30 to 40 feet in three sections across an 80-foot-wide rock escarpment. Turn off U.S. 101 at Sappho, 12 miles north of Forks and 17 miles west of Fairholm. Follow the northbound secondary road for 2 miles to an unsigned turnout 0.1 mile past Beaver Creek bridge. A short, unimproved path leads to the cataract.

Beaver Falls

7. Clallam Bay

Passing motorists probably miss the following cataracts as they admire the Clallam Bay portion of the Strait of Juan de Fuca, the passage connecting Puget Sound with the Pacific Ocean.

Hoko Falls ✫✫   ②

Form: punchbowl   *Magnitude:* 28 (h)   *Watershed:* lg
Elevation: 210 feet   *USGS Map:* Hoko Falls (1984)

The normally calm waters of the Hoko River rush 5 to 10 feet at a narrow reach where erosion-resistant rock constricts the stream. Follow S.R. 112 to the seaside village of Clallam Bay. Continue on S.R. 112 for 4.1 miles, then turn left (south) toward Ozette Lake. Proceed 6.3 miles to a bridge over the Hoko River, parking on the far side. Fishermen's paths lead down to a view near the base of the falls.

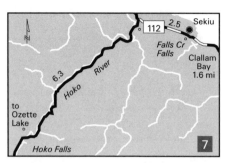

Others: *Falls Creek Falls* (u) ☆ USGS Clallam Bay (1984 nl). A low stream flow reduces the scenic quality of this 20- to 25-foot tumble along Falls Creek. Follow S.R. 112 to the seaside village of Clallam Bay. Continue 1.6 miles west to the hamlet of Sekiu, parking at an unsigned turnout on the north (right) side of the road. Walk down a jeep trail a short distance, passing beneath the highway and progressing to the base of the falls.

8. Cape Flattery

One of the most rugged sections of the Washington coast is Cape Flattery, where the Strait of Juan de Fuca meets the Pacific Ocean. While most visitors take to the sea for fishing excursions, the scenic beauty of the cape's coast, accented by several minor waterfalls, also merits an afternoon boat ride. Charter or launch your own craft at Neah Bay, located about 5 miles east of the cape. Early summer is the best time of the year to view the falls, as stream discharge is usually adequate and the weather conditions most often favorable for boating.

Beach Creek Falls (u) ☆ USGS Cape Flattery (1984 nl). Beach Creek trickles 30 to 40 feet directly into the Strait of Juan de Fuca. Proceed 3.6 miles west of Neah Bay to a small cove and its small cataract. As with the following pair of descents, you should have a large-scale nautical map if you are navigating your own boat.

Titacoclos Falls ☆ USGS Cape Flattery (1984). This 100- to 120-foot drop tends to be seasonal, seldom flowing from mid- to late summer. Deserves a higher rating during peak periods. Look for the falls about 0.4 mile west of Beach Creek Falls.

Flattery Creek Falls (u) ☆ USGS Cape Flattery (1984 nl). Water slides 45 to 60 feet into a crevasse at the head of Hole-in-the-Wall Cove. Accessible only by small-craft boaters experienced in navigating rocky embayments. Proceed 1 mile past Titacoclos Falls to Cape Flattery, and enter Hole-in-the-Wall. After dropping anchor, walk up the drainage a short distance to view this previously unnamed cataract. An ankle-deep wade may be required part

of the way. Intriguing ruins of early twentieth-century buildings can also be seen in the cove.

9. Olympic Coast

For safe access to the following waterfall hikers or backpackers must be aware of tide conditions. Some of the beaches are inundated by the Pacific at high tide. Appropriate information for coastal hiking, such as tide tables, can be obtained at the Mora or Kalaloch Ranger Stations of Olympic National Park.

Strawberry Bay Falls (u) ☆☆

Form: horsetail   *Magnitude:* 29 (l)   *Watershed:* vsm
Elevation: 80 feet   *USGS Map:* Toleak Point (1982 nl)

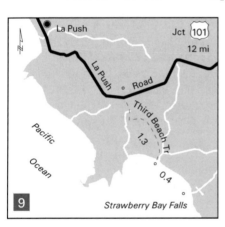

An unnamed creek pours 100 to 120 feet into the surf. Five miles north of Forks turn left off U.S. 101, heading toward La Push and the Pacific Coast. After 8 miles, turn left (south), staying on La Push Road, and continue 4 miles to Third Beach Trailhead. Hike 1.3 miles to the ocean, then 0.4 mile south to the nearest beach-side view of the falls. Closer vantages are possible from wave-cut rocks, but for safety's sake walking on the rocks must be restricted to time periods when the tide is receding.

10. Enchanted Valley

This entry is for all the waterfall enthusiasts who also like to backpack. Marvel at the Enchanted Valley, located in the southern part of Olympic National Park. The most popular trailhead for accessing the valley, Graves Creek, is 23 miles east of Quinault, off U.S. 101, near the ranger station.

Valley of 10,000 Waterfalls (u) ☆☆☆☆

Form: many horsetails and tiers *Magnitude:* not calculable
Watershed: sm (g) *Elevation:* 3400 to 4200 feet
USGS Map: Chimney Peak (1990 nl and ns)

Many visitors and long-time residents of the Olympic Peninsula prefer the name "Valley of 10,000 Waterfalls" to the more common "Enchanted Valley." Although the number of falls may be exaggerated in the name, you would be hard-pressed to keep track of the scores of waterfalls that can be

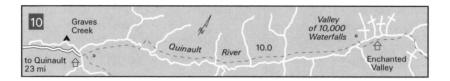

seen during a single day's journey in this valley. Practically every tributary encountered along Enchanted Valley Trail breaks into a waterfall as it enters the glacially carved valley of the Quinault River. Varied vegetation completes

Strawberry Bay Falls

the serene scenery of the gorge. Secure a backcountry permit at the Graves Creek or Dosewallips Ranger Stations. Most of the falls are within 0.3 mile of the Enchanted Valley Ranger Station, which is 10 miles from the trailhead and is open during the summer if you need information or assistance.

11. Quilcene

The following entry is located within Olympic National Forest in the vicinity of Quilcene Ranger Station.

Falls View Falls (u) ★★

Form: horsetail   *Magnitude:* 26 (l)   *Watershed:* vsm
Elevation: 280 feet   *USGS Map:* Mount Walker (1985 ns)

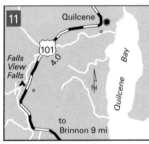

An unnamed creek drops 80 to 120 feet into the Big Quilcene River. The flow is greatest during the wet season from autumn to spring. It may disappear entirely during droughts. The cataract is also known as *Campground Falls* (u).

Turn off U.S. 101 at Falls View Camp, 4 miles south of Quilcene and 9 miles north of Brinnon. A short trail at the south end of the campground leads to a fenced vista high above the canyon floor.

12. Dosewallips

Kudos to a local resident for pointing out this otherwise obscure, yet entertaining spectacle. It is likely situated on private land but was accessible to the public when last visited.

Rocky Brook Falls (u) ★★★★

Form: horsetail   *Magnitude:* 71   *Watershed:* med
Elevation: 500 feet   *USGS Map:* Brinnon (1985 ns)

Water thunders 100 to 125 feet over a massive scarp. If you also plan on taking a day trip to Dosewallips Falls (described next), save this one for last. Drive 1 mile north of Brinnon on U.S. 101, then turn left (west) at Road #261, signed Dosewallips Recreation Area. Proceed west for 3 miles and park at the unsigned turnout on the west side of Rocky Brook bridge. A well-worn trail quickly leads to the base of the falls.

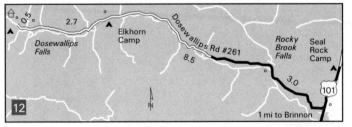

Dosewallips Falls ☆☆☆

Form: cascade   *Magnitude:* 53   *Watershed:* lg
Elevation: 1400 feet   *USGS Map:* The Brothers (1985 nl)

Water pours 100 to 125 feet over and around boulders along the Dosewallips River. Located within Olympic National Park. Continue driving 11.2 miles westward past Rocky Brook bridge (described previously) along Dosewallips Road (#261). A signed turnout will be seen near the base of the cataract, 0.7 mile beyond the park boundary.

13. Lake Cushman

Cushman Falls ☆☆

Form: horsetail   *Magnitude:* 44   *Watershed:* sm
Elevation: 850 feet   *USGS Map:* Lightning Peak (1990 nl)

An unnamed creek slides 25 to 35 feet, nearly spraying onto the road. Located on a strip of private property adjacent to Olympic National Park. Depart U.S. 101 at the hamlet of Hoodsport; the turnoff is signed Olympic National Park–Staircase Area. Lake Cushman State Park is in 7.2 miles. In another 2 miles turn left onto Road #24 toward the Staircase Area and reach the waterfall in 2.4 miles.

Cushman Falls

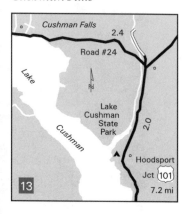

14. Wynoochee Lake

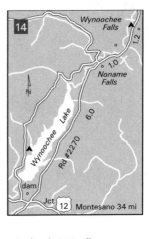

The south-central portion of Olympic National Forest, being remote from travelers' facilities, is one of the lesser-frequented areas of the Olympic Peninsula. The most reliable access to the following pair of cataracts is from the south. Depart U.S. 12 at Devonshire Road, 1.5 miles west of Montesano. After 0.1 mile, turn left (north) on Wynoochee Road #22 and drive 34 miles to Wynoochee Dam.

Wynoochee Falls ☆☆

Form: tiered   *Magnitude:* 44
Watershed: med
Elevation: 1010 feet   *USGS Map:* Wynoochee Lake (1990 nl)

This pretty double punchbowl tumbles 25 to 35 feet along the Wynoochee River. At Wynoochee Dam turn north onto Road #2270. In 6.0 miles pass the turnoff to Noname Falls (described below). Proceed 1.2 miles farther and turn left onto Road #260 into an old National Forest campground. Proceed to the north end of the camp, then walk along any of the several footpaths, all of which lead to the falls in 50 to 100 yards.

Others: *Noname Falls*(u) ☆ USGS Wynoochee Lake (1990 ns). An unnamed creek drops 40 to 60 feet in two major steps. Since no labeled features occur in

Wynoochee Falls

the immediate vicinity, I have "no name" for the falls. Six miles north of Wynoochee Dam, bear right at a fork and proceed 1 more mile to a roadside view of this entry.

15. Shelton

Goldsborough Creek Falls (u) ★★   ② 🏃
Form: block   *Magnitude:* 37   *Watershed:* lg (d)
Elevation: 130 feet   *USGS Map:* Shelton (1981 nl)

    Goldsborough Creek pours 8 to 12 feet over a wide reach of the stream just below a small overflow dam. The property is owned by Simpson Timber, which allowed access, but no fishing, when this entry was field-truthed.

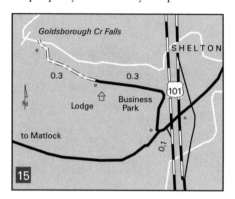

    Depart the divided highway of U.S. 101 on the south side of Shelton at the Matlock Exit. Drive west for just 0.1 mile, then turn right at the sign for Goldsborough Business Park. Proceed 0.3 mile, parking just beyond the Moose Lodge. Walk down the dirt road 0.3 mile to the falls, avoiding the side roads.

16. Kamilche

Kennedy Falls ★★   ③ 🏃
Form: tiered   *Magnitude:* 38   *Watershed:* med
Elevation: 240 feet   *USGS Map:* Kamilche Valley (1981)

    Kennedy Creek drops to an emerald-tinted gorge in two major tiers. The upper portion of this small, but pleasant waterfall tumbles 5 to 10 feet into a pool. A short distance downstream, the creek pours 20 to 30 feet into the narrow gorge.

    Turn off U.S. 101 onto Old Olympia Highway 2.5 miles south of the Kamilche/S.R. 108 Exit and 4.2 miles northwest of the junction of U.S. 101 and S.R. 8. Drive 0.7 mile to the dirt road south of Kennedy Creek. Turn west and stay on the main route for 2.7 miles, bearing right (toward the creek) at all

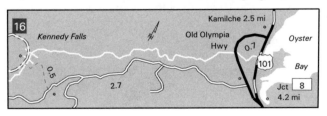

major forks. Park along the side of the road at its junction with an unsigned jeep trail and hike for 0.5 mile to the creek. The best views of the falls are from the north side of the valley. Walk a short distance upstream to a fairly easy ford above the upper descent, then progress downstream to a clear, unguarded vista. This site is most likely on private land.

17. Olympia

Four cataracts highlight a leisurely 30-minute stroll through the landscaped setting of Tumwater Falls Park. Located on the grounds of the Pabst Brewery (formerly the Olympia Brewery). Depart I-5 at Exit 103. Visitor parking is one block east of the freeway. After visiting the falls, take a tour of the brewery and enjoy a complimentary glass of beer or soda in the hospitality room.

Tumwater Falls ★★★   ① 🏃

Form: punchbowl   *Magnitude:* 41   *Watershed:* lg (d)
Elevation: 60 feet   *USGS Map:* Tumwater (1994 nl)

This 40-foot waterfall has become famous over the years by having its likeness shown on the labels of the brewery's Olympia brands. First called *Puget Sound Falls* by European settlers in 1829, it was renamed *Shutes River Falls* in 1841. In 1845 Michael Troutman Simmons led a party of American settlers to the vicinity. He coined the name Tumwater based on a Chinook word. The Chinook called running water *tumtum* because they thought its sound was like the throb of a heart.

From the parking lot walk downstream 0.2 mile to a vista overlooking the falls. A footbridge crosses above the descent.

Olympia Falls (u) ★★   ① 🏃

Form: tiered   *Magnitude:* 46   *Watershed:* sm (?)
Elevation: 100 feet   *USGS Map:* Tumwater (1994 ns)

Purified water is returned to the Deschutes River from the brewery in a nice display descending a total of 40 to 60 feet. Cross the river at

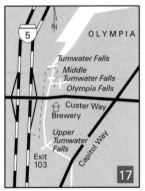

Tumwater Falls (described previously), walk upstream a short distance; the trail passes between the upper and lower portions of this waterfall.

Others: *Upper Tumwater Falls* (u) ★ USGS Tumwater (1994 nl). The form of this 10- to 20-foot drop along the Deschutes River has been modified to harness water power, reducing its scenic value. This entry is located near the picnic area adjacent to the visitor parking area for the brewery.

Middle Tumwater Falls (u) ★ USGS Tumwater (1994 ns). Water tumbles 15 to 25 feet along the

Deschutes River. Walk a short distance downstream from Olympia Falls (described previously). The reason for the river's French name, "River of the Falls," is now apparent as you complete your tour of the area.

Tumwater Falls

Olympia Falls

18. Mima Prairie

Most of the rolling terrain of the Black Hills is managed by the Washington Department of Natural Resources as Capitol State Forest. The most interesting feature in this area is on the eastern fringe of the forest at Mima Mounds, a small prairie composed of numerous small hummocks. It is theorized that these 5- to 10-foot-high "pimpled mounds" were formed thousands of years ago by rodent activity and/or processes related to glaciation.

The following modest waterfall also occurs in the vicinity.

Mima Falls ☆ USGS Littlerock (1986). Mima Creek tumbles 20 to 25 feet; a wooden bench above the cataract offers the best vantage. The scenic rating may increase during periods of peak discharge. Depart S.R.

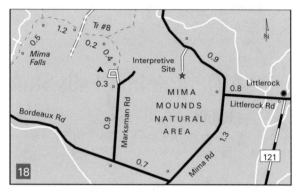

121 at the village of Littlerock on 128th Ave/Littlerock Road, signed for Mima Mounds. Continue 0.8 mile to a T intersection and turn left on Mima Road. (Turning right will take you to the Mima Mounds interpretive area.) Go 1.3 miles and turn right onto Bordeaux Road. Proceed 0.7 mile, then turn right on Marksman Road; reach the entrance to Mima Falls camp, signed Mima Falls Trailhead, in 0.9 miles.

Drive 0.3 mile to a small parking area. Mima Porter Trail #8 starts here and follows gentle terrain most of the way; the trick is making the correct turns at its various junctions. The first junction, signed for a variety of destinations, is met in 0.4 mile. Continue straight rather than bearing right. The path crosses a dirt road in another 0.2 mile. Look for a sign stating "Mima Falls 1.7 miles." In 1.2 miles after passing the sign, bear left at another trail junction and continue for 0.5 mile to the falls.

19. Porter

Porter Falls ☆☆   ② 🚶

Form: punchbowl   *Magnitude:* 32   *Watershed:* med
Elevation: 400 feet   *USGS Map:* Malone (1986 nl)

This largest in a series of small cataracts along West Fork Porter Creek drops 8 to 12 feet just above the stream's confluence with North Fork Porter Creek. Located within Capitol State Forest. Leave U.S. 12 at the hamlet of Porter on unsigned Porter Creek Road. Drive 2.7 miles, where the road turns into a graveled surface. Continue another 0.5 mile to the Porter Creek entrance to Capitol State Forest. Stay on this road, now called B-Line, for another 0.6 mile to a generic trail sign immediately before the entrance to Porter Creek Camp. Park here, where

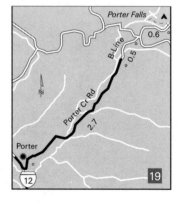

an interpretive sign describes the logging railroad that played a large role in the history of the area. The 0.5-mile trail parallels North Fork for 0.3 mile before ending at the falls.

20. Rainbow Falls State Park

Rainbow Falls ☆☆

Form: punchbowl   *Magnitude:* 24 (h)   *Watershed:* lg
Elevation: 400 feet   *USGS Map:* Rainbow Falls (1986)

A large pool at the base of this 5- to 10-foot waterfall along the Chehalis River serves as a popular swimming hole. Drive to Rainbow Falls State Park, which is adjacent to S.R. 6, about 3 miles east of Doty and 12 miles west of Adna. Views of the falls can be had from the bridge over the river at the park entrance. Within the park, interpretive trails guide the visitor through stands of virgin timber.

MOUNT RAINIER REGION

The region within and surrounding Mount Rainier National Park is among the most scenic in North America. While the mountain itself, called *Takhoma* by the Yakama Indians, is the centerpiece of the area, many other attractions await discovery. Of the 150 waterfalls known to occur within the area, 56 are mentioned in this chapter.

This is a land of fire and ice. The oldest rocks predate Mount Rainier itself. Between 30 million and 60 million years ago, the region was part of a large, low-lying coastal zone scattered with terrestrial and subterranean volcanoes, which deposited thick accumulations of lava over a wide area. Ten million to thirty million years later, continued volcanic activity forced molten material, *magma,* toward the surface of the earth. Most of this magma cooled before it could pour from the volcanoes' vents as lava. It solidified to become bedrock, which was later thrust to the surface by internal earth forces or exposed by erosion.

Because of this complex history the landscape along the periphery of Mount Rainier comprises many different types of rocks that streams erode at unequal rates. *Silver Falls* occurs where the Ohanapecosh River intersects resistant vertical layers of basalt before continuing its course along relatively weak volcanic *breccia,* which was formed when lava intermingled with sandstone and siltstone. At *Lower Stevens Falls* magma was injected into an older rock complex and the resulting bedrock proved to be more resistant than the neighboring material.

Mount Rainier formed some 1 million to 5 million years ago and is composed of interlayered andesitic lava and volcanic ash from repeated eruptions. One large lava flow blocks the northward course of Maple Creek, diverting the stream eastward. Coincidentally, a vertical break in the local

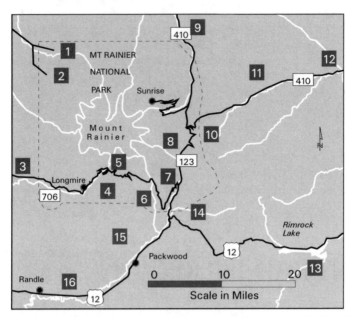

topography, called a *fault*, is positioned along the redefined route of the stream. *Maple Falls* presently plummets down this fault.

The abundance of waterfalls in the region is due not only to the processes described above but also to the large-scale landscape modifications achieved by glaciers. A total of twenty-seven named glaciers surround Mount Rainier today; 10,000 years ago these awesome phenomena, the earth's greatest erosive agents, extended to much lower elevations.

A topographic feature called a *step* is common to the higher valleys of this area. It occurs where an alpine glacier gouges its valley floor unevenly. *Clear Creek Falls* and *Sylvia Falls* lie along breaks probably formed in this manner. Waterfalls that drop from *hanging valleys* are also common around Mount Rainier. Hanging valleys formed when small, tributary glaciers could not erode their valleys as deeply as the large, main glaciers. Therefore, the floor of a smaller glacial valley will be high above that of a main glacial valley where the two meet. *Comet Falls* and *Spray Falls* are dramatic examples of this type.

I. Carbon River

Vacationers visiting the region for the first time usually overlook this northwestern portion of Mount Rainier National Park, favoring instead better known locations like Sunrise and Paradise. Local residents call it "Our Own Little Corner of the Mountain." But wherever you are from, you will be welcomed. Drive to the city of Buckley on S.R. 410, then go south along S.R. 165 through the historic mining towns of Wilkeson and Carbonado. About 3 miles south of Carbonado, the road forks. Bear left and follow the highway along the Carbon River for another 9 miles to the park entrance, where the road turns to gravel.

Ranger Falls ☆☆☆☆   ③ 🥾
Form: tiered   *Magnitude:* 70   *Watershed:* sm
Elevation: 2800 feet   *USGS Map:* Mowich Lake (1971)

This entry tumbles a total of 100 to 125 feet along Ranger Creek. The form is eye-catching because the lower portion splits into twin falls. Proceed for 3 miles beyond the park entrance to Green Lake Trailhead. The trail ascends moderately for about 1 mile to a marked spur leading to the falls.

Chenuis Falls ☆☆   ① 🥾
Form: cascade   *Magnitude:* 17 (l)   *Watershed:* med
Elevation: 2180 feet   *USGS Map:* Mowich Lake (1971)

Water slides 70 to 100 feet across rock layers along Chenuis Creek. Drive 0.5 mile past Green Lake Trailhead (described previously) to a parking turnout adjacent to the Carbon River. The falls is only 0.2 mile away. A log bridge provides access across the river.

Ipsut Falls ☆☆☆   ① 🥾
Form: tiered   *Magnitude:* 38   *Watershed:* sm
Elevation: 2600 feet   *USGS Map:* Mowich Lake (1971)

This double falls along Ipsut Creek totals 40 to 60 feet. Please do not stray from the trail as the creek is the source of water for the campground. Drive just past Ipsut Camp to the trailhead at the end of the park road. Bear right (south) and hike along the Wonderland Trail a little way past the trailhead, to a signed spur trail leading to the falls.

Carbon Falls (u) ☆☆   ③ 🥾
Form: tiered   *Magnitude:* 50
Watershed: vsm
Elevation: 3300 feet   *USGS Map:*
Mowich Lake (1971 nl)

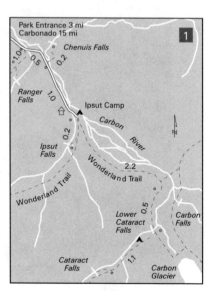

The only view of a tributary creek tumbling toward the Carbon River is from across the valley. This waterfall is best viewed during the afternoon, if it is not overcast. Its rating decreases during the low water periods of late summer.

Hike 2.2 miles from the Ipsut Camp trailhead along the Wonderland Trail. Soon after you leave the forested area and catch sight of the slopes across the river, the waterfall comes into view: first the lower falls, then the upper portion.

Cataract Falls ☆☆☆   ③ 🚶

Form: segmented   *Magnitude:* 63   *Watershed:* sm
Elevation: 4020 feet   *USGS Map:* Mowich Lake (1971)

Cataract Creek drops a total of 50 to 75 feet. In 1988, a major blowdown of trees blocked access to the spur trail and the descent. Before embarking, check with a ranger on the current status of the route.

Proceed 0.5 mile along the Wonderland Trail past the viewing area for Carbon Falls (described previously), 2.7 miles from the trailhead. Pass Lower Cataract Falls (described later) and at the trail junction follow the right (west) fork. The left fork goes to the toe of Carbon Glacier, which extends to a lower elevation than any other glacier in the continental United States. Hike 1.1 miles to a signed spur trail which quickly leads to the falls.

Cataract Falls

Others: *Lower Cataract Falls* (u) ☆ USGS Mowich Lake (1971 ns). Cataract Creek tumbles a total of 50 to 75 feet. Proceed 0.5 mile along the Wonderland Trail past the viewing area for Carbon Falls (described previously). This entry can be seen from a footbridge crossing on the way toward Carbon Glacier.

2. Mowich Lake

Drive to the city of Buckley via S.R. 410 and turn south on S.R. 165 toward Wilkeson and Carbonado. Three miles past Carbonado, turn right on the gravel extension of S.R. 165. This road, which has imposing views of Mount Rainier, ends at Mowich Lake, just inside the boundary of Mount Rainier National Park, in 16 miles.

Spray Falls ☆☆☆☆☆   ③ 🏃

Form: fan   *Magnitude:* 98   *Watershed:* sm (g)
Elevation: 5100 feet   *USGS Map:* Mowich Lake (1971)

This enormous display descends 300 to 350 feet along Spray Creek and is 50 to 80 feet wide. It is fed mostly from meltwaters of snowfields in Spray Park. Reach the falls by taking a substantial but not overly difficult hike of 2.3 miles. Embark upon the Wonderland Trail at the southeast end of Mowich Lake and proceed for 0.4 mile. Turn left onto Spray Park Trail and follow it for 1.6 miles. Finally, turn right at Spray Falls Trail. You will be rewarded with an exciting view of the spectacle 0.3 mile farther.

Spray Falls

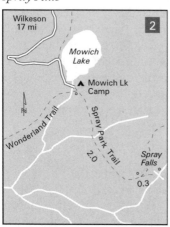

3. Eatonville

Eatonville lies just outside Mount Rainier National Park on S.R. 161, northeast of S.R. 7. The following entry is located within Charles L. Pack Experimental Forest.

Little Mashel Falls ★★   ③, and 🚶

Form: horsetail   *Magnitude:* 28   *Watershed:* lg
Elevation: 920 feet   *USGS Map:* Eatonville (1990)

The Little Mashel River slides steeply 25 to 30 feet over a rock escarpment. Not recommended for children, as it is in an undeveloped locale with no guardrails. From downtown Eatonville take Center Street East for 2.2 miles to a large unsigned turnout on the right side of the road. Park at the far end. Find a well-worn path and follow it down the hill to a set of railroad tracks. Cross the tracks and continue along the path to the creek. Proceed downstream to a concrete slab above the falls. Make your way down the least steep part of the escarpment, which is situated to your left, to airy views from the base of the cataract.

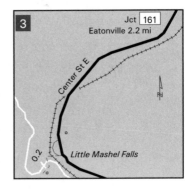

4. Nisqually River

The south-central part of Mount Rainier National Park has a wealth of waterfalls. The area is bounded on the west by Cougar Rock Campground and on the east by the entrance to the Paradise area.

Carter Falls ★★★   ② 🚶

Form: horsetail   *Magnitude:* 61   *Watershed:* med (g)
Elevation: 3650 feet   *USGS Map:* Mt. Rainier West (1971)

This 50- to 80-foot entry is named for Harry Carter, who built much of the early Paradise Trail. Drive along S.R. 706 to Cougar Rock Campground, located 8 miles east of the Nisqually entrance. Embark eastward on the Wonderland Trail, which you can access just across the highway from the camp entrance. A sign directs you toward the falls, but you must first cross the Nisqually River on one of two footbridges. Hike 1.3 miles up the trail to the falls.

Madcap Falls ★★   ② 🚶

Form: cascade   *Magnitude:* 22   *Watershed:* med (g)
Elevation: 3800 feet   *USGS Map:* Mt. Rainier West (1971)

The Paradise River tumbles 20 to 30 feet. The USGS topographic map shows this feature about 0.2 mile farther upstream, but nothing resembling falls could be found when I field-truthed this entry. Continue a short distance past Carter Falls (described previously) to an unsigned spur trail. Take it 0.1 mile to views of this cascade, a total of 1.4 miles from the trailhead.

Narada Falls ☆☆☆☆

Form: horsetail *Magnitude:* 91 *Watershed:* sm (g)
Elevation: 4400 feet *USGS Map:* Mt. Rainier West (1971)

This popular tourist attraction veils 168 feet along bedrock before plunging another 73 feet to its base. A branch of the Theosophical Society of Tacoma named the fails after their guru, Narada, in 1893. Drive to the signed parking area located along S.R. 706 about 1 mile west of the entrance to the Paradise area. Alternatively, one may continue hiking 1.5 miles along the Wonderland Trail past Carter Falls (described previously).

Middle Van Trump Falls (u) ☆☆

Form: plunge *Magnitude:* 61 (h) *Watershed:* sm (g)
Elevation: 4520 feet *USGS Map:* Mt. Rainier West (1971 nl)

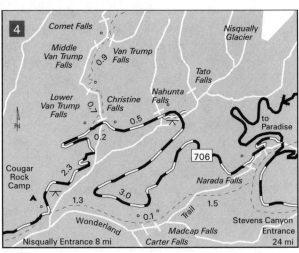

Van Trump Creek possesses several series of falls. Four major descents are described in this and the next two capsule summaries. This particular waterfall drops 40 to 50 feet and is easily seen from a few feet off the trail. Drive 2.3 miles east of Cougar Rock Campground to the signed Comet Falls Trailhead. The trail is steep but safe, ascending 1,400 feet in 1.6 miles. It is usually free of snow after mid-July. The roar of *Lower Van Trump Falls* (u), USGS Mt. Rainier West (1971 nl), will be heard after the first 0.7 mile. The shape of the canyon hides it from view. The Middle Falls will be encountered in an additional 0.8 mile.

Van Trump Falls (u) ☆☆☆

Form: tiered *Magnitude:* 54 (h) *Watershed:* sm (g)
Elevation: 4600 feet *USGS Map:* Mt. Rainier West (1971 nl)

Van Trump Creek crashes 60 to 90 feet in tiered fashion. Do not give up hiking at Middle Van Trump Falls (described previously). This double drop is only 0.2 mile farther, and you are less than 100 yards away from the best of them all.

Comet Falls ☆☆☆☆☆

Form: plunge   *Magnitude:* 106 (h)   *Watershed:* sm (g)
Elevation: 5100 feet   *USGS Map:* Mt. Rainier West (1971)

This spectacular 320-foot plunge is a classic example of a waterfall descending from a hanging valley, an escarpment that occurs where a tributary glacier did not erode as deeply as its larger relative.

The viewpoint for this descent is just beyond Van Trump Falls (described previously), 1.6 miles from the trailhead. If you haven't had enough aerobic

Comet Falls

exercise by now, Comet Falls Trail continues steeply for another mile toward the top of the cataract.

Christine Falls ✫✫✫

Form: plunge   *Magnitude:* 57   *Watershed:* sm (g)
Elevation: 3680 feet   *USGS Map:* Mt. Rainier West (1971)

The stone masonry of the highway bridge forms a picturesque frame for this 40- to 60-foot drop along the lower reaches of Van Trump Creek. Drive along S.R. 706 eastward past Comet Falls Trailhead for 0.2 mile to the turnout on the east side of the bridge. Stairs lead quickly down to a view of this entry.

Tato Falls ✫✫

②🚶

Form: horsetail   *Magnitude:* 45   *Watershed:* sm (g)
Elevation: 4280 feet   *USGS Map:* Mt. Rainier West (1971)

Only a moderately distant view is available of this 40- to 60-foot display as it drops along an unnamed tributary of the Nisqually River. Park at an old gravel spur road 0.5 mile east of Van Trump Creek bridge on S.R. 706. Walk along the gravel spur 0.3 mile to its end. Look upvalley and to the left for the falls. Surrounding vegetation obscures closer views.

Others: *Nahunta Falls* ✫ USGS Mt. Rainier West (1971). An unnamed tributary of the Nisqually River steeply cascades 150 to 175 feet. It reduces to a trickle during low discharge periods of late summer. Park at an old gravel spur 0.5 mile east of Van Trump Creek bridge on S.R. 706 and look up the side of the slope.

5. Paradise

At 5,800 feet of elevation, Paradise is the highest point to which you can drive on Mount Rainier's southern face. Travel 15 miles east from the

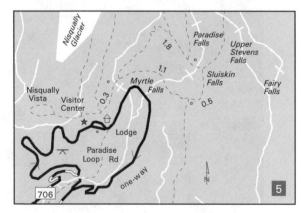

Nisqually entrance or 24 miles west from the Stevens Canyon entrance along the park's extension of S.R. 706. The contemporary-looking visitors center and the traditionally rustic Paradise Inn are located about 1.5 miles off the main road and are accessible via the Paradise Loop Road.

Myrtle Falls ★★★   ① 🚶

Form: fan   *Magnitude:* 34 (l)   *Watershed:* sm (g)
Elevation: 5560 feet   *USGS Map:* Mt. Rainier East (1971 ns)

This entry provides one of the signature views of Mount Rainier, as Edith Creek tumbles 60 to 80 feet in the foreground. Find the Skyline Trail

Myrtle Falls

which begins next to Paradise Inn. Walk an easy 0.3 mile to a stairway, descending to the overlook for a superb view.

Sluiskin Falls ☆☆☆   ③, 🚶 or 🚶

Form: fan   *Magnitude:* 40 (l)   *Watershed:* sm (g)
Elevation: 5920 feet   *USGS Map:* Mt. Rainier East (1971)

This 300-foot slide along the Paradise River is named for an Indian guide who aided Hazard Stevens and P. B. Van Trump in the first recorded climb of Mount Rainier in 1870. Just past Myrtle Falls (described previously), take the southern loop of the Skyline Trail to its junction with Lakes Trail, 1.4 miles from the trailhead. Bear left at the trail junction. Proceed another 0.5 mile, passing in succession the Paradise Glacier Trailhead, the Stevens-Van Trump historic monument, and a footbridge crossing the Paradise River. Proceed a few hundred yards farther to a view of the top portion of the falls. Short side spurs from the trail provide full views. Children and nervous adults should stay on the main trail, since the spurs end abruptly at cliffs. Either return the way you came or continue on for 2.1 miles to complete the northern portion of the loop.

Others: *Paradise Falls* (u) ☆ USGS Mt. Rainier East (1971 nl). A moderately distant view of a 30- to 50-foot descent near the headwaters of Paradise River. From the footbridge near Sluiskin Falls (described previously) look upstream to see the falls.

6. Stevens Canyon

It is no exaggeration to say that the National Park Service's eastward extension of S.R. 706 is one of the most scenic roads ever engineered. The Stevens Canyon stretch is not as convoluted as other sections of the route, but its construction was just as daring an undertaking. The view across the canyon from the Wonderland Trail confirms that judgment. The fine line of the highway can be seen cut into the side of Stevens Ridge over 400 feet above the canyon floor.

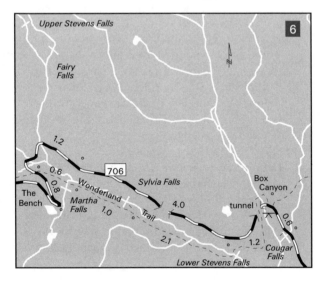

Martha Falls ★★★★   ②,

Form: fan   *Magnitude:* 80   *Watershed:* sm
Elevation: 3680 feet   *USGS Map:* Mt. Rainier East (1971)

Water spills 126 to 150 feet along Unicorn Creek. It can be viewed at a moderate distance from the highway or close-up from the trailside. Sightseers in cars can drive along S.R. 706 to the Martha Falls wayside, located 2 miles northeast of The Bench and 4 miles west of Box Canyon. Hikers can access the Wonderland Trail where it intersects the highway 0.8 mile north of The Bench. Embark upon the trailhead on the east side of the road, where the path winds moderately down 0.6 mile to a footbridge overlooking the falls.

Sylvia Falls ★★★

Form: fan   *Magnitude:* 38 (l)   *Watershed:* med (g)
Elevation: 3080 feet   *USGS Map:* Mt. Rainier East (1971)

Stevens Creek tumbles 80 to 100 feet over a rock step within Stevens Canyon. Continue along the Wonderland Trail past Martha Falls (described previously) for an additional mile. Look for an unsigned, but well-worn, spur trail that quickly leads to a vantage of the descent.

Lower Stevens Falls (u) ★★

Form: cascade   *Magnitude:* 23   *Watershed:* med (g)
Elevation: 2580 feet   *USGS Map:* Mt. Rainier East (1971 nl)

Water cascades 30 to 40 feet over granite bedrock along Stevens Creek. Hike 1.2 miles south from Box Canyon on the Wonderland Trail, or continue 2.1 miles past Sylvia Falls (described previously) for a total of 3.7 miles from the westward trailhead, to the footbridge above the falls.

Cougar Falls ★★★   ③

Form: plunge   *Magnitude:* 65   *Watershed:* med
Elevation: 2800 feet   *USGS Map:* Mt. Rainier East (1971)

This impressive 100- to 125-foot plunge shoots through a tight gorge. Recommended for adults only. Drive southeast from Box Canyon along S.R. 706 for 0.6 mile to the unsigned turnout immediately northwest of the Nickel Creek bridge. Walk down the primitive trail to good direct views of the falls in 0.1 mile. Stay away from the bare rock surfaces near the creek. There are no guardrails along the precipitous rim, which slopes sharply into the steep canyon!

Others: *Fairy Falls* ★ USGS Mt. Rainier East (1971). One of the highest recorded falls in the world is not highly regarded because there are no close views of it. Two silvery white threads drop from Stevens Basin, plummeting 700 feet as two large horsetails. Drive to the turnout at The Bench, located 5.5 miles east of Paradise or 6 miles west of Box Canyon. Look up the valley toward Stevens Basin, which is situated below and to the right (east) of your

Lower Stevens Falls

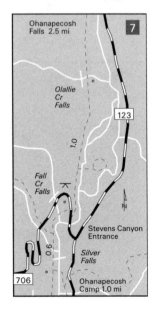

view of Mount Rainier. Fairy Falls can also be viewed from the Skyline Trail (see the Myrtle Falls entry and map in the previous chapter subsection).

Upper Stevens Falls (u) ☆ USGS Mt. Rainier East (1971 nl). Stevens Creek drops 200 to 300 feet. For a distant view, drive to The Bench and look just to the left of Fairy Falls.

7. Upper Ohanapecosh

This popular area near the southeast entrance of Mount Rainier National Park boasts hot springs and a stand of forest giants in addition to waterfalls. Walk a short distance from Ohanapecosh Campground to the natural setting of the hot springs. Feel dwarfed by the Grove of the Patriarchs between the Stevens Canyon entrance and Olallie Creek.

Silver Falls ☆☆☆

Form: punchbowl   *Magnitude:* 55 (h)   *Watershed:* lg
Elevation: 2000 feet   *USGS Map:* Chinook Pass (1987)

Rushing water thunders 30 to 40 feet into a pool. Limit your views to those available from the trail and designated vantages. While the falls do not look dangerous, the tumultuous river has claimed the lives of many who failed to heed the posted warnings.

From the Stevens Canyon entrance drive 0.3 mile south along S.R. 123 to the East Side Trailhead on the right (west) side of the road. A short trail leads down to the bottom of the gorge and the falls along the Ohanapecosh River. A pair of trails from Ohanapecosh Campground also provide a leisurely 1-mile stroll to the falls. There are three smaller descents immediately upstream and one downstream from the main falls.

Fall Creek Falls (u) ☆☆

Form: horsetail   *Magnitude:* 24 (l)   *Watershed:* vsm
Elevation: 2280 feet   *USGS Map:* Chinook Pass (1987 ns)

Fall Creek drops 30 to 50 feet, nearly spraying onto the highway before flowing beneath it. It deserves a lower rating during the low-water periods of late summer. A car-window glimpse of this entry can be gained from S.R. 706 just 0.2 mile from the Stevens Canyon entrance. If you wish to linger, stop at the parking area near the entrance and walk up the road.

Others: *Olallie Creek Falls* (u) ☆ USGS Chinook Pass (1987 nl). A modest 30- to 50-foot cascade along Olallie Creek. Hike north along the East Side Trail from the parking area near the Stevens Canyon entrance or from Silver Falls (described previously). One mile north of the highway, the East Side Trail crosses Olallie Creek, with the cataract visible upstream from the footbridge.

8. Chinook Creek

This pleasant collection of waterfalls lies along a sparsely used, but easily accessible trail system within Mount Rainier National Park. Drive to the Owyhigh Lakes Trailhead next to S.R. 123, located 6.5 miles north of the Stevens Canyon entrance and 4.5 miles south of Cayuse Pass. Alternatively, hikers can continue north past Olallie Creek (refer to the previous subsection) along the East Side Trail.

Deer Creek Falls (u) ★★★   ② 🚶

Form: cascade   *Magnitude:* 45   *Watershed:* med
Elevation: 3000 feet   *USGS Map:* Chinook Pass (1987 nl)

Deer Creek cascades steeply 60 to 80 feet on the way to its confluence with Chinook Creek. Wind down Owyhigh Lakes Trail, reaching Deer Creek in 0.2 mile. Look back upstream into the small gorge to see the falls.

Chinook Creek Falls (u) ★★   ③ 🚶

Form: cascade   *Magnitude:* 54   *Watershed:* med
Elevation: 3120 feet   *USGS Map:* Chinook Pass (1987 nl)

This series of steep cascades totaling 75 to 100 feet descends from Chinook Creek. Views will be partially obstructed by trees in the foreground. From Deer Creek Falls (described previously), continue hiking a short distance farther to the East Side Trail. Turn right at the junction and proceed 0.2 mile, passing the junction with Owyhigh Lakes Trail. Go 0.5 mile farther, where the falls will be seen just before the trail switchbacks uphill.

Kotsuck Creek Falls (u) ★★★★   ③, 🚶 and 🚶

Form: segmented   *Magnitude:* 65   *Watershed:* sm
Elevation: 3520 feet   *USGS Map:* Chinook Pass (1987 nl)

Kotsuck Creek zigzags 125 to 150 feet over a bulbous escarpment. The best views, however, require a short bushwhack not recommended for children. From its junction with the East Side Trail (described previously), ascend moderately along Owyhigh Lakes Trail. An uninspiring view at the top of the falls will be reached in 1.4 miles. For a better vista, retrace your steps down the trail, then carefully make your way through the woods to the canyon rim facing the falls.

Stafford Falls ★★★   ② 🚶

Form: punchbowl   *Magnitude:* 48   *Watershed:* lg
Elevation: 2700 feet   *USGS Map:* Chinook Pass (1987)

Water plummets 30 to 40 feet into a large pool along Chinook Creek. Follow the East Side Trail south from its junction with the Deer Creek access (described previously). An easy 1.5 miles later, an unsigned but well-worn spur trail quickly leads to this pretty descent.

Ohanapecosh Falls (u) ★★★★   ③ 🚶

Form: tiered   *Magnitude:* 56   *Watershed:* med (g)
Elevation: 2400 feet   *USGS Map:* Chinook Pass (1987 nl)

This tiered punchbowl waterfall drops 50 to 75 feet along the grayish waters of the Ohanapecosh River. The color of the water is due to ground-up rock called *glacial flour* being carried by this glacier-fed stream. Continue south past Stafford Falls (described previously) for 1.6

miles to the point where the East Side Trail crosses the Ohanapecosh River, a total of 3.5 miles from S.R. 123, or 2.5 miles north of Olallie Creek Falls (described in the previous subsection). The best view is just south of the footbridge, a few feet off the trail.

9. Camp Sheppard

Camp Sheppard is a Boy Scouts of America site, but visitors are welcome to use the trail system. In fact, the Boy Scouts blazed the pathways for that purpose. The entrance to the camp is along S.R. 410, about 11 miles south of Greenwater and 5 miles north of Mount Rainier National Park.

Skookum Falls ☆☆

Form: tiered   *Magnitude:* 32 (l)   *Watershed:* vsm
Elevation: 2920 feet   *USGS Map:* Sun Top (1986 nl)

Skookum Creek can be seen from a moderate distance as silvery threads descending 150 to 200 feet in two primary tiers. Located within White River Ranger District of Mount Baker–Snoqualmie National Forest. Before entering Camp Sheppard, drive 1.4 miles north of the Boy Scout camp along S.R. 410 to an unsigned turnout. A cross-valley view of the cataract can be gained from this point.

Others: *Snoquera Falls* ☆ USGS Sun Top (1986 nl). The impressiveness of this thin 200- to 300-foot waterfall decreases from spring to autumn. From the parking area of Camp Sheppard, follow Moss Lake Nature Trail to the east side of a small lake. Take the designated Snoquera Falls Loop Trail #1167 to the falls in 1.5 miles. Alternatively, hike from the north end of Trail #1167 via White River Trail #1199.

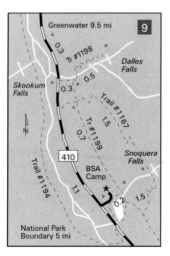

Dalles Falls (u) ☆ USGS Sun Top (1986 ns). Each portion of this double waterfall can be viewed separately. Both tiers are reduced to trickles during the low-water periods of late summer. Continue hiking past Snoquera Falls along Snoquera Falls Trail #1167 (described previously) to its north end, where Dalles Creek Trail #1198 is met. This trail ascends steeply but safely through switchbacks to the top of The Dalles Gorge. In 0.3 mile, a short spur trail leads to the lower falls. In 0.2 mile more, the upper falls can be seen from the main trail. The return hike along White River Trail #1199 is 1.5 miles to the parking area, or 3.2 miles via the Snoquera Falls route.

10. Dewey Lake

The following obscure entry is located within William O. Douglas Wilderness, administered by Wenatchee National Forest.

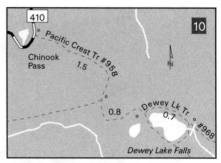

Dewey Lake Falls (u) ☆ USGS Cougar Lake (1988 ns). The outlet from Dewey Lake trickles down a 25- to 35-foot escarpment. Departing from Chinook Pass, follow Pacific Crest Trail #958 eastward 2.3 miles to Dewey Lake Trail #968 and turn left. Hike past the north end of the lake to the falls in 0.7 mile.

11. Rainier Valley

For an excellent example of a glacial trough shaped by the enormous erosive powers of an alpine glacier, look down from Chinook Pass and admire the characteristic steep-sided, U-shaped form of Rainier Valley. The glacier has long since disappeared, and the Rainier Fork American River flows along the valley floor. The pass was also formed by glacial activity and is what is known geomorphically as a *col,* a notch eroded in a ridge by glaciers flowing from either side.

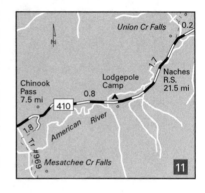

Mesatchee Creek Falls ☆☆☆   ④

Form: horsetail   *Magnitude:* 72   *Watershed:* sm
Elevation: 3840 feet   *USGS Map:* Norse Peak (1988 nl)

Water shimmers 100 feet along Mesatchee Creek. Located within William O. Douglas Wilderness, administered by Wenatchee National Forest. Drive 7.5 miles east from Chinook Pass on S.R. 410 and turn south at Wenatchee National Forest Road #1710. Drive 0.3 mile to the end of this gravel route to the trailhead for Mesatchee Creek Trail #969. After crossing Morse Creek and the American River, the trail steepens considerably and reaches an open vista of the descent after 1.5 miles.

Union Creek Falls ☆☆☆   ②

Form: horsetail   *Magnitude:* 64   *Watershed:* med
Elevation: 3520 feet   *USGS Map:* Goose Prairie (1988)

This picturesque 40- to 60-foot drop along Union Creek is located within Norse Peak Wilderness, administered by Wenatchee National Forest. Turn into the parking and picnic area at Union Creek Trail #956, located 10

Mesatchee Creek Falls

miles east of Chinook Pass. Follow the trail about 0.2 mile to a well-traveled but unmarked spur that quickly leads to the cataract.

12. Naches

The following three waterfalls are situated within the rain shadow of the Cascades in ponderosa pine and Douglas-fir forests administered by Naches Ranger District, Wenatchee National Forest, and thus are best visited during a wet spell. The point of departure for all three is the junction of S.R. 410 and Little Naches Road #19, located 23.5 miles east of Chinook Pass and 38 miles northwest of Yakima.

West Quartz Creek Falls ☆☆   ② 🚶

Form: plunge   *Magnitude:* 35 (l)   *Watershed:* vsm
Elevation: 3160 feet   *USGS Map:* Mount Clifty (1987 ns)

Low volume West Quartz Creek plummets 150 to 175 feet into a canyon. Drive about 2.7 miles north along Little Naches Road #19 and turn left onto Road #1902, proceeding 0.4 mile to gravel Road #1920. Turn left again and drive 1.1 miles, then bear right onto Road #1922 and go 0.7 mile to the creek crossing. Walk down the trail 0.1 mile to trailside views back into the falls. Be careful at the unfenced canyon rim, which drops a sheer 200 feet.

Lower Devil Creek Falls (u) ☆☆   ② 🚶

Form: tiered   *Magnitude:* 16 (l)   *Watershed:* med
Elevation: 2720 feet   *USGS Map:* Cliffdell (1987 nl)

By itself, this 20- to 30-foot falls would deserve a lower rating, but the unique geology of this area is not to be missed. The cataract is viewed from within a recess shaped like an amphitheater. Immediately downstream is Boulder Cave, which was formed when a landslide blocked the course of Devil Creek and the stream eventually eroded a tunnel through the debris. A flashlight is required to explore the cavern.

Drive south on S.R. 410 for 3.3 miles beyond the junction with Little Naches Road #19. Depart the main road here, turning right to cross the bridge over the Naches River, then turn right again, heading north on Naches River Road #1704. Park in 1.2 miles at Boulder Cave Picnic Area. Hike an easy 0.5 mile along the canyon rim, then drop down to the base of the descent.

Others: *Horsetail Falls* ☆ USGS Cliffdell (1987). Water from an unnamed tributary descends 40 to 50 feet from cliffs toward the Little Naches River. This is a pretty falls during early spring and late autumn, but it is otherwise only a trickle.

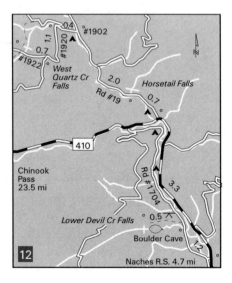

Drive about 0.7 mile north of S.R. 410 along Little Naches Road #19, then turn right (east) onto a short turnout.

13. Rimrock Lake

The Rimrock Lake area is administered by Tieton Ranger District, Wenatchee National Forest. Tieton Ranger Station, the primary reference point for the following falls, is located 34 miles west of Yakima or 17 miles east of White Pass on U.S. 12.

Clear Lake Falls ✭✭

Form: tiered   *Magnitude:* 33   *Watershed:* lg
Elevation: 2960 feet   *USGS Map:* Spiral Butte (1988 ns)

Water tumbles 40 to 60 feet at the outlet from Clear Lake and flows toward Rimrock Lake. Ten miles west of the ranger station turn south off U.S. 12 onto Tieton Road #12. Drive 0.8 mile to Clear Lake Road #740 and turn left. The pair of cascades is 0.4 mile away and is divided by a bridge spanning the drainage.

South Fork Falls ✭✭✭

Form: block   *Magnitude:* 66   *Watershed:* lg
Elevation: 3840 feet   *USGS Map:* Pinegrass Ridge (1988 nl)

A misty vista makes this modest 30- to 40-foot curtain along the South Fork Tieton River an unforgettable experience. Drive 0.5 mile west of

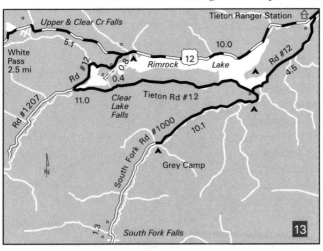

the ranger station, then turn south on Tieton Road #12. After 4.5 miles, turn left (south) on South Fork Road #1000. Continue for 11.4 miles (1.3 miles past the bridge over Bear Creek) to an unsigned turnout and a moderately steep trail that leads to the river in 0.2 mile.

Upper Clear Creek Falls (u) ✭✭✭✭

Form: fan   *Magnitude:* 74   *Watershed:* med
Elevation: 4000 feet   *USGS Map:* Spiral Butte (1988 nl)

Every waterfall collector should see this unusual configuration. One side of the 60- to 80-foot falls horsetails, while the other side veils

South Fork Falls

downward into a pool adjacent to the main portion of the creek. Drive 2.5 miles east of White Pass along U.S. 12 to the signed Clear Creek Falls parking area. Take the short trail to the right (west) a few yards past the parking area to the fenced vista high above the falls.

Clear Creek Falls ☆☆☆☆☆
Form: plunge   *Magnitude:* 99   *Watershed:* med
Elevation: 3800 feet   *USGS Map:* Spiral Butte (1988)
        Enjoy a grand canyon-rim view of this spectacular 300-foot plunge along Clear Creek. From the Clear Creek Falls parking area take the short trail to the left to the fenced viewpoint.

14. Lower Ohanapecosh
        Vacationers tend to zip past the northeast portion of Packwood Ranger District, Gifford Pinchot National Forest, on their way to Mount Rainier during the summer and to White Pass during the winter. Slow down. Better yet, stop and explore. The fine scenery includes, of course, waterfalls.

Lava Creek Falls ✮✮✮

Form: horsetail   *Magnitude:* 86   *Watershed:* med

Elevation: 2600 feet   *USGS Map:* Ohanapecosh Hot Springs (1989 nl)

These braids of water rushing 200 to 250 feet down the facing canyon wall are hard to see on sunny mid-days. Drive along U.S. 12 to an obscurely marked turnout 7.6 miles west of White Pass or 4.8 miles east of the junction with S.R. 123. A viewpoint overlooks the Clear Fork Cowlitz River canyon.

Upper Falls (u) ✮✮

Form: cascade   *Magnitude:* 35   *Watershed:* med

Elevation: 2180 feet   *USGS Map:* Ohanapecosh Hot Springs (1989 ns)

Rushing water skips 25 to 35 feet across slabs of bedrock on Summit Creek. From U.S. 12, 1.3 miles east of the junction with S.R. 123, turn north on Summit Creek Road #4510. Drive 2 miles farther and park at the unmarked turnout on the north side of the road. Follow the well-worn trail about 40 yards to these cascades.

Thunder Falls ✮✮✮   ③, 🚶 and 🚶

Form: fan   *Magnitude:* 72   *Watershed:* med

Elevation: 2120 feet   *USGS Map:* Ohanapecosh Hot Springs (1989 ns)

Close-up views of this 80-foot cataract spreading outward along Summit Creek are possible. From Upper Falls (described previously) continue along the path in the downstream direction. The way becomes steep toward the end, so it is recommended only for nimble hikers.

Fish Ladder Falls ✮✮✮   ④ 🚶

Form: horsetail   *Magnitude:* 48   *Watershed:* med

Elevation: 2760 feet   *USGS Map:* Ohanapecosh Hot Springs (1989)

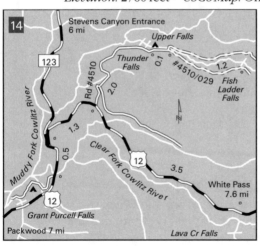

Peer from a canyon-rim vantage to enjoy this pristine 60-foot drop roaring along Summit Creek. Drive 0.1 mile past the trailhead for Thunder Falls (described previously) and bear right on dirt Road #4510/029. When last traveled, most of the 1.2-mile route was overgrown with shrubs. Park at a dry ravine near the end of the road. Walk up the route a short distance

Thunder Falls

and bear right at the junction, which continues 0.1 mile to the top of a small knoll at a fire pit. Bushwhack another 0.1 mile through a clearcut to an open vista hundreds of feet above the falls at an unguarded cliff. You may need to walk along the wooded canyon rim in one direction or the other to find the unmarked viewpoint.

Others: *Grant Purcell Falls* ✰ USGS Ohanapecosh Hot Springs (1989). Purcell Creek slides 75 to 100 feet across sloping bedrock. Enter La Wis Wis Campground, on the west side of U.S. 12, 0.5 mile south of its junction with S.R. 123. Park at the C-Loop Tent Site Area. A sign directs you to the trail, which leads shortly to the stream and its waterfall.

15. Johnson Creek

Rainbow Falls ✰✰   ③ 🏃

Form: plunge   *Magnitude:* 21 (t)   *Watershed:* vsm
Elevation: 2900 feet   *USGS Map:* Wahpenayo Peak (1989 nl)

    This 100-foot drop from an unnamed tributary of Johnson Creek is reduced to a trickle in late summer. Located in Packwood Ranger District, Gifford Pinchot National Forest. Leave U.S. 12 at Skate Creek Road #52, across from the Packwood Ranger Station. In 9 miles, just after Road #52 crosses Skate Creek for the second time, turn right (northeast) onto

Dixon Mountain Road #5260. Drive 1.7 miles farther and park along the road. Scramble 100 yards up the small draw to the base of the falls.

16. Silverbrook

Davis Creek Falls ☆☆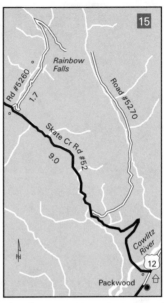

Form: horsetail   *Magnitude:*34
Watershed: med
Elevation: 1260 feet *USGS Map:*
Purcell Mtn (1989 ns)

Davis Creek tumbles 30 to 50 feet into a tight gorge within Randle Ranger District, Gifford Pinchot National Forest. Drive 5.7 miles east of Randle or 10 miles west of Packwood on U.S. 12. Turn north on County Road #90, which later turns into Davis Creek Road #63. In 1 mile, a bridge crosses 146 feet above the creek and its impressive gorge. Park across the bridge and find an obscure, unmarked trailhead about 20 yards north of the span. The trail is extremely short, soon ending at the unprotected rim of the gorge.

Hopkins Creek Falls (u) ☆☆   ① 🚶

Form: horsetail   *Magnitude:* 24 (l)   *Watershed:* sm
Elevation: 1600 feet   *USGS Map:* Purcell Mtn (1989 nl)

Water tumbles 50 to 75 feet in a narrow spot along Hopkins Creek. Likely located on and accessible via private property. Turn off U.S. 12 onto Silverbrook Road, 5.5 miles east of Randle or 11.4 miles west of Packwood. Park across the road from the first driveway to the right (east). The unmarked trailhead is obscured by vegetation. Search at the intersection of the road and the driveway. Once the trailhead is found, its well-worn path leads easily and quickly to the base of the cataract.

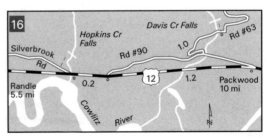

GIFFORD PINCHOT COUNTRY

Gifford Pinchot National Forest is named after the pioneer of professional forestry in the United States. Pinchot was the first chief of the U.S. Forest Service, from 1898 to 1910, serving under presidents McKinley, Roosevelt, and Taft. During his tenure, the entire forest service system and administrative structure were developed. Pinchot's leadership in the conservation movement of this period was important in developing a policy of preserving and managing the public lands of our nation.

There are 80 waterfalls known to occur within this region; 38 are referred to in this chapter. In addition, Wayne Parsons has informed me that over 150 falls have been inventoried within Gifford Pinchot National Forest. Most of them are small and inaccessible.

The waterfalls of this region are the result of many different combinations of geologic forces, including volcanism, mountain-building, and glaciation. For more information, see the introduction to the chapter on Mount Rainier.

With the establishment of Mount St. Helens National Volcanic Monument following the catastrophic eruption of the volcano on May 18, 1980, the region is more popular with tourists than ever before. But in addition to the Monument, there are many other recreational opportunities in the area, including, of course, waterfalls.

I. Cowlitz River

Cowlitz Falls ☆ USGS Cowlitz Falls (1993). More like rapids than falls, as the Cowlitz River descends 5 to 10 feet along its broad expanse. Access is

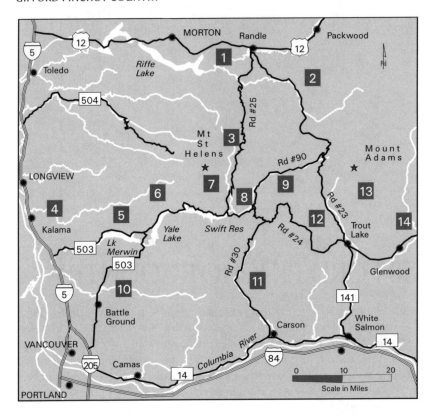

likely on private property. Leave U.S. 12 at Savio Road, located 2.5 miles west of Randle and 13 miles east of Morton. Proceed south on Kiona Road and drive 2.5 miles to Falls Road. Turn right (west) and drive 6 miles farther to a point where many spur roads join Falls Road. Turn left and continue south on a spur, then bear left (east) on a dirt road above the Cowlitz River. Park along a wide stretch of road about 0.9 mile from the maze of route intersections. Walk down the short, steep slope to a view of the cascades from a rocky bank next to the river.

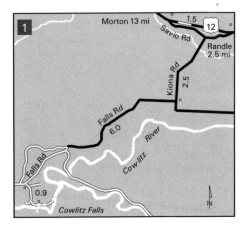

2. North Fork Cispus River

Several falls occur along tributaries to the North Fork Cispus River, with
their flows decreasing to a trickle as summer progresses. All are located within
Randle Ranger District.

Yozoo Creek Falls ★★

Form: fan   *Magnitude:* 18 (l)   *Watershed:* vsm
Elevation: 3000 feet   *USGS Map:* Blue Lake (1970 ns)

A roadside vantage is offered of water veiling 25 to 40 feet from
Yozoo Creek. Turn south off U.S. 12 onto Randle–Lewis River Road #25
about 1.3 miles west of Randle Ranger Station; after 1 mile, turn left (east)
on Randle–Trout Lake Road #23. Drive 10.5 miles, then bear left on North
Fork Cispus Road #22. After 5.8 miles, turn right on Timonium Road #78 and
continue for 3.4 miles to reach the falls.

Others: *Initial Falls* (u) ★ USGS Blue Lake (1970 ns). An unnamed stream
slides 25 to 35 feet down the mountainside. This is the first cataract that will
be encountered along the right (south) side of the Timonium Road #78
(described previously), 2.7 miles past the junction with North Fork Cispus
Road #22.

Grouse Creek Falls ★ USGS Blue Lake (1970 ns). Grouse Creek slides 40
to 50 feet next to the forest road. Proceed 0.9 mile past Yozoo Creek Falls
(described previously).

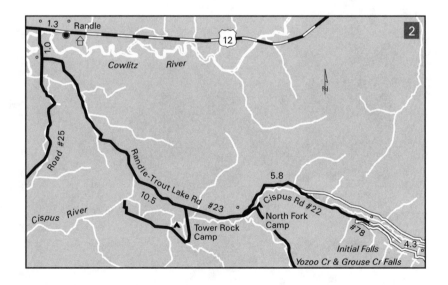

3. Mount St. Helens

The following cataracts are all in close proximity to the volcano. All but Iron Creek Falls are situated in the blast zone of the 1980 eruption.

Harmony Falls ☆☆   ④ 🚶

Form: fan   *Magnitude:* 15 (l)   *Watershed:* vsm
Elevation: 3480 feet   *USGS Map:* Spirit Lake East (1984)

This waterfall, which formerly fell 50 feet into Spirit Lake, was significantly altered in appearance by the catastrophic eruption of Mount St. Helens in 1980. The appearance of the falls will continue to change as its watershed matures along with successional changes in the accompanying vegetative cover.

Turn south off U.S. 12 about 1.3 miles west of the Randle Ranger Station onto Randle–Lewis River Road #25. Follow Road #25 for 20 miles until you reach Spirit Lake–Iron Creek Road #99, then turn right (west). In just under 5 miles enter the National Volcanic Monument and continue on Road #99 to Harmony Viewpoint, 4.2 miles south of the route's junction with Road #26.

Harmony Falls

The current 40- to 60-foot cataract is located at the end of Harmony Falls Trail, a moderately steep hike of 1 strenuous mile.

Iron Creek Falls ☆☆☆   ② 🚶

Form: punchbowl   *Magnitude:* 48   *Watershed:* med
Elevation: 2740 feet   *USGS Map:* French Butte (1965 ns)

Iron Creek hurtles 25 to 35 feet into a small pool. Formerly accessible only to bushwhackers, this entry is now reachable by a short path constructed by the Randle Ranger District. Look for a signed turnout along the east side of Randle–Lewis River Road #25 (described previously), located 0.4 mile past the junction with Big Creek Road #2517 and 0.4 mile before Spirit Lake–Iron Creek Road #99.

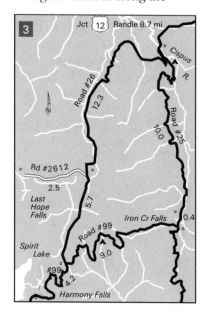

Others: *Last Hope Falls* ☆ USGS Spirit Lake East (1984 ns). A distant cross-valley view of water steeply cascading 70 feet from an unnamed tributary into the headwaters of Green River. Located outside the National Volcanic Monument, but within another part of Randle Ranger District devastated by the eruption of Mount St. Helens. At Cispus River on Road #25 (described previously) turn right onto Road #26. Proceed 12.3 miles, then turn right onto Road #2612. Vantages of the falls are at the 2.5-mile end of the gravel road. Polar Star Mine is nearby, on your side of the valley. Look, but do not enter!

4. Kalama River Road

Marietta Falls ☆☆   🚂 or 🚗

Form: plunge   *Magnitude:* 30 (l)   *Watershed:* sm
Elevation: 60 feet   *USGS Map:* Kalama (1990)

Marietta Creek tumbles 75 to 100 feet into the Kalama River. Depart I-5 onto Kalama River Road, located 0.5 mile north of the town of Kalama.

Drive 4 miles east to a vantage point across the river from the falls. Unfortunately the only safe roadside view is from the car window, as there are no parking turnouts. For better views, bring an inner tube or canoe and

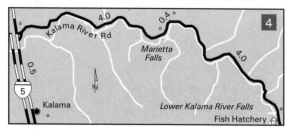

float down the main river. Launch your craft from access points 0.4 mile upstream from the falls.

Others: *Lower Kalama River Falls* ✫ USGS Woolford Creek (1993). The most enjoyment to be gained at this otherwise modest 15- to 25-foot cascade is watching fish negotiate it. Drive 8.4 miles east on Kalama River Road (described previously) to the marked turnoff to Kalama Falls Salmon Hatchery. The view is from the top of the falls at the end of the road.

5. Lake Merwin

Lake Merwin is the first of three reservoirs along the Lewis River. The other two are Yale Lake and Swift Reservoir. The valley sides are steep, with three waterfalls accessible in the area. All are outside the National Forest. Turn off I-5 at Woodland and drive east on S.R. 503.

Marble Creek Falls (u) ✫✫   ②, 🚶 and 🚶
Form: horsetail   *Magnitude:* 37   *Watershed:* sm
Elevation: 540 feet   *USGS Map:* Ariel (1994 nl)

Marble Creek descends 40 to 60 feet in an undeveloped area. Take S.R. 503 east 11.4 miles past Woodland, 1.2 miles beyond the junction signed for Merwin Dam, to Marble Creek. Park at the turnout on the east side of the culvert. Walk upstream through the lush meadow, then along a short footpath through a wooded tract.

Lower Marble Creek Falls (u) ✫✫   ②, 🚤 or 🚶
Form: plunge   *Magnitude:* 44   *Watershed:* sm
Elevation: 270 feet   *USGS Map:* Ariel (1994 nl)

Marble Creek pours 25 to 35 feet into Lake Merwin. A wooden deck offers a moderately distant view which is partly obscured when the surrounding vegetation is in leaf. Boaters have clearer views.

From the turnout for Marble Creek Falls (described previously), backtrack westward 1.2 miles along S.R. 503 to Merwin Village Road, signed for Merwin Dam. Drive 0.8 mile to the picnic area at the end of the road, park,

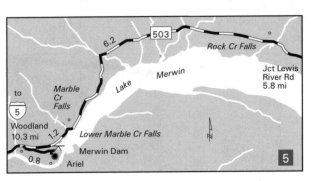

and head uplake until you reach the signed Marble Creek Trailhead. Maintained by Pacific Power and Light, the 0.4-mile route ends near the cataract.

Rock Creek Falls ☆☆

Form: horsetail   *Magnitude:* 72 (h)   *Watershed:* med
Elevation: 480 feet   *USGS Map:* Amboy (1993 nl)

Peer down into a rugged gorge to see this 75- to 100-foot cataract as well as the creek making a 180-degree bend around a rock outcrop near the falls. Drive S.R. 503 east 17.6 miles past Woodland (6.2 miles past Marble Creek Falls, described previously) and park on the east side of the Rock Creek bridge. When traffic is clear, walk across the steel-girded span. Continue 200 yards farther to modest vantage points of the gorge and its otherwise hidden descent.

6. Kalama Falls

Kalama Falls ☆☆

Form: punchbowl   *Magnitude:* 57   *Watershed:* lg
Elevation: 1300 feet   *USGS Map:* Cougar (1983)

The falls and the trail to it are owned by Weyerhaeuser Company, which invites visitation by the public. At the northeastern extreme of S.R. 503,

turn east on Lewis River Road #90 and go 4.4 miles to Merrill Lake Road #81. Drive north 6.3 miles, then turn left (west) on Kalama River Road #7500. Continue 1.7 miles farther, as shown on the accompanying map.

Kalama Falls

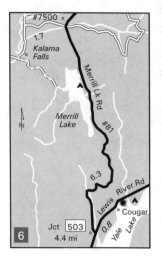

Park at any available turnout. A short trail leads down to the Kalama River, then upstream to the base of the falls.

7. Lava Canyon

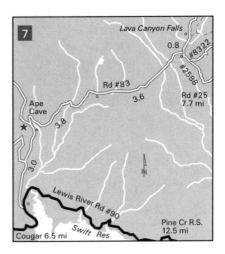

Understandably, most accounts have focused upon the destructive consequences of the 1980 eruption of Mount St. Helens. It is not so well known that the volcano also contributed to creating some new geographic features. Lava Canyon and its series of waterfalls, for instance, were unveiled when glacial meltwaters and mudflows sent forth by the eruption scoured away sediments that had long obscured a previous lava flow.

Lava Canyon Falls (u) ★★★   ② 🚶

Form: plunge   *Magnitude:* 46   *Watershed:* med
Elevation: 2440 feet   *USGS Map:* Smith Creek Butte (1983 nl)

The Muddy River rumbles through Lava Canyon. Part of Mount St. Helens National Volcanic Monument. Drive 6.5 miles eastward past the community of Cougar along Lewis River Road #90 (described previously). Turn

Lava Canyon Falls

left on Forest Road #83 and proceed 11.2 miles to a parking area for the canyon. Walk 0.4 miles to a footbridge overlooking the falls.

8. Eagle Cliff

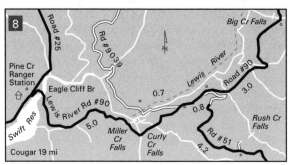

Located in close proximity to Mount St. Helens National Volcanic Monument, three of the following quartet of waterfalls are described in National Forest literature as points of interest. All of them are situated within a portion of Gifford Pinchot National Forest administered by the National Monument office.

Curly Creek Falls ★★★★

Form: tiered   *Magnitude:* 66 (h)   *Watershed:* med
Elevation: 1120 feet   *USGS Map:* Burnt Peak (1965 ns)

Despite its modest size, the natural arch that has been formed between the tiers of its 50- to 75-foot drop puts Curly Creek Falls on everyone's must-see list. Look closely; stream erosion is in the process of constructing a second arch from the bedrock. At the northeastern extreme of S.R. 503, turn east on Lewis River Road #90. Follow Lewis River Road #90 for 5 miles past the Eagle Cliff Bridge (19 miles east of Cougar). Turn left (west) on Road #9039 and drive about 0.7 mile to a parking area on the near side of the Lewis River. Walk across the bridge and follow the trail downstream for 0.3 mile to a view of the falls from across the river.

Miller Creek Falls ★★

Form: plunge   *Magnitude:* 52   *Watershed:* sm
Elevation: 1120 feet   *USGS Map:* Burnt Peak (1965 ns)

Miller Creek pours 40 to 60 feet into the Lewis River. Continue 0.1 mile beyond Curly Creek Falls (described previously). Find the cataract on the opposite side of the river from the trail.

Big Creek Falls ★★★★

Form: plunge   *Magnitude:* 76 (h)   *Watershed:* med
Elevation: 1600 feet   *USGS Map:* Burnt Peak (1965 ns)

The view from the rim of this natural gorge is breathtaking as Big Creek plummets 125 feet into an obscured pool. Be careful—there is no protection at the top of these sheer cliffs. Drive 3.8 miles beyond Road #9039 (described previously) along Lewis River Road #90, a total of 8.8 miles east from Eagle Cliff Bridge. Park on the north side of the marked crossing of Big Creek. Follow the path downstream a short distance along the south side of the gorge.

Rush Creek Falls ☆☆☆☆   ⑤

Form: fan   *Magnitude:* 89 (h)   *Watershed:* lg
Elevation: 1960 feet   *USGS Map:* Burnt Peak (1965 ns)

This is the toughest bushwhack in this book. Only those adults with a penchant for physical challenge should attempt to visit this 100- to 125-foot cataract. From Big Creek Falls (described previously), backtrack 3 miles along Lewis River Road #90 to Road #51. Proceed 4.2 miles along this route to a turnout next to County Stockpile 2–7, located 0.1 mile from mile marker 3. Park here. Walk a short distance past the stockpile and through a clear-cut to the valley rim. Carefully make your way down the steep slope, through the prickly devil's club ground cover that you will inevitably encounter. It is a 0.3-mile scramble. *Warning:* As you approach the creek, be sure to choose a route downstream from the falls, as the slopes are too treacherous adjacent to and immediately below the main cataract and the minor falls at its base.

9. Lewis River

The scenic quality of the following falls within Mount Adams Ranger District improves as one progresses downstream.

Twin Falls ☆☆

Form: tiered   *Magnitude:* 64   *Watershed:* sm
Elevation: 2660 feet   *USGS Map:* Steamboat Mtn (1970)

Twin Falls Creek is named for the successive 15- to 20-foot punchbowls that occur above its confluence with the Lewis River. Drive along Lewis River Road #90 for 17.6 miles past Big Creek Falls (described previously), a total of 26.4 miles northeast of Eagle Cliff Bridge. Proceed down the access road to Twin Falls Camp and drive 0.3 mile to its end. The view of the falls is from across the Lewis River.

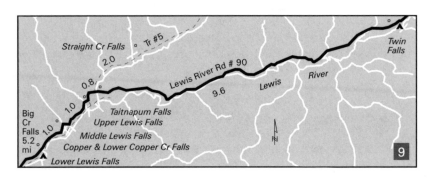

Rush Creek Falls

Straight Creek Falls ★★ ③ 🚶

Form: cascade   *Magnitude:* 33 (h)   *Watershed:* med
Elevation: 1980 feet   *USGS Map:* Quartz Creek Butte (1965 ns)

This pleasant series of cascades along Straight Creek totals 30 to 60 feet. The highlight when the author surveyed this entry was the appearance of several elk along the trail. Drive along Lewis River Road to the parking area for Quartz Creek Trailhead #5, located 16.8 miles northeast of Eagle Cliff Bridge and 9.6 miles southwest of the access road to Twin Falls Camp (described previously). Hike 2 miles, passing a logged area in 1.7 miles. Walk across the log bridge over Straight Creek, then pick up your own path upstream to a viewpoint.

Upper Lewis Falls ✫✫✫

Form: block   *Magnitude:* 65   *Watershed:* lg
Elevation: 1620 feet   *USGS Map:* Quartz Creek Butte (1965)

The Lewis River thunders 35 feet over a massive slab of bedrock. This waterfall and those described in the next four entries are all interconnected by the recently expanded Lewis River Trail system. For access, find Upper Falls Trail next to Lewis River Road as indicated by a sign 0.8 mile southwest of Quartz Creek Trail #5 (described previously). The path is moderately steep but only 0.3 mile long. At its end are the falls and the junction with Lewis River Trail.

Copper Creek Falls ✫✫

Form: punchbowl   *Magnitude:* 44   *Watershed:* vsm
Elevation: 1680 feet   *USGS Map:* Quartz Creek Butte (1965 ns)

A sharp 40- to 60-foot drop along Copper Creek. It can be viewed by descending beneath a footbridge. Drive 1 mile southwest of Upper Falls Trail (described previously) along Lewis River Road to the parking area for an unnamed trail that leads down to the Lewis River. After walking along the path for several hundred yards, look back toward the footbridge framing the cataract.

Middle Lewis Falls ✫✫

Form: block   *Magnitude:* 56   *Watershed:* lg
Elevation: 1560 feet   *USGS Map:* Quartz Creek Butte (1965)

This 30-foot descent along the Lewis River is the least inspiring of the three Lewis Falls. Take the trail to Copper Creek Falls (described previously). Continue another 0.5 mile to Lewis River Trail and views of this cataract.

Lower Copper Creek Falls (u) ✫✫

Form: block   *Magnitude:* 29   *Watershed:* vsm
Elevation: 1600 feet   *USGS Map:* Quartz Creek Butte (1965 ns)

Copper Creek slides steeply into the Lewis River. A footbridge along Lewis River Trail passes over this 20- to 30-foot drop. Walk a short distance downstream from Middle Lewis Falls (described previously) to this entry.

Lower Lewis Falls ✫ ✫ ✫ ✫

Form: block   *Magnitude:* 67   *Watershed:* lg
Elevation: 1480 feet   *USGS Map:* Spencer Butte (1965)

Water crashes 35 feet over a broad expanse of the Lewis River in an especially scenic block form. Drive along Lewis River Road to Lewis River Campground, located 1 mile south of Copper Creek (14 miles northwest of Eagle Cliff Bridge) and 5.2 miles north of Big Creek Falls. Park in the southeast part of the campground. A short trail leads to good vistas overlooking the falls.

10. East Fork Lewis River

Four small waterfalls tumble along the East Fork Lewis River. Follow the marked route 3 miles from the town of Battle Ground to Battle Ground Lake State Park. Continue 2.8 miles northbound from the state park, passing the hamlet of Heisson, to Lucia Falls Road.

Lower Lewis Falls

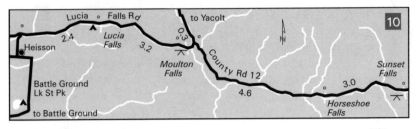

Lucia Falls ★★

Form: block   *Magnitude:* 44 (h)   *Watershed:* lg
Elevation: 400 feet   *USGS Map:* Yacolt (1990)

The park surrounding this 15- to 25-foot waterfall is privately developed and has periodically been closed to the public. When last visited, there was an admittance fee. Drive 2.4 miles east along Lucia Falls Road and turn into Lucia Falls Park and Cafe.

Sunset Falls ★★

Form: block   *Magnitude:* 60 (h)   *Watershed:* lg
Elevation: 980 feet   *USGS Map:* Gumboot Mtn (1986 nl)

The East Fork Lewis River splashes 20 feet within Wind River Ranger District. From Lucia Falls follow Lucia Falls Road east for 3.5 miles to its end and turn right (southeast) onto County Road #12, which rises 100 to 200 feet above the East Fork. Drive 7.6 miles farther to the Sunset Picnic Area. Walk a short distance upstream to the descent.

Others: *Moulton Falls* ★ USGS Yacolt (1990). The East Fork Lewis River slides 15 to 25 feet within a public park. Continue east 3.2 miles past Lucia Falls (described previously) along Lucia Falls Road to the park.

Horseshoe Falls ★ USGS Dole (1994). This crescent-shaped 15- to 20-foot waterfall, situated on private property posted no trespassing, would earn a higher rating if closer views were possible. The waterfall is visible from County Road #12, 4.6 miles southeast of Lucia Falls Road.

II. Wind River Road

Three of the most impressive waterfalls of the region are located within Wind River Ranger District and drainage basin.

Panther Creek Falls ★★★★

②

Form: segmented   *Magnitude:* 74   *Watershed:* med
Elevation: 1790 feet   *USGS Map:* Big Huckleberry Mtn (1983 ns)

This 50- to 75-foot waterfall is unique because it is actually two waterfalls dropping side by side from Panther Creek and Big Creek. From S.R. 14 turn north onto Wind River Road #30. Pass Carson in 1 mile and after another 5.8 miles turn right (east) on Old State Road. Almost immediately, take

Panther Creek Falls

a left (north) onto Panther Creek Road #65. Drive 7.4 miles up this road and find a safe place to park near its junction with Road #6511. Walk about 100 yards up Panther Creek Road #65 to a faint unsigned path that drops sharply down (the most difficult part), then quickly leads to an unfenced vista overlooking the falls.

Falls Creek Falls ★★★★★   ③

Form: tiered   *Magnitude:* 99 (h)   *Watershed:* lg
Elevation: 2200 feet   *USGS Map:* Termination Point (1983)

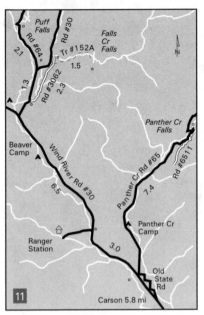

This fantastic triple tiered waterfall totals 250 feet and is so outstanding one must wonder how it was given such a generic name. Several vantages are afforded toward the end of the trail, although the shape of the cataract is such that all three tiers cannot be viewed together.

Drive north on Wind River Road #30 and continue 9.5 miles past Panther Creek Road #65 (described previously) to Road #3062–057. Turn right and proceed 2.3 miles to Lower Falls Creek Trail #152A. The trail crosses Falls Creek in 0.8 mile. Half a mile beyond is a steeply sloping cascade, which can be forded easily during high-water periods, after which, the upper and middle portions of the falls soon come into view. The trail ends in front of the middle and lower falls 0.2 mile farther.

Puff Falls ★★★   ④

Form: plunge   *Magnitude:* 65   *Watershed:* med
Elevation: 1560 feet   *USGS Map:* Termination Point (1983 ns)

Dry Creek leaps 120 feet into a pool, which makes a good secluded swimming hole if you can bear the chilly water. Proceed 1.3 miles past Road #3062–057 (described previously) along Wind River Road #30 to Dry Creek Road #64. Turn left onto #64 and proceed 2.1 miles to the point where the road crosses the creek. Proceeding upstream to the falls, also known as *Dry Creek Falls*, is not overly difficult, but the 0.8-mile route is slow going and requires perseverance.

12. Trout Lake

The point of departure for these attractive waterfalls, all located within Gifford Pinchot National Forest, is Mount Adams District Ranger Station, located 0.5 mile west of Trout Lake on S.R. 141.

Little Goose Creek Falls ★★★

Form: segmented   *Magnitude:* 80   *Watershed:* med
Elevation: 3000 feet   *USGS Map:* Sleeping Beauty (1970 ns)

Peer into a canyon, looking down upon this 75- to 100-foot trip-let descending from Little Goose Creek. Be careful at the rim; there is no fence and the sheer cliffs are dangerously abrupt! Drive about 1 mile west of the ranger station, then turn right (north) on Trout Lake Creek Road #88. After 8.3 more miles, park on the far (northwest) side of the gorge where the paved road leaves the creek. Although there is no trail, viewpoints at the canyon rim are easily and quickly reached.

Langfield Falls ★★★★

Form: fan *Magnitude:* 86 *Watershed:* med
Elevation: 3400 feet   *USGS Map:* Sleeping Beauty (1970)

Mosquito Creek veils 110 feet, deep within the forest. The water-fall is named after a retired ranger who is credited with its discovery. Drive along Trout Lake Creek Road #88 for 4.4 miles past Little Goose Creek Falls (described previously) to a marked turnout for Langfield Falls. A short trail leads to a viewpoint in front of the descent.

13. Mount Adams

These high-country waterfalls are all accessible from the Yakama In-dian Reservation, adjacent to Mount Adams Wilderness. The best visiting pe-riod is from late summer to early autumn. The roads are rough and slow but usually navigable by passenger vehicles. Proceed north from Trout Lake along Road #23 for 1.3 miles, then bear right onto Road #80. Bear right again after 0.6 miles, this time onto Road #82. Stay on this route for 8.5 miles, then turn left (north) on Mount Adams Road #8290.

Bird Creek Falls ★★

Form: tiered   *Magnitude:* 16 (h)   *Watershed:* sm (g)
Elevation: 4800 feet   *USGS Map:* King Mtn (1971 ns)

A series of 5- to 10-foot cascades and punchbowls adjacent to both sides of the road on the way to Mount Adams. From the junction of Forest Roads #82 and #8290, proceed 2.7 miles north along #8290 to an unmarked turnout at the creek.

Crooked Creek Falls ★★★   ③🏃

Form: horsetail   *Magnitude:* 50
Watershed: sm (g)
Elevation: 6100 feet   *USGS Map:* Mount
Adams East (1970)

Water pours 35 to 50 feet from a small cliff, then steeply cascades along the stream course. Lots of flowering plants and miniature waterfalls make the 1-mile hike absolutely charming. Proceed northward past Bird Creek Falls (described previously) along Road #8290 for 1.9 miles. Turn left at Mirror Lake and drive 1 mile to Bird Lake and the trailhead at the end of this access road.

Hellroaring Falls ★★   ④, 🏃 or 🚗

Form: segmented   *Magnitude:* 68
Watershed: sm (g)
Elevation: 6800 feet   *USGS Map:* Mount
Adams East (1970 nl)

Distant views of several 100- to 150-foot cataracts, unofficially named *Hellroaring Basin Falls* in the previous edition of this book, are dwarfed by the specter of Mount Adams in the background. A roadside vista is afforded from Hellroaring Falls overlook, which is located 2 miles beyond Mirror Lake. A better, yet still-distant vantage is available from Hellroaring Viewpoint, a moderately strenuous 1-mile hike. The shortest trail to the viewpoint starts at Bird Creek Picnic Area. Reach the picnic site by backtracking 0.9 mile from the overlook along Road #8290.

14. Glenwood

Outlet Falls ★★★★★   🚗

Form: plunge   *Magnitude:* 74
Watershed: med
Elevation: 1600 feet   *USGS Map:* Outlet Falls (1970)

Outlet Creek roars toward Klickitat Canyon in an exciting 120- to 150-foot plummet. The gorge-rim vista into the cataract and its large natural amphitheater is unguarded, making it very dangerous. From BZ Corner,

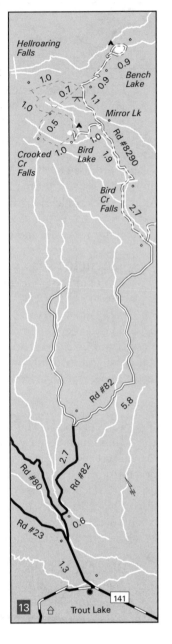

which is north of White Salmon on S.R. 141, drive northeast for 20 miles on BZ Corner–Glenwood Road to the town of Glenwood (alternatively drive 17 miles

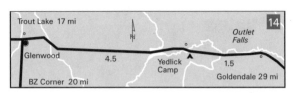

east of Trout Lake on Trout Lake–Glenwood Road). Proceed 6 miles east of Glenwood to a parking area and viewpoint, which is obscurely marked.

Outlet Falls

THE INLAND EMPIRE

The eastern half of the state of Washington is known locally as the Inland Empire. The name was popularized in the late 1800s, when the region ceased to be part of the frontier. Since then it has grown into a substantial producer of agricultural products, timber, minerals, and hydroelectric power. Railroads played a vital role in developing the Inland Empire and establishing Spokane as its center of commerce. The region's rail passenger service is still known as "The Empire Builder."

There are 52 falls recognized within this region; 26 of them are described on the following pages. Waterfalls are distributed throughout the Inland Empire, being found in the Selkirk Mountains, Okanogan Highlands, and the Channeled Scablands.

The Selkirks are composed of old sedimentary rocks that range from 80 million to 500 million years old. Recent folding and faulting, 1 million to 3 million years ago, was followed by glaciation, giving the range its present appearance.

The Okanogan Highlands, a complex metamorphic mixture of schists and gneisses, were formed and uplifted 50 million to 75 million years ago. Glaciation and stream erosion have sharpened the peaks and valleys. Most of the falls in this mountainous terrain formed where rivers flow over rocks of variable erodibility, creating escarpments wherever an outcrop of resistant bedrock eroded more slowly than weaker rocks downstream.

The Channeled Scablands, west and southwest of Spokane, are a uniquely eroded province of the Columbia Plateau where waterfall development has paralleled scabland formation. Toward the end of the last Ice Age, 10,000 to 13,000 years ago, glacial Lake Missoula occupied an area in western Montana roughly half the size of Lake Michigan. This glacial lake was created when a natural ice dam blocked the valley's drainage at Clark Fork in northern Idaho. The ice dam broke repeatedly, each time liberating staggering volumes of water, which spread across the Columbia Plateau and portions of the Palouse Hills. These events, called the Spokane Floods, scoured the landscape and created waterfalls that drop from the rims of the Columbia and Snake River canyons.

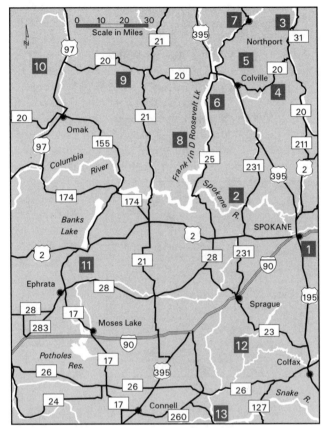

Many of the cataracts of the Scablands have since disappeared, but the evidence of their magnitude is clearly visible. Famous *Dry Falls* was so powerful that its plunge pools remain, although several thousand years have passed since its waters thundered over the adjacent rock walls!

The Spokane Floods also created a descent along Trail Lake Coulee called *Summer Falls*. It became a dry cataract once the floodwaters ceased, but the torrent was resurrected at one point by an irrigation project whose outlet follows the coulee (streambed). But alas! A new dam has reduced Summer Falls to a trickle. Nature giveth and taketh away, and so have humans.

The Palouse River originally flowed into the Columbia River, but the Spokane Floods caused it to divert its course into a fracture in the basaltic bedrock near the present site of Washtucna. The new river course flowed south and eventually plunged into the Snake River. The waterfall has since eroded its way 7.5 miles upstream, creating a canyon 400 to 800 feet deep from the Snake River to the present location of *Palouse Falls*.

1. Spokane

A renaissance occurred in downtown Spokane when the city hosted Expo 74, an international fair. The resulting national image boost has had a lasting effect. The former fair site is now Riverfront Park. It includes gardens, exhibits, an impressive opera house, and several falls along the Spokane River.

Spokane Falls ★★★★

Form: cascade   *Magnitude:* 82 (h)   *Watershed:* lg (d)
Elevation: 1830 feet   *USGS Map:* Spokane NW (1986)

Take an exciting gondola ride above these falls, where the Spokane River absolutely roars 60 to 100 feet downward as white water foams. Turn off I-90 at the U.S. 2/U.S. 395/Division Street Exit. Turn north at the end of the ramp and drive eight blocks north to Spokane Falls Boulevard. Proceed six blocks westward to the entrance for Riverfront Park. When the park's aerial tramway is not operating, there is another good vista of the falls near City Hall, two blocks west of the park.

Others: *Upper Falls* (u) ★ USGS Spokane NW (1986 nl). Walkway bridges cross just above this wide pair of 15- to 30-foot falls where Canada Island splits the Spokane River. Two smaller falls can be found farther upstream within the park. *Canada Island Falls* (u) ★ USGS

Upper Falls

Spokane NW (1986 ns) is situated just above the east end of the island. *Diversion Dam Falls* (u) ☆ USGS Spokane NW (1986 ns) occurs upstream of the Washington Street bridge. Visitor maps show the locations of sixteen viewpoints for all of the falls in the park. Once at Riverfront Park (described previously), go to the northwest corner, where a small pavilion provides a vista of the cataracts. Bird's eye views are also available from the walkways over the river.

2. Spokane Indian Reservation

Do not bring your rod and reel to the following waterfalls. The Spokane Indian Reservation, like most Native American lands, prohibits public fishing in its streams.

Chamokane Falls ☆☆

Form: segmented   *Magnitude:* 35   *Watershed:* lg
Elevation: 1500 feet   *USGS Map:* Long Lake (1973)

Water tumbles 25 to 35 feet along Chamokane Creek near some picnic tables. At Reardon turn north off U.S. 2 onto S.R. 231. Drive 13.6 miles to Martha–Boardman Road, located about 0.7 mile past the bridge over the Spokane River. Turn left and follow the dusty road 1.3 miles, then bear right (north) on Road #13. Proceed another 0.7 mile and turn right on a dirt road. Watch for an old sign tacked to a tree at a turnoff 0.3 mile farther. Park at this junction and walk toward the creek. Hike 0.5 mile down to the end of this road and find a small picnic area with the cataract a short distance upstream.

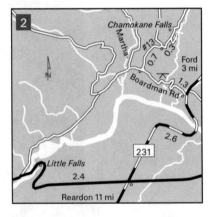

Little Falls ☆☆☆

Form: cascade   *Magnitude:* 51 (h)   *Watershed:* lg (d)
Elevation: 1400 feet   *USGS Map:* Little Falls (1973 ns)

The Spokane River pours from the uniquely V-shaped Little Falls Dam, then cascades downward 20 to 30 feet over a jumble of boulders. From Reardon, travel northward for 11 miles, then turn left (west) onto the access road signed for Little Falls. Drive 2.4 miles to an unsigned turnout on the near (east) side of the river. There are good views adjacent to the bridge.

3. Boundary Dam

The following descent is one of the largest in eastern Washington, but unless visited by watercraft, is accessible only to bushwhackers. Other visitors can still enjoy attractions such as Boundary Dam and Gardner Cave.

Pewee Falls ☆☆☆☆   ④, 🏃 or

Form: horsetail   *Magnitude:* 78   *Watershed:* med
Elevation: 2270 feet   *USGS Map:* Boundary Dam (1986)

Pewee Creek ribbons 150 to 200 feet down a vertical rock wall into Boundary Dam Reservoir. Talk about your misleading names! This starkly beautiful waterfall was actually originally called *Periwee Falls* in 1895 by a French-Canadian hunter and prospector, but the name was later shortened.

Turn northward off S.R. 31 onto Crawford Park Road #2975, which is located about 1 mile southwest of the town of Metaline Falls. Drive 11 miles to a boat launch site just below Boundary Dam. Boaters can follow the shoreline southward along the west shore of the lake approximately 1.5 miles to the falls.

Bushwhackers can gain a hilltop vista of the cataract as follows: Backtrack 1.2 miles by car from the boat ramp to an unsigned

Pewee Falls

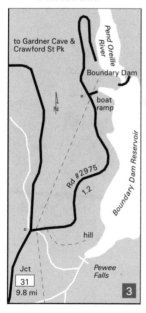

parking spot just west of the powerlines. Walk back up the road a short distance in order to avoid a marsh, then turn left, following the powerlines into the woods. After a few hundred yards, bear left (east) and progress 0.3 mile toward the top of a small knob. *Warning:* Do not attempt to get close to the waterfall, its stream, or the lake. Slopes in this area are dangerously unstable and cannot be walked upon.

4. Park Rapids

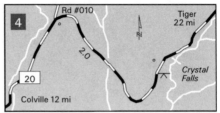

Formerly located on private land, the following waterfall is now a part of day-use Crystal Falls State Park.

Crystal Falls ☆☆☆

Form: tiered   *Magnitude:* 75 (h)   *Watershed:* lg
Elevation: 2780 feet   *USGS Map:* Park Rapids (1986)

The Little Pend Oreille River shoots 60 to 80 feet in tiered fashion. Look for a marked turnout along S.R. 20 approximately 14 miles east of Colville and 22 miles southwest of the ghost town of Tiger.

5. Colville

The small city of Colville developed from old Fort Colville, a U.S. Army outpost from 1859 to 1882. The following falls are nearby.

Marble Creek Falls (u) ☆☆

Form: horsetail   *Magnitude:* 41   *Watershed:* sm
Elevation: 3120 feet   *USGS Map:* Gillette Mountain (1986 nl)

Marble Creek descends 25 to 35 feet. Located within Colville National Forest. Drive 1.2 miles east of Colville along S.R. 20 and turn left (north) on signed County Road 700. After 2 miles, bear right onto Alladin Road and proceed 11 miles. Look for obscurely marked Forest Road #200 to the left (west). Park along this primitive route, which quickly deteriorates into a well-worn path that leads in a short distance to the falls.

Douglas Falls ☆☆☆

Form: fan   *Magnitude:* 71   *Watershed:* lg
Elevation: 1800 feet   *USGS Map:* Colville (1986)

Mill Creek veils downward 60 feet within historic Douglas Falls Grange Park (Washington State Department of Natural Resources). In 1855, R. H. Douglas harnessed the cataract for a grist mill, which he later converted into a sawmill. Failing to negotiate a lumber contract with Fort Colville, Douglas abandoned the project, but not his entrepreneurship. He turned his talents to the production of distilled spirits!

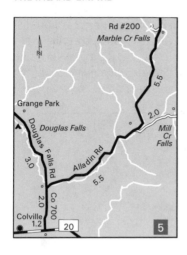

From the junction of County Road 700 and Alladin Road (described previously), bear left onto Douglas Falls Road. It is 3 additional miles to the entrance of the park. The falls can be seen from an enclosed viewpoint adjacent to the picnic and playground areas.

Others: *Mill Creek Falls* (u) ☆ USGS Park Rapids (1986 nl). Water tumbles 30 to 50 feet along a wide breadth of South Fork Mill Creek. From the junction of County Road 700 and Alladin Road, drive 5.5 miles and turn right onto a gravel road. After 2 more miles park at an unsigned turnout near the bridge crossing South Fork Mill Creek. Make your way downstream through the woods to a view of the rapids.

6. Kettle Falls

Kettle Falls is now only the name of a town. A cascade once tumbled nearby along the Columbia River, but the river's once mighty waters have been pacified by Grand Coulee Dam, which created Franklin D. Roosevelt Lake. However, two other waterfalls still exist in the vicinity.

Meyers Falls ☆☆☆

Form: fan   *Magnitude:* 60   *Watershed:* lg (d)
Elevation: 1510 feet   *USGS Map:* Kettle Falls (1969)

The Colville River crashes down 60 to 100 feet although some of the water is diverted to run a small Washington Water Power facility beneath

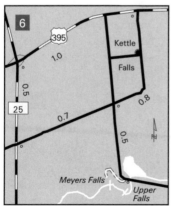

the falls. The cataract is named for Louther Walden Meyers, a pioneer who lived here in the 1860s.

Turn off U.S. 395 and drive south through Kettle Falls. After 0.8 mile, turn left (south) on a paved road, then right on a dirt road 0.5 mile farther. Park at the unsigned parking area and walk down the road a short distance to good vantages. Please respect the landowner's privacy by not driving down the access road and by making your midday visit brief.

Meyers Falls

Others: *Upper Falls* (u) ☆ USGS Kettle Falls (1969 ns). The Colville River drops 15 to 20 feet into a small rock basin. Pass this waterfall on your way to Meyers Falls (described previously).

7. Northport

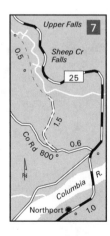

Sheep Creek Falls ★★★★ ③ 🏃

Form: fan *Magnitude:* 63 (h) *Watershed:* lg
Elevation: 1600 feet *USGS Map:* Northport (1982)

Sheep Creek explodes 125 to 150 feet over a sharp escarpment. Drive north along S.R. 25 to the village of Northport. Cross the Columbia River and turn left (west) on County Road 800. Continue approximately 0.8 mile to the first dirt road to the right (north). Park here and hike along this route about 1 mile to the canyon rim. An old railroad grade picks up from here and passes above and adjacent to the falls in another 0.5 mile.

Upper Falls ☆☆   ③
Form: block   *Magnitude:* 59 (h)   *Watershed:* lg
Elevation: 1800 feet   *USGS Map:* Northport (1982)

Sheep Creek roars 40 to 60 feet downward below a collapsed railroad trestle. Continue 0.5 mile on the railroad grade along the canyon rim beyond Sheep Creek Falls (described previously) to the Upper Falls near the end of the route, 2 miles from the county road.

8.   Franklin D. Roosevelt Lake

Both the following waterfalls can be accessed by boat, and one can be easily reached by land. Given the great length of the reservoir, nautical maps should be taken along to aid in lake orientation. They can be obtained at the marinas in Kettle Falls or Seven Bays, where boat rentals are also available.

Hawk Creek Falls ☆☆   or
Form: punchbowl   *Magnitude:* 46   *Watershed:* lg
Elevation: 1320 feet   *USGS Map:* Olsen Canyon (1985 nl)

This nice 35- to 50-drop next to Hawk Creek Campground is sheltered in a narrow crevice. Depart S.R. 25 at the sign for Seven Bays.

Hawk Creek Falls

Proceed 7.3 miles to an access road for the lake and turn right, reaching the camp and falls in 0.7 mile. Boaters may also gain a view by proceeding to the head of the embayment of Hawk Creek.

Others: *Quillisacut Creek Falls* (u) ☆ USGS Rice (1985 nl). Low streamflows limit the impressiveness of this 20- to 30-foot cataract. Try visiting right after wet weather. From the boat ramp and picnic area immediately north of Barnaby Island, head almost due east to a cove along the eastern shore of the lake. After dropping anchor, follow a jeep trail 0.3 mile to a very short path leading to the base of the falls.

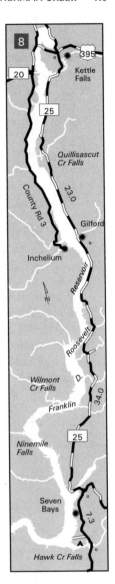

9. Sherman Creek

Both of the following entries are located within Colville National Forest.

Upper Sherman Creek Falls ☆☆

Form: horsetail   *Magnitude:* 26   *Watershed:* med
Elevation: 3800 feet   *USGS Map:* Sherman Peak (1985 nl)

Sherman Creek drops 15 to 25 feet next to the highway. Take S.R. 20 eastward for 5 miles beyond Sherman Pass to an unsigned turnout preceding the falls. Walk along the highway for a short distance to a vantage of the cataract.

Lower Sherman Creek Falls ☆☆ ③,🚶or🚗

Form: horsetail   *Magnitude:* 42   *Watershed:* lg
Elevation: 3090 feet   *USGS Map:* So Huckleberry Mountain (1985 nl)

Water drops 35 to 50 feet along Sherman Creek; requires a short, steep bushwhack for the best views. Continue eastward past the Upper Falls (described previously) for 3.4 miles to another unsigned turnout. A moderately distant vista is available from the road. Close-up vantages require a scramble down the slope to the creek.

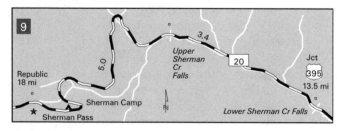

10. Conconully

Conconully is a small resort town 22 miles northwest of Omak in north-central Washington. The following falls are located in the vicinity.

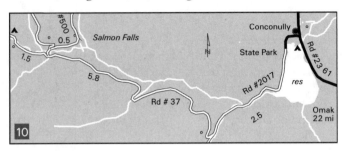

Salmon Falls ☆☆   ③, 🏃 and 🏃

Form: tiered   *Magnitude:* 38   *Watershed:* lg
Elevation: 3130 feet   *USGS Map:* Conconully West (1989)

West Fork Salmon Creek drops 300 feet over a 0.2-mile length of the stream. Located within Okanogan National Forest. Starting at the hamlet of Conconully, drive west on Road #2017, which becomes Forest Road #37 after 2.5 miles. Proceed another 5.8 miles, then bear right onto Road #500. Go another 0.5 mile to a jeep trail on the right. Park here. Walk down this dirt road for 0.3 mile to several paths leading to the various descents. Be careful! The ground tends to be somewhat steep and crumbly.

11. Coulee City

One of the engineering feats of the modern world was the construction of Grand Coulee Dam. One of the engineering feats of planet Earth is just to the south at Dry Falls.

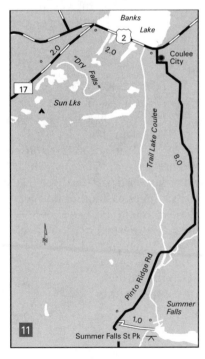

Dry Falls ☆☆☆☆

Form: block   *Magnitude:* 174 (10,000 years ago: h, today: 0)
Elevation: 1510 feet   *USGS Map:* Coulee City (1965)

At one time the largest waterfall ever known plunged 400 feet over cliffs in five sweeping horseshoes totaling 3.5 miles in width! The discharge was 40 times mightier than Niagara Falls. Follow U.S. 2 west from Coulee City, and turn south on S.R. 17. Stop at the scenic turnout, viewpoint, and interpretive site 2 miles farther.

Summer Falls ★★

Form: punchbowl   *Magnitude:* 20 (t)   *Watershed:* lg (d)
Elevation: 1490 feet   *USGS Map:* Coulee City (1965)

Water once thundered 70 to 100 feet from Trail Lake Coulee, formerly an outlet for Banks Lake Reservoir. Unfortunately, most of the water has been diverted to generate hydroelectric power so the falls have been reduced dramatically. Drive 8 miles south of Coulee City along Pinto Ridge Road. Turn left (east) at the marked access road to Summer Falls State Park. The picnic area and the waterfall are in 1 mile. There is a memorial at the state park for three teenagers who, in 1978, drowned because of whirlpool action and forceful undertow in the basin beneath the once-powerful falls.

12. Rock Creek Coulee

Rock Creek Falls ★★

Form: block   *Magnitude:* 50   *Watershed:* lg
Elevation: 1700 feet   *USGS Map:* Texas Lake (1964)

This cooling 10- to 15-foot sheet of water in a sagebrush setting along Rock Creek is located on private property. Fortunately, as the posted signs indicate, permission to hike can be obtained from the adjacent landowner. From Ewan drive west along S.R. 23 for about 1.3 miles. Find a dusty back road to the left (south). Walk along this route for 1.5 miles to the stream and the falls.

Summer Falls

13. Palouse Canyon

The third, and largest, waterfall described below is part of a state park, but the other two are located on federal land leased for grazing. When visiting the latter, for the sake of safety and to avoid suspicion, you should inform a county patrolman in Washtucna before embarking on your hike.

Little Palouse Falls ☆☆☆   ②

Form: block   *Magnitude:* 66   *Watershed:* lg
Elevation: 1000 feet   *USGS Map:* Palouse Falls (1981)

Where the Palouse River takes a 90-degree turn, the stream widens to 200 feet and drops 15 feet into a large circular basin. Here during the Spokane Floods the river was diverted into a rock fracture.

From Washtucna drive east along S.R. 26 for 2.4 miles (alternatively, from Hooper drive 6.6 miles west). Park just west of the historical marker. Follow a dirt road 1.2 miles south until it deteriorates into a trail above the falls. This route is a small portion of the historic Mullan Road, which extended 624 miles between Fort Benton, Montana, and Walla Walla, Washington. Immigrants poured westward over it during the 1860s and 1870s.

Palouse Falls ☆☆☆☆☆

Form: plunge   *Magnitude:* 86   *Watershed:* lg
Elevation: 770 feet   *USGS Map:* Palouse Falls (1981)

The Palouse River hurtles 185 feet into Lower Palouse Canyon in a thundering display. The Wilkes Expedition of 1841 called this descent *Aputapat Falls.* In 1875 W. P. Breeding erected a flour mill at the falls, envisioning a vibrant Palouse City at the site, but it never came to be.

From Washtucna follow S.R. 260 south to S.R. 261, turn left, and drive 9 miles southeast to the marked access road to Palouse Falls State Park. You can

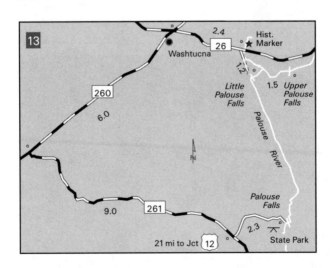

also reach the park entrance from the south by turning west onto S.R. 261 from U.S. 12 about 15 miles north of Dayton. The picnic area and falls are 2.3 miles from the entrance.

Others: *Upper Palouse Falls* (u) ★ USGS Palouse Falls (1981 nl). The Palouse River separates into five different channels, each dropping 22 feet. Make your way upstream for 1.5 miles past Little Palouse Falls (described previously). No trails here, so you must hike along the canyon rim. This entry gets a low rating due to poor vantages from the north side of the river.

Palouse Falls

THE COLUMBIA GORGE

The Columbia Gorge is a haven for waterfall lovers. Although it is the smallest of the fourteen regions in this book, it has the greatest density of waterfalls. There are 108 recognized falls in this area of 1,700 square miles. Descriptions of 62 are given in this chapter. The others cannot be viewed either because no trails lead to them or because they are in watersheds in which travel is restricted.

The majority of the falls along the Oregon side of the gorge were formed by the same geological events that shaped the region. Two major lava flows, which covered much of the Pacific Northwest, impacted this area, one over 30 million years ago and the other about 15 million years ago.

As the layers of lava cooled, they mainly formed a type of rock called basalt. The Cascade Mountains were formed when this bedrock material was uplifted by internal earth forces. Because basalt is relatively resistant to erosion by running water, the rise of the Cascades diverted the course of most rivers. But the Columbia River was powerful enough to erode through the rising bedrock to shape the Columbia Gorge. The small streams that flow into the Columbia from the adjacent upland cannot effectively erode the basalt, so their courses are interrupted by the sharp, vertical breaks of the gorge, resulting in spectacular waterfalls.

Because landslides have modified the steepness of relief on the Washington side these great waterfalls are limited to the south side of the gorge, with those on the Washington side being smaller and fewer in number than those in Oregon. Sections 1 through 12 below cover the Oregon side of the Gorge, sections 13 through 18 the Washington side.

A federal law that went into effect in 1986 designated most of this region, over 225,000 acres, as the Columbia River Gorge National Scenic Area. The first of its kind, the National Scenic Area legislation was the

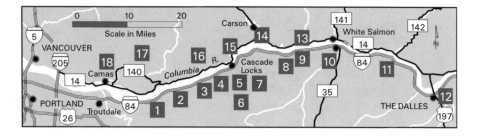

result of two primary concerns: first, to protect and provide for the enhancement of the scenic, cultural, recreational, and natural resources of the area and, second, to protect and support the economy of the Gorge by encouraging growth to occur in existing urban areas, and by allowing future economic development outside these areas where it is compatible with Gorge resources.

I. Bridal Veil

The Columbia Gorge Scenic Highway is accessible from I-84 (formerly I-80) for eastbounders at Troutdale (Exit 17), Lewis and Clark State Park (Exit 18), Corbett (Exit 22), or Bridal Veil (Exit 28). Westbounders can access the area at Dodson (Exit 35) or Warrendale (Exit 37).

Latourell Falls ☆☆☆☆☆

Form: plunge   *Magnitude:* 83   *Watershed:* sm
Elevation: 400 feet   *USGS Map:* Bridal Veil (1994)

This 249-foot waterfall along Latourell Creek is within Guy W. Talbot State Park, the land for which was donated to the state of Oregon in 1929 by Mr. and Mrs. Guy W. Talbot. The waterfall was named in August 1887, after Joseph Latourell, a prominent local settler. From Exit 28 on I-84 drive 3.4

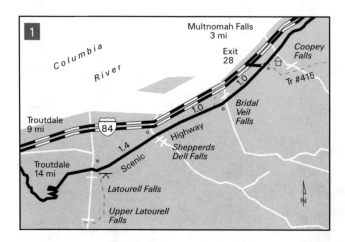

miles west on the Scenic Highway to the day-use park. It is a very short walk from the picnic area to the viewpoint.

Upper Latourell Falls ✯✯✯   ③ 🚶

Form: plunge   *Magnitude:* 65   *Watershed:* sm
Elevation: 680 feet   *USGS Map:* Bridal Veil (1994)

It is possible to walk behind this 75- to 100-foot cataract on Latourell Creek. Continue along the trail past Latourell Falls (described previously) for 0.8 mile to the upper falls.

Latourell Falls

Shepperds Dell Falls (u) ☆☆

Form: tiered   *Magnitude:* 30 (l)   *Watershed:* sm
Elevation: 200 feet   *USGS Map:* Bridal Veil (1994 nl)

A roadside view of a pair of falls is available by looking upstream from the bridge crossing at Shepperds Dell State Park. The lower tier is of the horsetail form and drops 40 to 60 feet. The 35- to 50-foot plunge of the upper portion is not as clearly visible. The day-use park is located 2 miles west of Exit 28 on the Columbia Gorge Scenic Highway.

Bridal Veil Falls ☆☆☆

Form: tiered   *Magnitude:* 59   *Watershed:* sm
Elevation: 200 feet   *USGS Map:* Bridal Veil (1994)

Bridal Veil Creek drops abruptly twice, the upper portion falling 60 to 100 feet and the lower portion 40 to 60 feet. Along the trail to the falls, you can look across the Columbia River to distant views of some seasonal cataracts descending from the Washington side of the gorge. Drive to a parking area located about 2.4 miles east of Latourell Falls (described previously), or 1 mile west of Exit 28 on the Columbia Gorge Scenic Highway. A short trail winds down to the base of the cataract.

Coopey Falls ☆☆

Form: horsetail   *Magnitude:* 59   *Watershed:* sm
Elevation: 360 feet   *USGS Map:* Bridal Veil (1994)

This waterfall drops 150 to 175 feet along Coopey Creek, which is named for Charles Coopey, who once owned the adjacent land. Located on the Columbia Gorge Scenic Highway just east of Exit 28.

A convent owned by the Franciscan Sisters of the Eucharist is located at the base of the falls. Meals are served to the public and guests are invited to stroll up to the falls. Partial views can also be gained above the descent by hiking 0.6 mile up nearby Angels Rest Trail #415.

2. Multnomah Falls

Multnomah Falls is the most famous waterfall in Oregon. In the same vicinity are several other falls that are worth a visit; all can be accessed from the Columbia Gorge Scenic Highway or from the rest area at Exit 31 on I-84.

Wahkeena Falls ☆☆☆☆

Form: tiered   *Magnitude:* 59   *Watershed:* sm
Elevation: 560 feet   *USGS Map:* Bridal Veil (1994)

Wahkeena Creek glistens 242 feet down the mountainside. It was once known as *Gordan Falls* and was renamed by the Mazamas outdoor recreation association in 1915. *Wahkeena* is a Yakama Indian word meaning "most beautiful." To view the falls, drive to the signed Wahkeena

Wahkeena Falls

Picnic Area 0.5 mile west of Multnomah Falls Lodge on the Columbia Gorge Scenic Highway.

Necktie Falls ★★

Form: horsetail   *Magnitude:* 49   *Watershed:* sm
Elevation: 800 feet   *USGS Map:* Multnomah Falls (1986 ns)

    This aptly named cataract veils 30 to 50 feet along Wahkeena Creek. Embark upon the moderately steep Wahkeena Trail #420 from Wahkeena Picnic Area (described previously). After 0.8 mile, a spur trail quickly leads to the falls.

Fairy Falls ★★★

Form: fan   *Magnitude:* 45   *Watershed:* sm
Elevation: 1000 feet   *USGS Map:* Multnomah Falls (1986 ns)

    Wahkeena Creek tumbles 20 to 30 feet in pleasant fashion. Continue 0.3 mile past the spur path for Necktie Falls (described previously) to the point where Wahkeena Trail #420 crosses in front of the base of this cataract.

Multnomah Falls ★★★★★

Form: plunge   *Magnitude:* 93   *Watershed:* med
Elevation: 620 feet   *USGS Map:* Multnomah Falls (1986 l)

    With a recorded height of 611 feet, Multnomah Falls is the fourth highest waterfall in the United States. The main portion drops 542 feet while *Lower Multnomah Falls* ★★★ USGS Multnomah Falls (nl) descends 69 feet. Near the base of the cataract is Multnomah Falls Lodge, which houses a gift shop, restaurant, and visitor center. Nearby is a plaque that tells about the falls in Native American folklore.

    Multnomah Falls Lodge can be accessed via the Columbia Gorge Scenic Highway or by walking from the rest area at Exit 31 of I-84.

Dutchman Falls (u) ★★

Form: block   *Magnitude:* 37   *Watershed:* sm
Elevation: 840 feet   *USGS Map:* Multnomah Falls (1986 ns)

    In this series of three falls along Multnomah Creek, the lower and upper falls drop 10 to 15 feet, while the middle section tumbles 15 to 20 feet. Embark upon Larch Mountain Trail #441, which begins to the left of Multnomah Falls Lodge (described previously). The steep trail offers a variety of views of Multnomah Falls in its 1-mile journey to a short spur path, which ends at a viewpoint at the top of the cataract. Look upstream to see the 10- to 15-foot descent of *Little Multnomah Falls* (u) ★ USGS Multnomah Falls (1986 ns). Continue along

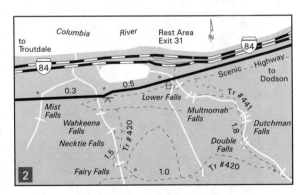

the main trail, where the trio comprising Dutchman Falls will be encountered over the next 0.2 to 0.3 mile.

Double Falls (u) ★★★   ④ 🚶

Form: tiered   *Magnitude:* 62   *Watershed:* sm
Elevation: 960 feet   *USGS Map:* Multnomah Falls (1986 ns)

While full trailside views are available of the 50- to 75-foot lower plunge, only the top of the upper 100- to 125-foot tier can be seen along

Multnomah Falls

Multnomah Creek. Continue along Larch Mountain Trail #441 for 0.3 to 0.4 mile past Dutchman Falls (described previously), a total of 1.6 or so miles from the trailhead.

Others: *Mist Falls* ✫ USGS Bridal Veil (1994). Water spirals down hundreds of feet from tiny Mist Creek. The falls can be viewed from the Columbia Gorge Scenic Highway 3 miles east of Bridal Veil and 0.8 mile west of Multnomah Falls. Peer up the cliffs near mile marker 19.

Upper Multnomah Falls (u)✫ USGS Multnomah Falls (1986 ns). This is the smallest of the falls along Multnomah Creek, tumbling 15 to 20 feet. Proceed along Larch Mountain Trail #441 for 0.2 mile past Double Falls (described previously). It is a total of 1.9 miles back to the trailhead at Multnomah Lodge.

3. Oneonta Gorge

The cool, moist north-facing slopes and sheltered drainages of the Oregon side of the Columbia Gorge provide an environment for lush, diverse vegetation. This setting is best experienced at Oneonta Gorge Botanical Area, 2 miles east of Multnomah Falls along the Columbia Gorge Scenic Highway. See the Bridal Veil subsection of this chapter for information on accessing the Scenic Highway.

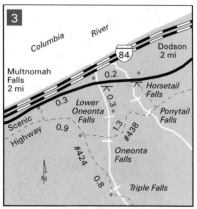

Lower Oneonta Falls (u) ✫✫✫   ④
Form: plunge   *Magnitude:* 49   *Watershed:* med
Elevation: 220 feet   *USGS Map:* Multnomah Falls (1986 ns)

Water plummets 50 to 70 feet into the narrow emerald-green Oneonta Gorge. Pick your way up Oneonta Creek from the signed entrance of the Botanical Area. Some brief wading or swimming will be required during high water along the 0.3-mile journey.

Oneonta Falls ✫✫   ④
Form: horsetail   *Magnitude:* 63   *Watershed:* med
Elevation: 400 feet   *USGS Map:* Multnomah Falls (1986)

Water slides steeply 60 to 75 feet along Oneonta Creek. Hike up moderately strenuous Oneonta Trail #424 for 0.9 mile to its junction with Horsetail Falls Trail #438. Follow Trail #438 for a few hundred yards to the footbridge overlooking the falls.

Lower Oneonta Falls

Triple Falls ★★★★★

Form: segmented   *Magnitude:* 71   *Watershed:* sm
Elevation: 560 feet   *USGS Map:* Multnomah Falls (1986)

This is a jewel of waterfalls, as three rivulets of Oneonta Creek plunge 100 to 135 feet. The trail provides an aerial view high above the cataract. Walk along Oneonta Trail #424 for 1.7 miles from the trailhead

(0.8 mile past the junction with Horsetail Falls Trail #438) to Triple Falls.

Horsetail Falls ★★★★
Form: horsetail   *Magnitude:* 82 (h)
Watershed: sm
Elevation: 240 feet   *USGS Map:*
Multnomah Falls (1986)

Horsetail Creek sprays 176 feet next to the Columbia Gorge Scenic Highway in a classic example of its namesake form. Drive to the signed turnout 2.5 miles east of Multnomah Falls Lodge (described previously).

Ponytail Falls ★★★ ③ 🚶
Form: horsetail   *Magnitude:* 76 (h)
Watershed: sm
Elevation: 240 feet   *USGS Map:*
Multnomah Falls (1986 ns)

Ponytail Falls

Horsetail Creek shoots 100 to 125 feet over a bulbous escarpment. The trail goes behind the base of the falls. It is also called *Upper Horsetail Falls.* Hike 0.4 mile from the Columbia Gorge Scenic Highway along Horsetail Falls Trail #438, which starts at Horsetail Falls (described previously).

4. Yeon State Park

John B. Yeon State Park is a day-use area located adjacent to the east end of the Columbia Gorge Scenic Highway, just before it returns to I-84 at Exit 37.

Elowah Falls ★★★★★ ② 🚶
Form: plunge   *Magnitude:* 83   *Watershed:* sm
Elevation: 400 feet   *USGS Map:* Tanner Butte (1994)

McCord Creek plummets 289 feet within John B. Yeon State Park. A committee of the Mazamas, an outdoor recreation association, named the falls in 1915. Begin on Gorge Trail #400, turning left at the first trail junction. A second junction occurs 0.2 mile from the parking area. For an aerial view of the falls, turn right on Elowah Falls Trail and take this moderately steep route 0.6 mile. To reach the base of the falls, stay on Trail #400 for 0.4 mile.

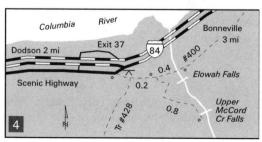

Elowah Falls

Upper McCord Creek Falls ★★★ ④ 🚶

Form: segmented   *Magnitude:* 39 (l)   *Watershed:* sm
Elevation: 480 feet   *USGS Map:* Tanner Butte (1994 nl)

McCord Creek tumbles 100 to 125 feet. Continue 0.2 mile past the upper viewpoint of Elowah Falls (described previously) to the end of Elowah Falls Trail.

5. Tanner Creek

Turn off I-84 at Bonneville Dam (Exit 40) and proceed south several hundred yards to the parking area for Tanner Creek Trail, which starts out as a dirt road. *Note:* Gorge Trail #400 does not pass the following water-falls.

Munra Falls (u) ☆☆   ① 🚶

Form: fan   *Magnitude:* 27 (l)   *Watershed:* vsm
Elevation: 80 feet   *USGS Map:* Bonneville Dam (1994 ns)

An unnamed creek drops 35 to 50 feet into Tanner Creek. The author has named the falls after nearby Munra Point. Walk 0.2 mile from the trailhead where the dirt road turns into a footpath.

Wahclella Falls ☆☆☆☆   ① 🚶

Form: tiered   *Magnitude:* 75 (h)   *Watershed:* med
Elevation: 420 feet   *USGS Map:* Tanner Butte (1994 nl)

The upper portion of this thunderous waterfall plunges 15 to 25 feet before veiling downward 50 to 70 feet into a pool. Also known as *Tanner Falls.* Wahclella is the name of a nearby Indian locality and was given to the falls in 1915 by a committee of the Mazamas, an outdoor recreation association.

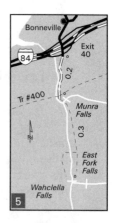

Proceed 0.3 mile past Munra Falls (described previously) along the Tanner Creek Trail to the path's end. *East Fork Falls* (u) ☆ USGS Tanner Butte (1994 nl), can also be seen stream-ing above the main cataract from a vantage on the west side of Tanner Creek.

6. Eagle Creek

Eagle Creek Trail is the author's favorite hike. A dozen waterfalls will be encountered as you take the mod-erately ascending 1,400-foot route over the 6-mile length of beautiful, narrow Eagle Creek Gorge. *Note:* The trail passes along exposed cliffs and children should be carefully super-vised.

Eastbound travelers can access the trailhead by turning off I-84 at Eagle Creek Park (Exit 41). West-bounders will have to make a U-turn at Bonneville Dam (Exit 40) to reach Exit 41. When departing, make a simi-lar turn at Cascade Locks (Exit 44) to get back on the westbound freeway.

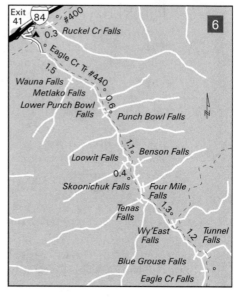

Wauna Falls (u) ★★

Form: cascade   *Magnitude:* 22   *Watershed:* vsm
Elevation: 480 feet   *USGS Map:* Bonneville Dam (1994 nl)

This minor cataract is the first of the dozen falls along Eagle Creek Trail #440. Named by the author after nearby Wauna Point. Look across the gorge at this descent along the first major tributary to Eagle Creek. It is located about 1.1 miles from the trailhead.

Metlako Falls ★★★★

Form: plunge   *Magnitude:* 73 (h)   *Watershed:* lg
Elevation: 240 feet   *USGS Map:* Bonneville Dam (1994)

This is the highest cataract on Eagle Creek, dropping 100 to 150 feet. It was named for the legendary Indian goddess of salmon in 1915 by a committee of the Mazamas, an outdoor recreation association. Continue 0.4 mile beyond Wauna Falls (described previously) to the signed vista for a partially obscured view of this entry.

Lower Punch Bowl Falls ★★★

Form: punchbowl   *Magnitude:* 19   *Watershed:* lg
Elevation: 340 feet   *USGS Map:* Tanner Butte (1994 ns)

Despite possessing only a modest 10- to 15-foot drop, this exquisite punchbowl and its upper counterpart (described next) have been made famous by photographers worldwide. Hike 0.6 mile beyond Metlako Falls (described previously), 2.1 miles from the trailhead of Eagle Creek Trail #440. Take the signed spur that quickly leads streamside in front of the descent.

Punch Bowl Falls ★★★★

Form: punchbowl   *Magnitude:* 48 (h)   *Watershed:* lg
Elevation: 360 feet   *USGS Map:* Tanner Butte (1994)

The larger of the pair of punchbowls, as Eagle Creek pours 20 to 40 feet into a large amphitheater. Continue along Eagle Creek Trail #440 for 0.1 mile beyond the spur to Lower Punch Bowl Falls (described previously). The trailside view is high above the descent.

Loowit Falls ★★

Form: horsetail   *Magnitude:* 21 (l)   *Watershed:* sm
Elevation: 720 feet   *USGS Map:* Tanner Butte (1994)

A cross-canyon view of the 50- to 60-foot drop of Loowit Creek into Eagle Creek Gorge. Hike 1 mile past Punch Bowl Falls (described previously) to the next viewpoint for this entry, a total of 3.2 miles from the Eagle Creek Trailhead. High Bridge crosses Eagle Creek a short distance farther and, soon after, the 10- to 20-foot base of *Benson Falls* (u) ★ USGS Tanner Butte (1994 nl) is visible from the trail.

Punch Bowl Falls

Skoonichuk Falls ☆☆   ③
Form: tiered   *Magnitude:* 61   *Watershed:* lg
Elevation: 640 feet   *USGS Map:* Tanner Butte (1994 nl)
    Eagle Creek drops a total of 50 to 70 feet as a pair of punchbowls.
Lack of unobstructed views prevents a higher scenic rating. Proceed 0.4
mile past High Bridge along Eagle Creek Trail #440 (described previously).
Besides trailside views, a very short spur trail goes to the top of the cataract.

Wy'East Falls (u) ☆☆   ④, 🚶 and 🚶
Form: plunge   *Magnitude:* 30 (l)   *Watershed:* vsm
Elevation: 1120 feet   *USGS Map:* Wahtum Lake (1979 nl)
    A small unnamed tributary drips 90 to 110 feet, a short distance off
Eagle Creek Trail #440. Named by the author after the nearby campsite. Walk
along Eagle Creek Trail for 1 mile beyond Skoonichuk Falls (described previously) to Wy'East Camp. Proceed another 0.3 mile to a stream crossing and a
mostly obscured view of the cataract. A fairly easy 0.1-mile bushwhack up
the drainage leads to an open vantage.

Tunnel Falls ☆☆☆☆☆   ④, 🚶🚶 or 🚶
Form: plunge   *Magnitude:* 67   *Watershed:* med
Elevation: 1200 feet   *USGS Map:* Wahtum Lake (1979)
    This exciting cataract is named for the passageway blasted though
the bedrock behind its 100-foot plummet. The scenery is further accentuated

by the fact that Eagle Creek Trail #440 is built into the gorge wall, half-way up the falls! This unmistakable feature is located 0.7 mile past Blue Grouse Camp, nearly 6 worthwhile miles from Eagle Creek Trailhead.

Eagle Creek Falls (u) ☆☆☆   ④, 🚶🚶 or 🚶
Form: tiered   *Magnitude:* 37   *Watershed:* med
Elevation: 1160 feet   *USGS Map:* Wahtum Lake (1979 nl)
    View a cornucopia of waterfall shapes as Eagle Creek descends in four distinct forms: punchbowl, cascades, plunge, and horsetail. Follow Eagle Creek Trail #440 for 0.2 mile past Tunnel Falls (described previously). Bathing rocks and a small punchbowl waterfall are located a short distance farther upstream.

Others: *Ruckel Creek Falls* (u) ☆ USGS Bonneville Dam (1994 ns). Ruckel Creek slides 30 to 50 feet beneath a footbridge that is an antiquated span of an abandoned portion of the old Columbia River Highway. Before embarking up Eagle Creek Trail, waterfall collectors may wish to visit this entry next to eastbound Gorge Trail #400. The trailhead is located just a short way along the access road to the campsites. The falls, which deserve a higher rating during high stream flows, are 0.3 mile away.

Eagle Creek Falls

Tenas Falls (u) ☆ USGS Tanner Butte (1994 ns). An unnamed tributary tumbles 15 to 25 feet into Eagle Creek. During the summer, it is partially obscured by the surrounding vegetation. Walk along Eagle Creek Trail #440 for 0.4 mile beyond Skoonichuk Falls (described previously). It is located just above 4½ Mile Bridge.
    Blue Grouse Falls (u) ☆ USGS Wahtum Lake (1979 nl). The trailside view of this 30- to 40-foot punchbowl along Eagle Creek is mostly obscured when the surrounding vegetation is in leaf. Named by the author after a campsite in the vicinity. Hike

0.6 mile past Wy'East Camp to Blue Grouse Camp. Proceed 0.6 mile beyond the camp to the falls, which is easier to find upon the return hike from the Tunnel Falls entry (described previously).

7. Cascade Locks

The following falls are accessible via Pacific Crest National Scenic Trail #2000. The trail's northern entry into Oregon is at Bridge of the Gods, located off I-84 at Cascade Locks (Exit 44). Alternate trailheads are at the Columbia Gorge Work Center and Herman Camp, situated off I-84 near Forest Lane–Herman Creek (Exit #47).

Dry Creek Falls (u) ★★★   ④ 🚶

Form: plunge   *Magnitude:* 49   *Watershed:* sm
Elevation: 1400 feet   *USGS Map:* Carson (1994 nl)

Dry Creek plunges 50 to 70 feet. The drainage is a part of the watershed for the city of Cascade Locks. Obey the signs posted near the falls. From Bridge of the Gods, hike 2 miles along the Pacific Crest Trail to Dry Creek. For those departing from the Work Center or Herman Camp, take the appropriate spur trail to the Crest Trail and go 2.3 miles westward to Dry Creek. Once at the drainage, follow a dirt road 0.3 mile upstream to the base of the descent.

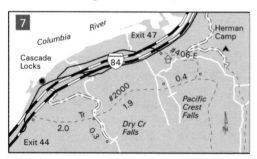

Others: Pacific Crest Falls (u) ★ USGS Carson (1994 nl). Look a fair distance up the drainage for an obscured view of water pouring 25 to 40 feet from an unnamed stream. Named by the author for the Pacific Crest Trail. From the Dry Creek drainage (described previously) hike 1.9 miles eastward, or hike 0.4 mile west from the junction of the Crest Trail and Herman Bridge Trail #406-E.

8. Wyeth

Gorton Creek Falls ★★★   ② 🚶

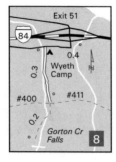

Form: horsetail   *Magnitude:* 70   *Watershed:* sm
Elevation: 500 feet   *USGS Map:* Carson (1994 ns)

Gorton Creek pours 120 to 140 feet from cliffs of the Columbia Gorge. Some vantages reveal a 20- to 30-foot upper tier along the stream. Depart I-84 at Wyeth (Exit 51) and drive 0.4 mile through Wyeth Campground. Proceed to route's end at the parking area for Wyeth Trail #411 and begin walking; after a few hundred yards the way becomes a dirt road. Do not take either of the two signed trails, but continue along the dirt road. In 0.3 mile the road again becomes a path, crossing the creek once. After another 0.2 mile, you will need to negotiate a few large boulders before reaching the base of the cataract.

9. Starvation Creek State Park

Turn off I-84 at the eastbound-only exit for day-use Starvation Creek State Park and rest area. Westbounders must make a U-turn at Wyeth (Exit 51) to enter, then make a similar turn at Viento Park (Exit 56) when leaving.

Starvation Creek Falls ★★★★

Form: horsetail   *Magnitude:* 62   *Watershed:* sm
Elevation: 280 feet   *USGS Map:* Mount Defiance (1994 nl)

The name of this 186-foot waterfall and its stream came from an event in December 1884. Two trains were snowbound nearby on the recently completed railroad. The stranded passengers called the area "Starveout," although no one perished during the incident. Walk a very short distance from the southeast side of the picnic area to view the falls.

Cabin Creek Falls ★★

Form: horsetail   *Magnitude:* 32 (l)   *Watershed:* vsm
Elevation: 300 feet   *USGS Map:* Mount Defiance (1994 nl)

Water trickles 175 to 200 feet from Cabin Creek. Starting at the rest area hike 0.3 mile west along Mount Defiance Trail #413 to a trailside view in front of the cataract.

Hole-in-the-Wall Falls ★★★

Form: cascade   *Magnitude:* 42   *Watershed:* sm
Elevation: 200 feet   *USGS Map:* Mount Defiance (1994 nl)

This 75- to 100-foot descent once sprayed onto the old highway, so the course of Warren Creek was diverted by blasting a tunnel through the adjacent basaltic cliff. Originally named *Warren Falls*. Walk 0.3 mile past Cabin Creek Falls (described previously) along Mount Defiance Trail #413.

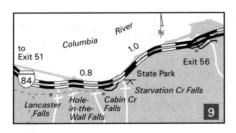

Lancaster Falls ☆☆   ③

Form: plunge   *Magnitude:* 29 (l)   *Watershed:* vsm
Elevation: 400 feet   *USGS Map:* Mount Defiance (1994)

This 200- to 250-foot cataract descends seasonally from Wonder Creek. It was named in 1970 after Samuel C. Lancaster, who designed the beautiful Columbia River Scenic Highway prior to World War I. Continue

Hole-in-the-Wall Falls

0.2 mile past Hole-in-the-Wall Falls (described previously) for a total of 0.8 mile along Mount Defiance Trail #413.

10. Hood River Valley

The area around Hood River is known for sailboarding and fruit orchards. The town and its surrounding valley can be accessed from I-84 via Exits 62 and 64 or from Mount Hood via S.R. 35.

Wah Gwin Gwin Falls ★★★

Form: plunge   *Magnitude:* 65   *Watershed:* med
Elevation: 280 feet   *USGS Map:* Hood River (1994)

This 207-foot plunge along Phelps Creek is located on the grounds of the luxuriant Columbia Gorge Hotel. *Wah Gwin Gwin* is a Native American phrase meaning "tumbling or rushing waters." Leave I-84 at West Hood River/ Westcliff Drive (Exit 62), turning left (west) at Westcliff Drive and reaching the hotel and falls in 0.2 mile.

Punchbowl Falls ★★★

Form: punchbowl   *Magnitude:* 41 (h)   *Watershed:* lg
Elevation: 840 feet
USGS Map: Dee (1994)

The Hood River drops 10 to 15 feet into a large pool flanked by sheer cliffs of columnar basalt. Drive to the lumber processing facility at Dee, located on S.R. 281. Turn right on Punchbowl Road and continue 1.4 miles to an unsigned parking area on the near (east) side of the river. Take a short walk down the dirt road to pathways leading to unguarded vistas at the rim of the small canyon.

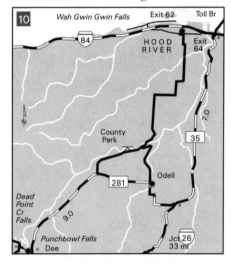

Dead Point Creek Falls (u) ★★

Form: tiered   *Magnitude:* 23 (l)   *Watershed:* med
Elevation: 840 feet   *USGS Map:* Dee (1994 nl)

Look across the Hood River to view this 40- to 50-foot double falls. It is located immediately downstream from Punchbowl Falls (described previously) and can be seen from the same viewpoints. The USGS topographic map erroneously labels this previously unnamed cataract as Punchbowl Falls.

11. Mosier

Mosier Creek Falls (u) ★★★   ①

Form: horsetail   *Magnitude:* 57   *Watershed:* lg
Elevation: 160 feet   *USGS Map:* White Salmon (1978 nl)

Mosier Creek slides into a small gorge, falling a total of 125 to 150 feet. Turn off I-84 at Mosier (Exit 69) and drive 0.6 mile east, passing the town of Mosier. A short, easy path on the right (east) side of Mosier Creek bridge leads to an unguarded overlook.

Others: *Rowena Dell Falls* (u) ★ USGS Lyle (1994 nl). A brief glimpse of this falls is possible while driving eastbound just prior to Rowena (Exit 76) along I-84.

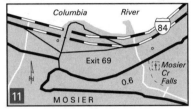

12. The Dalles

Turn off I-84 at The Dalles East/U.S. 197 (Exit 87). Drive south 0.2 mile, then turn right (west) and go 0.2 mile to Southeast Frontage Road.

Cushing Falls ★★

Form: punchbowl   *Magnitude:* 13   *Watershed:* lg
Elevation: 140 feet   *USGS Map:* Petersburg (1994)

This modest 10- to 15-foot drop along Fifteenmile Creek occurs in a setting that is markedly drier than those of its counterparts to the west. The eastern flank of the Columbia Gorge is characterized by a climatological phenomenon called the "rain-shadow effect." The rain shadow results from the fact that most of the region's precipitation falls on the western, windward side of the Cascade Mountains. Drive 1 mile along Southeast Frontage Road, then turn left and continue for 0.4 mile. Cross the bridge and turn right on an unimproved road. The descent is a very short, easy walk heading upstream.

Others: *Petersburg Falls* (u) ★ USGS Petersburg (1994 nl). This small series of 5- to 10-foot cascades along Fifteenmile Creek was named by the author after a nearby unincorporated hamlet. Proceed 2.5 miles past the junction for Cushing Falls, staying on Southeast Frontage Road (described previously). Turn left and drive 0.4 mile along Fifteenmile Road. Park just before the bridge and walk a short distance to the creek and its rapids.

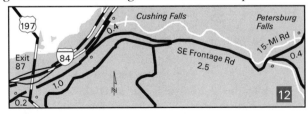

Petersburg Falls

13. Dog Creek

Dog Creek Falls (u) ★★

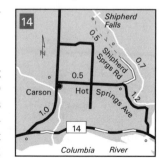

Form: fan   *Magnitude:* 32 (h)   *Watershed:* sm
Elevation: 120 feet   *USGS Map:* Mount Defiance (1994 nl)

Motorists zipping along S.R. 14 are not likely to notice this 15- to 25-foot waterfall. Stop at the unsigned parking area just west of mile marker 56, located 6 miles east of Carson and 10 miles west of Bingen. Walk a short distance upstream to a view.

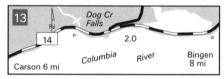

14. Carson

The Carson area is best known for St. Martin Hot Springs, but the owners of the springs have periodically closed the waters to the public. The less well known Shipherd Falls was, however, open to visitation at the time of the author's last visit.

Shipherd Falls ★★   ② 🚶

Form: tiered   *Magnitude:* 55   *Watershed:* lg
Elevation: 160 feet   *USGS Map:* Carson (1994)

This 40- to 60-foot series of cascades along the Wind River is next to a fishway, gauging station, and (locked) footbridge. Follow Hot Springs Avenue 0.5 mile east from Carson or 1.2

miles north from S.R. 14 to Shipherd Springs Road and turn north, following the graveled route 0.7 mile farther. A trail at the road end leads to a pair of views in 0.3 mile and 0.5 mile.

15. Rock Creek

Rock Creek Falls (u) ★★★   ① 𝕏
Form: block   *Magnitude:* 39 (l)   *Watershed:* lg
Elevation: 240 feet   *USGS Map:* Bonneville Dam (1994 nl)

A short, well-worn path leads to side views of Rock Creek, shimmering as it drops 35 to 50 feet over a wide ledge. Turn off of S.R. 14 onto Second Street either in Stevenson, or 1 mile west of town. Turn west off Second Street onto Ryan Allen Road. In 0.2 mile, turn right on Iman Cemetery Road. Continue on this road to its end in 0.7 mile. Look for a path leading down to the stream.

Rock Creek Falls

Steep Creek Falls (u) ★★

Form: horsetail *Magnitude:* 48 *Watershed:* sm
Elevation: 1160 feet *USGS Map:* Bonneville
Dam (1994 nl)

Gain a roadside view of Steep Creek tumbling 30 to 40 feet into Rock Creek. Follow the directions to Rock Creek Falls (described previously) but instead of turning on Iman Cemetery Road, continue along Ryan Allen Road for 1 more mile. Turn left on Red Bluff Road and drive 5.5 miles to the point where the gravel road crosses Rock Creek next to the cataract.

16. Beacon Rock State Park

·The 600-foot projection of Beacon Rock is one of the major landmarks of the Columbia River Gorge. Beacon Rock State Park is located next to S.R. 14 about 18 miles east of Washougal and 4 miles west of North Bonneville.

Rodney Falls ★★ ③ 🚶

Form: tiered *Magnitude:* 51 *Watershed:* sm
Elevation: 1000 feet *USGS Map:* Beacon Rock
(1994)

Hardy Creek plunges and cascades a total of 100 to 150 feet in two major sections. Drive 0.3 mile from the highway to the picnic area of Beacon Rock State Park. Begin hiking along Hamilton Mountain Trail. After a moderate climb of nearly 1.25 miles, you will encounter two short spur paths. The lower spur provides a view of the lower tier of the falls. Proceed on the main trail to a footbridge crossing and another short spur to the upper portion.

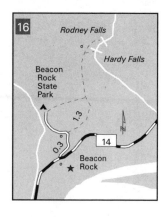

Hardy Falls ★★★ ③ 🚶

Form: horsetail *Magnitude:* 63
Watershed: sm
Elevation: 800 feet *USGS Map:*
Beacon Rock (1994)

The more scenic of two descents along Hardy Creek, this one pours 80 to 120 feet downward. Instead of taking the lower spur to Rodney Falls (described previously), choose the upper way to the far right. This spur leads quickly to a viewpoint for this entry.

17. Dougan Camp

Dougan Falls ☆☆

Form: tiered   *Magnitude:* 32   *Watershed:* lg
Elevation: 640 feet   *USGS Map:* Bobs Mtn (1994)

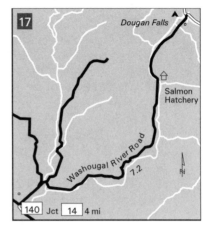

This stairstep series of block-type falls totals 30 to 60 feet along the Washougal River. Water also slides 20 to 30 feet into the river from nearby Dougan Creek. Located on public land maintained by the state of Washington. Turn north off S.R. 14 onto S.R. 140, 10 miles east of Washougal or 12 miles west of North Bonneville. Drive up the hill and after 4 miles, turn right (north) onto Washougal River Road. The waterfall is 7.2 miles farther, where the road crosses the river for a second time.

18. Camas

Lacamas Park, located within the lumber town of Camas, harbors three modest falls. From downtown, drive 1.4 miles north on S.R. 500 from its junction with Business S.R. 14. Turn left into the parking area.

Dougan Falls

The Potholes ★★   ②

Form: punchbowl   *Magnitude:* 30   *Watershed:* lg (d)
Elevation: 240 feet   *USGS Map:* Camas (1993 ns)

      Rivulets of Lacamas Creek pour 15 to 20 feet along a wide expanse of bedrock. Views are obscured when the foliage is in leaf. Walk past the park's small playground and turn right, taking a path following tiny Round Lake. Cross a footbridge over a generator, then in 0.3 mile walk over the concrete dam. Parallel the lake for another 0.2 mile, then select the middle trail at a three-pronged fork. Proceed 0.1 mile to a grassy area above the cataract.

Lower Falls ★★   ②, ⋏ or ⋏

Form: segmented   *Magnitude:* 29   *Watershed:* lg (d)
Elevation: 120 feet   *USGS Map:* Camas (1993 nl)

      Lacamas Creek slides 25 to 35 feet over an escarpment in two segments. Continue past The Potholes (described previously), following Lacamas Creek downstream. In 0.6 mile reach a footbridge over the top of the falls. Better views require a bit of a bushwhack. Backtrack from the bridge, looking for a faint path where the trail begins to leave the creek. Follow it down to open views below the base of the falls.

Others: *Woodburn Falls* ★ USGS Camas (1993 ns). Water trickles 35 to 45 feet along an unnamed intermittent creek. At The Potholes (described previously) find the service road and hike up it for 0.3 mile, passing a trail sign and a path to the left that goes back to Round Lake. Do not turn here; rather continue another 0.1 mile to an unsigned path to the right. Take this path for 0.3 mile until it ends directly in front of the small cataract.

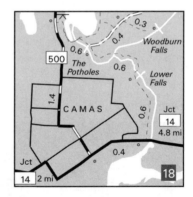

NORTHERN COAST RANGE

The Coast Range extends from the northwestern lobe of Oregon southward to California. For convenience, the region has been divided into two chapters, entitled "Northern Coast Range" and "Southern Coast Range." This chapter describes waterfalls found in association with the moist, montane environment stretching from the Columbia River, between Portland and Astoria, to an arbitrarily chosen southern limit along U.S. 20, which connects Newport and Corvallis.

During the author's travels along the coast, evidence was found suggesting that the Pacific Northwest has an enormous number of unmapped waterfalls. The density of mapped falls in the northern Coast Range is comparable to the other regions of the Northwest (U.S. Geological Survey topographic maps show 62, of

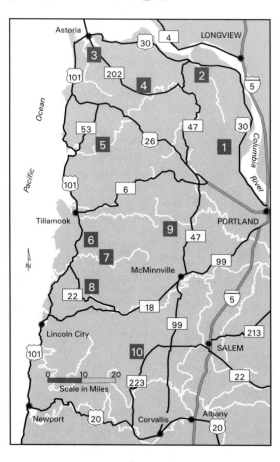

145

which 15 are described in the following pages). However, it appears likely that many more falls occur in the area. Cal Baker, an employee of Siuslaw National Forest, has surveyed and recorded 99 drops exceeding five feet just in the Hebo Ranger District alone. Much of Idaho, Oregon, and Washington is more rugged and wild than the Coast Range, so if a similar proportion of falls are unlisted in those areas, the entire Northwest probably has over 10,000 falls versus the 1,319 I have personally mapped. It would require an encyclopedia-sized document to describe every waterfall!

1. Scappoose

Bonnie Falls ★★

Form: segmented   *Magnitude:* 44
Watershed: lg
Elevation: 330 feet   *USGS Map:*
Chapman (1990)

North Scappoose Creek tumbles 15 to 25 feet over a basalt escarpment. Turn off U.S. 30 at the north end of Scappoose and drive 4.3 miles northwest along Scappoose–Vernonia Road. A small parking turnout immediately precedes the falls. A fish ladder has been built next to them.

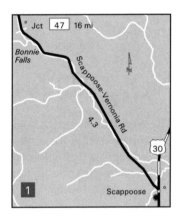

2. Beaver Creek

Motorists driving along old U.S. 30 pass by two waterfalls between Rainier and Clatskanie. The route has changed, so few travelers see them unless they turn off the main highway. Drive 6.2 miles west from Rainier on U.S. 30 to the marked Delena turnoff, located 1.2 miles west of the turnoff to Vernonia.

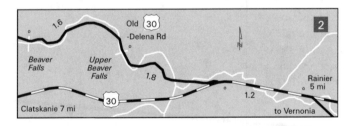

Beaver Falls ★★★   ①

Form: block   *Magnitude:* 64   *Watershed:* lg
Elevation: 230 feet   *USGS Map:* Delena (1985)

Water pours 60 to 80 feet from Beaver Creek. Be careful. There are no guardrails at the viewpoint from the top of the waterfall. Turn westward off U.S. 30 onto Old Highway 30/Delena Road and drive 3.4 miles to an un-signed parking area to the left (south). Walk down the short dirt road to a path leading shortly to side views above the descent.

Others: *Upper Beaver Falls* (u) ✫ USGS Delena (1985 ns). A modest 10- to 15-foot cataract along Beaver Creek. Follow the directions for Beaver Falls (discussed previously), but drive just 1.8 miles on Delena Road. The falls are situated beside the road.

3. Olney

Youngs River Falls ✫✫✫   ① 🏃

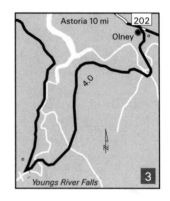

Form: fan   *Magnitude:* 54   *Watershed:* lg
Elevation: 90 feet   *USGS Map:* Olney (1973)

The Youngs River curtains 30 to 50 feet into the Klaskanine Valley. The author remembers seeing a commercial showing Clydesdales high-stepping near the base of the falls. Drive 10 miles southeast from Astoria on S.R. 202, or 20 miles northwest from Jewell. At Olney, turn south on the paved road marked for the falls. Continue 4 miles to the wide, unmarked parking area at a hairpin turn in the road. A short, easy trail leads down to a streamside vantage.

4. Jewell

Fishhawk Falls ✫✫   ② 🏃

Form: fan   *Magnitude:* 33   *Watershed:* med
Elevation: 770 feet   *USGS Map:* Vinemaple (1984)

Fishhawk Creek ripples 40 to 60 feet downward within Lee Wooden County Park. Located between Jewell and Fishhawk Falls is Jewell Meadows Wildlife Area. Elk and deer are often seen browsing in this state game refuge. There are marked viewpoints next to the highway.

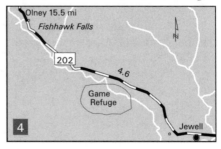

Drive 4.4 miles northwest from Jewell along S.R. 202 to the park. Trails lead upstream to the base of the falls in 0.2 mile. You can also drive 0.2 mile farther to an unsigned viewpoint above the descent.

5. Nehalem River Road

Take a leisurely drive down winding Nehalem River Road to two minor falls. The road faithfully follows the meandering river for 27 miles through Tillamook State Forest between U.S. 26 and S.R. 53.

Little Falls ☆ USGS Elsie (1984). Fishing access paths lead to the falls, where water cascades 5 to 10 feet over the 75- to 100-foot breadth of the Nehalem River. Turn off U.S. 26 near Elsie at the southbound turn marked Spruce Run County Park. Drive 5.2 miles to the park, then 1 mile farther to a sharp right (west) turn in both the road and the river. Park where the road widens.

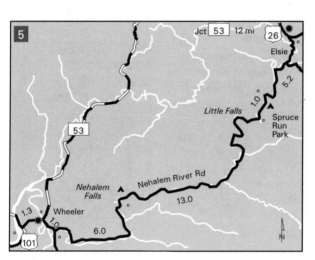

Nehalem Falls ☆ USGS Foley Peak (1985). The Nehalem River slides 5 to 10 feet within Nehalem Falls Park. Turn northeast off U.S. 101 onto S.R. 53 near Wheeler. In 1.3 miles turn right (southeast) on Nehalem River Road and drive 7 miles to the entrance to Nehalem Falls Park. Stop along the road about 100 yards inside the entrance and park.

6. Tillamook

Compared to the relatively modest falls of this region, the following entry will surely impress. Buy some crackers and the famous Tillamook cheese and take in the highest waterfall of the entire Coast Range.

Munson Creek Falls ☆☆☆☆   ②

Form: tiered   *Magnitude:* 75   *Watershed:* sm
Elevation: 760 feet   *USGS Map:* Beaver (1985)

This fine-lined cataract drops 266 feet as a triple horsetail. The descent and its stream are named after Goran Munson, a native of Michigan who settled nearby in 1889. Turn off U.S. 101 about halfway between Tillamook and Beaver at the sign for Munson Creek Falls County Park. Follow the signs 1.6 miles to the parking area and trailhead. The easily hiked Lower Trail traverses through a lush forest to the base of

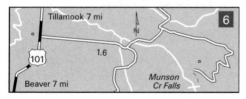

Munson Creek Falls

the falls. For full views, follow the Upper Trail for 0.5 mile to an excellent gorge vista. The steep trails were built as part of youth programs in 1960–62 and 1978–79.

7. Blaine

Clarence Creek Falls (u) ★★

Form: horsetail   *Magnitude:* 27   *Watershed:* med
Elevation: 560 feet   *USGS Map:* Blaine (1984 nl)

    Clarence Creek slides 46 feet next to the road. Turn left (north) off U.S. 101 at Beaver onto the Blaine–Little Nestucca River Road #85. Drive 11.8 miles, then turn left (north) on Clarence Creek Road #83. The gravel route ascends steeply, then levels off to a gentle slope in 0.9 mile at the falls.

Niagara Falls ★★★

Form: segmented   *Magnitude:* 26 (l)   *Watershed:* sm
Elevation: 680 feet   *USGS Map:* Niagara Creek (1979 ns)

    This is actually two waterfalls, as Pheasant Creek plunges 80 to 100 feet beside a tributary that cascades down 120 to 130 feet within Siuslaw National Forest. The falls' moniker is not derived from its famous eastern counterpart but from nearby Niagara Point and the Niagara Creek drainage basin. Its impressiveness decreases as summer progresses.

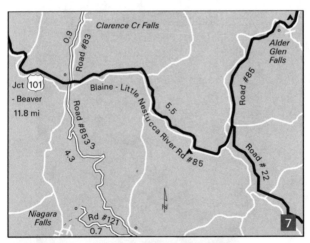

    Follow the directions for Clarence Creek Falls (described previously), but instead of turning left on Clarence Creek Road #83, turn right (south) on Road #8533. Proceed 4.3 miles to Road #8533–121 and turn right; the trailhead is located 0.7 mile along this secondary route. The trail ends in 0.7 mile at the base of the waterfall. The author recalls being almost struck by a boulder here and later found out it had been dislodged by an earthquake.

Niagara Falls

Others: *Alder Glen Falls* (u) ⭐ USGS Dovre Peak (1984 ns). An unnamed creek tumbles 15 to 25 feet into the Nestucca River. Located within Nestucca Recreation Area. Drive 5.5 miles east of Road #8533 (described previously) along Blaine–Little Nestucca River Road #85 to Alder Glen Camp. The cataract is situated across the river from the north end of this Bureau of Land Management campground.

8. Dolph

Gunaldo Falls ⭐⭐   ③ 🚶

Form: fan   *Magnitude:* 66   *Watershed:* med
Elevation: 520 feet   *USGS Map:* Dolph (1985 ns)

An unnamed tributary sprays 66 feet into Sourgrass Creek. Drive toward Dolph Junction, located where S.R. 22 and Little Nestucca River Road meet 11 miles south of Hebo and 14.2 miles northwest of Valley Junction. Take S.R. 22 from Dolph southeast for 1.2 miles to a wide expanse of the road immediately preceding a dirt road to the right (south). Listen for the falls. Scramble down the adjacent slope to the stream.

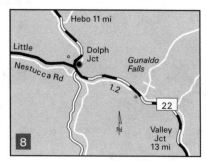

9. Cherry Grove

Cherry Grove is a small community nestled in the eastern foothills of the Coast Range. Two small waterfalls descend nearby along the refreshing waters of the Tualatin River.

Lee Falls ⭐⭐   ② 🚶

Form: segmented   *Magnitude:* 37   *Watershed:* lg
Elevation: 390 feet   *USGS Map:* Turner Creek (1979)

The Tualatin River pours 10 to 20 feet from a rocky escarpment adjacent to the gravel road. Turn west off S.R. 47 at Patton Valley Road 6 miles south of Forest Grove and 11 miles north of Yamhill. Drive 6 miles to Cherry Grove, staying on the main road through the village. At a sweeping curve to the right, the route

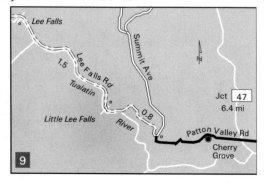

Lee Falls

becomes Summit Avenue. Continue to the end of the paved surface and turn left (west) on a dirt road, located 0.4 mile west of town. A gate prevents further driving, so hike the rest of the way (2.3 miles) to the falls.

Others: *Little Lee Falls* ☆ USGS Turner Creek (1979). The Tualatin River splits into three parts before cascading 6 to 10 feet into a large pool. Pass this falls 0.8 mile past the gate on the route to *Lee Falls* (described previously).

10. Falls City

Falls City Falls (u) ☆☆

Form: block   *Magnitude:* 57   *Watershed:* lg
Elevation: 380 feet   *USGS Map:* Falls City (1974 nl)
     The Little Luckiamute River sharply drops 25 to 35 feet into a tight gorge. Located within Michael Harding Park, where only partially obscured

side views are possible. Turn off S.R. 223 onto a road signed for Fall City, 6 miles south of Dallas and 20 miles north of U.S. 20. Drive 4 miles to town. After crossing a bridge over the river, turn right at the South Main Street sign and drive 0.1 mile to the park.

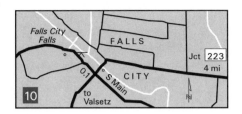

Falls City Falls

SOUTHERN COAST RANGE

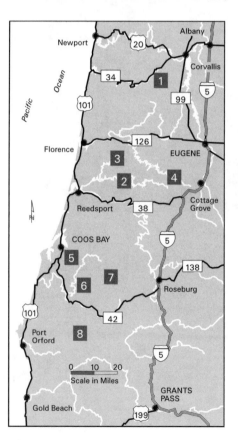

The southern portion of Oregon's Coast Range extends from the north along S.R. 34, which connects Waldport and Corvallis, south to the California border, where the range transitions into the Klamath Mountains. There are 93 waterfalls mapped in this region; 24 of them are included here.

The landscape of the Southern Coast Range is geomorphically youthful. Its geology includes each of the three major classes of rocks. *Igneous* rocks, such as basalt, are common, as are *sedimentary* layers of sandstone and siltstone. Heat and pressure have transformed some of these rocks into the third category, *metamorphic* rocks, of which gneiss and quartzite are examples. Each type of rock has a varying degree of resistance to the erosive effects of running water.

This region was once characterized by low relief, but between 1 million and 3 million years ago internal earth forces uplifted and deformed the flat, coastal plains. The courses of most of the rivers flowing to the Pacific Ocean from the western flank of the Cascade Mountains were altered by this evolution of the Coast Range. Only two waterways, the Rogue River and the Umpqua River, were powerful enough to maintain their passages to the sea. On these two rivers falls were shaped where rising bedrock with a slow rate of erosion met the less resistant streambeds.

Additional descents formed where tributary creeks connected with larger rivers. As uplifting progressed, smaller streams generally eroded the rock beneath them less effectively than did the main channels. Therefore, a vertical drop is often seen near a tributary's confluence with the larger waterway. *Elk Creek Falls* is an example.

1. Alsea

Alsea is located near three waterfalls along the eastern flank of the Coast Range. The town is 25 miles southwest of Corvallis and 40 miles east of Tidewater on S.R. 34.

Fall Creek Falls ☆☆
Form: punchbowl   *Magnitude:* 14   *Watershed:* lg
Elevation: 160 feet   *USGS Map:* Grass Mtn (1984 nl)

Although Fall Creek drops only 5 to 10 feet, a fish ladder has been constructed to bypass it. Follow S.R. 34 west of Alsea for 13 miles and turn right (north) on Fall Creek Road. Look for the cataract to the left in 1.2 miles.

Alsea Falls ☆☆ ① 🚶
Form: cascade   *Magnitude:* 30   *Watershed:* med
Elevation: 780 feet   *USGS Map:* Glenbrook (1984)

South Fork Alsea Creek cascades 30 to 50 feet downward. This entry is located within Alsea Falls Picnic Area. A short trail leads to the river at

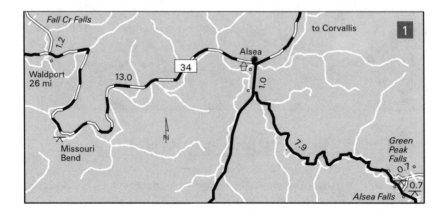

the base of the descent. Turn off S.R. 34 at Alsea and drive south for 1 mile. Then turn left (east) and continue 8.6 miles to the picnic area. The route is marked all the way from town.

Green Peak Falls ★★   ⑤ 🚶

Form: fan   *Magnitude:* 55   *Watershed:* med
Elevation: 740 feet   *USGS Map:* Glenbrook (1984)

Water veils 30 to 40 feet downward along the South Fork Alsea River. Recommended for nimble adults only. Enter Hubert K. McBee Memorial Park, located 0.7 mile northwest of Alsea Falls Picnic Area (described previously). Drive through the park for 0.5 mile to a junction with a dirt road. Park next to the road in slightly less than 0.2 mile. Short but very steep paths lead down to the river. Use the vegetative ground cover for hand- and footholds to help you carefully make your way down. Scrambling back up to the road will not be as difficult.

2. Smith River

Smith River Falls ★★

Form: block   *Magnitude:* 54   *Watershed:* lg
Elevation: 70 feet   *USGS Map:* Smith River Falls (1984)

This 5- to 10-foot drop along the otherwise placid Smith River is located on publicly accessible Federal Bureau of Land Management property. The features are named for Jedediah Strong Smith, an early nineteenth-century fur trader and explorer.

North of Reedsport turn east off U.S. 101 onto Smith River Road. Continue east for 22 miles, passing the junction with North Fork Road #48 (do not turn at the junction) at 11 miles. The waterfall, which is less impressive in summer, is located just before Smith River Falls Campground.

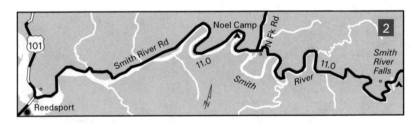

3. Mapleton Ranger District

Three scenic waterfalls are nestled deep within Mapleton Ranger District, Siuslaw National Forest. Each is accessible via the superbly designed

Smith River Falls

Kentucky Falls Trail. Take the Smith River Road (described previously) east from U.S. 101 for 11 miles to North Fork Road #48; turn north and continue 7.6 miles to Road #23, then turn right (east). After an additional 10.5 miles, turn left (northwest) on Road #919 and proceed 2.8 miles to the trailhead.

Upper Kentucky Falls ★★★

Form: segmented   *Magnitude:* 66   *Watershed:* sm
Elevation: 1400 feet   *USGS Map:* Baldy Mtn (1984 ns)
A trailside view of the first 80- to 100-foot descent of Kentucky Creek. The first 0.7 mile along the trail to the small gorge of Kentucky Creek is moderately gentle hiking. At the trail's end is a cliff-side vantage of the falls.

Lower Kentucky Falls ★★★★

Form: tiered   *Magnitude:* 48   *Watershed:* sm
Elevation: 920 feet   *USGS Map:* Baldy Mtn (1984 ns)
Kentucky Creek plunges 50 to 60 feet before diverging into a pair of 15- to 20-foot horsetails. A viewing platform has been built near the base of the falls. Kentucky Creek Trail (described previously) steepens considerably in the portion from the upper falls to its end 1.3 miles farther, 2 miles from the trailhead.

North Fork Falls ☆☆☆   ③ 大

Form: fan   *Magnitude:* 26 (l)   *Watershed:* med
Elevation: 820 feet   *USGS Map:* Baldy Mtn (1984)

     The North Fork Smith River curtains 60 to 80 feet over a large escarpment. During periods of low discharge, these falls appear in a segmented

Lower Kentucky Falls

form. This entry is also visible from the end of Kentucky Creek Trail (described previously). The cataract can be seen in tandem with Lower Kentucky Falls from selected vantages.

4. Lorane

Siuslaw Falls ★★   ①

Form: block   *Magnitude:* 22   *Watershed:* lg
Elevation: 570 feet   *USGS Map:* Letz Creek (1984)

Water stairsteps 5 to 10 feet over a 70-foot wide expanse of the Siuslaw River. From Cottage Grove drive 13 miles northwest on the Cottage Grove–Lorane Road to the hamlet of Lorane. Continue west on Siuslaw River Road for 8.8 miles to an unnamed county park. Stop at 0.5 mile along the park access road. The falls is a short walk away. Look for a fish ladder along the south side of the falls.

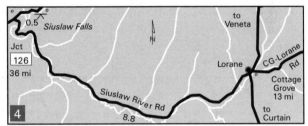

5. Millicoma River

Waterfalls are abundant on the various tributaries of the Millicoma River. Unfortunately, most of them are inaccessible. But all is not lost. The most impressive falls of the area and indeed of the region are the star attractions at Golden and Silver Falls State Park. Turn left off U.S. 101 south of downtown Coos Bay, on a road signed for Eastside and the state park. Drive through Eastside and on to the logging community of Allegany in 14 miles. The day-use state park is at the road's end 10 miles farther.

Silver Falls ★★   ①

Form: segmented   *Magnitude:* 21 (t)   *Watershed:* sm
Elevation: 520 feet   *USGS Map:* Golden Falls (1990)

Silver Creek trickles 80 to 120 feet over an unusual dome-shaped projection of weathered bedrock. Follow the marked trail from the picnic area a gently sloped 0.3 mile to the falls.

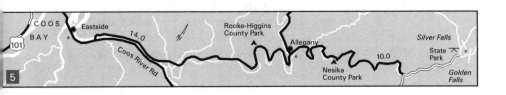

Golden Falls ★★★

Form: horsetail   *Magnitude:* 34   *Watershed:* med
Elevation: 480 feet   *USGS Map:* Golden Falls (1990)

Glenn Creek plummets 126 to 160 feet over a rock wall. It is named after Dr. C. B. Golden, First Grand Chancellor of the Knights of Pythias of Oregon. Take the second marked trail from the end of the park road, an easy 0.3 mile to the base of the falls.

6. Fairview

Laverne Falls ★ USGS Daniels Creek (1971). A modest series of miniature falls, ranging from 3 to 6 feet, along the North Fork Coquille River. Located within Laverne County Park. Leave S.R. 42 at Coquille and drive 9 miles northeast to Fairview. Continue north 5.6 miles past the community to the county park. Look for the rapids near the camping area, located downstream from the park entrance.

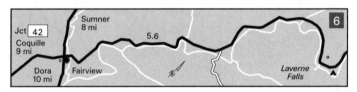

7. East Fork Coquille River

There are many small waterfalls along the scenic East Fork Coquille River, and the historic Coos Bay Wagon Road follows beside it. Be careful when driving this narrow route: Logging trucks have replaced horse-drawn buggies! Be sure to find a safe place to park off the road when you locate each descent. The Wagon Road can be accessed from the west at Fairview and from the east at Tenmile.

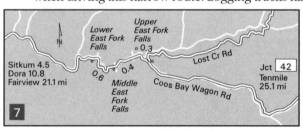

Lower East Fork Falls (u) ★★

Form: cascade   *Magnitude:* 19   *Watershed:* lg
Elevation: 880 feet   *USGS Map:* Sitkum (1990 nl)

The East Fork Coquille River tumbles 15 to 20 feet along a bend in the stream. The farthest downstream of a trio of descents, this waterfall is located 4.5 miles east of Sitkum, 10.8 miles east of Dora, and 26.4 miles west of Tenmile.

Middle East Fork Falls (u) ★★

Form: segmented   *Magnitude:* 36   *Watershed:* lg
Elevation: 920 feet   *USGS Map:* Sitkum (1990 nl)

    Water pours 15 to 20 feet over a small rock escarpment. Drive 0.6 mile upstream from the lower falls (described previously).

Others: *Upper East Fork Falls* (u) ★ USGS Sitkum (1990 nl). This low-lying 5- to 10-foot descent occurs where the East Fork Coquille River spreads downward next to a small, primitive campsite off the main road. Drive 0.4 mile upstream from the middle cataract (described previously).

8. Siskiyou National Forest

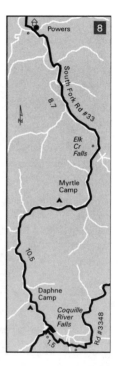

Siskiyou National Forest is a largely primitive portion of southwest Oregon's Coast Range. Many waterfalls here are currently inaccessible and unmapped. Also, seasonal descents are often seen along canyon roads during moist periods. Two of the most scenic cataracts are listed here; both are located within Powers Ranger District.

Elk Creek Falls ★★★   ② 🚶

Form: tiered   *Magnitude:* 32 (l)   *Watershed:* sm
Elevation: 480 feet   *USGS Map:* China Flat (1986)

    Elk Creek drops 80 to 120 feet over a bluff, next to which is a picnic table. Not as impressive during dry spells. Turn south off S.R. 42 onto South Fork Coquille River Road #33, 3 miles southeast of Myrtle Point. Drive 19 miles to the ranger station at Powers, then continue 8.7 miles south to the parking area for Elk Creek Falls Trail #1150. Follow the path to the left, toward the stream. It is a short stroll to the falls.

Coquille River Falls ★★★   ④ 🚶

Form: segmented   *Magnitude:* 46   *Watershed:* lg
Elevation: 1280 feet   *USGS Map:* Illahe (1989)

    This waterfall is superb year-round, as water crashes 40 to 60 feet along the Coquille River. At trail's end, miniature falls can also be seen sliding into the river from Drowned Out Creek. Drive 10.5 miles past Elk Creek Falls (described previously) and turn left (east) on Road #3348 soon after crossing the river. Continue for 1.5 miles to the trailhead. Coquille River Trail #1257 steadily switchbacks down the steep valley side for 0.5 mile to a streamside vantage below the falls.

Others: The lower Rogue River cuts through the Klamath Mountains portion of the Coast Range, creating a 2,000-foot-deep canyon. A 35-mile stretch of it is designated a Wild River, a federal classification intended to provide river recreation in a primitive setting and to preserve the natural, untamed integrity of the river and its surrounding environment. The following waterfalls and rapids can be found along this portion of the river, either by hiking or rafting: *Grave Creek Falls* and *Rainie Falls,* both USGS Mt Reuben (1989); *Upper Black Bar Falls* and *Lower Black Bar Falls,* both USGS Bunker Creek (1989); *Kelsey Falls,* USGS Kelsey Peak (1989 ns); *Stair Creek Falls,* USGS Marial (1989); *Tate Creek Falls,* USGS Marial (1989 nl); and *Flora Dell Falls,* USGS Illahe (1989 ns).

Coquille River Falls

THE MIDDLE CASCADES

This chapter describes waterfalls located in an area that ranges from Mount Hood, located a few miles south of the Columbia Gorge, through the Cascades to Mount Washington, 75 miles to the south. There are 136 cataracts known to occur throughout the region, with 48 of them mentioned here.

The major peaks of the Cascades are actually volcanoes. The appearance of each snow-topped mountain shows the relative time since it last experienced volcanic activity. The smooth slopes of Mount Hood (11,236 feet) indicate its youth, while Mount Jefferson (10,496 feet) is slightly older and hence more rugged. Three Fingered Jack (7,841 feet) and Mount Washington (7,802 feet) have very jagged features, suggesting that their volcanic activity ceased even longer ago,

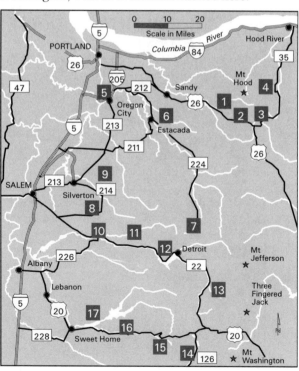

allowing glacial erosion to greatly modify the once-smooth form of these peaks.

Glaciation created most of the waterfalls associated with the volcanic mountains of the high Cascades. The alpine glaciers that top these peaks today once extended to lower elevations. Today, streams descend from adjacent rock walls into these glacially carved valleys. *Switchback Falls* is an example. Some cataracts are found on valley floors where glaciers eroded unevenly, as at *Gooch Falls,* or where the present stream cuts over a highly resistant rock escarpment, as at *Downing Creek Falls.*

The many falls along the western flank of the Cascades reflect the circumstances of the development of the entire range. About 20 million to 30 million years ago, lava flows and accumulations of ashfalls alternately covered the region. The lava hardened to become *basaltic* bedrock, while the volcanic ash mixed with dust to create rock layers called *tuffaceous sandstone.* Twelve million years ago the area was uplifted and folded, forming the Cascade Range. As streams carved courses from the high Cascades westward, their flowing waters eroded the softer sandstone much more rapidly than the resistant basalt. Good examples of this process are the descents at Silver Falls State Park and along the McKenzie River, which plunge over ledges of basalt. Recesses beneath the falls are open amphitheaters where sandstone layers have been eroded away by the running water.

I. Mount Hood Wilderness
One of twelve wilderness areas in Oregon, Mount Hood Wilderness, preserving over 35 square miles of pristine sanctuary, is just a few miles from metropolitan Portland.

Ramona Falls ☆☆☆   ③ 🧍
Form: fan   *Magnitude:* 54   *Watershed:* sm (g)
Elevation: 3520 feet   *USGS Map:* Bull Run Lake (1980)
        The Sandy River veils 60 to 80 feet downward. Located within Mount Hood Wilderness in the Zigzag Ranger District, Mount Hood National Forest. Turn north off U.S. 26 at Zigzag onto Lolo Pass Road #18. In 3.7 miles bear right on Muddy Fork Road #1825, driving to its end in 4 miles. Sandy River Trail #797 begins at the road's end. Hike 2 miles to the falls.

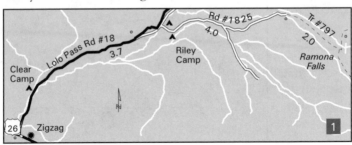

2. Zigzag River Drainage

All of the following cataracts are in the southwest sector of Mount Hood Wilderness in the Zigzag Ranger District of Mount Hood National Forest.

Devil Canyon Falls (u) ☆☆

Form: plunge   *Magnitude:* 54   *Watershed:* sm
Elevation: 2840 feet   *USGS Map:* Government Camp (1980 nl)

An unnamed stream plunges 60 to 76 feet within Devil Canyon. Only a distant view is possible. Drive 1.6 miles east of Rhododendron along U.S. 26 to Zigzag Mountain Road #27-2627 and turn north. The road soon deteriorates into a dirt surface, but is usually navigable by automobiles during the summertime. Drive 4 miles to an overlook of the Zigzag River Valley and the falls, 0.6 mile up the canyon.

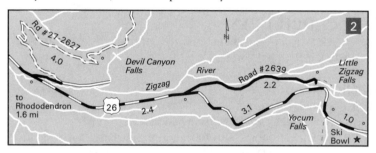

Yocum Falls ☆☆

Form: cascade   *Magnitude:* 48   *Watershed:* sm
Elevation: 3360 feet   *USGS Map:* Government Camp (1980)

Camp Creek slides over 100 feet down into the valley. The waterfall is named after Oliver C. Yocum, who in 1900 opened a hotel and resort in nearby Government Camp. Drive along U.S. 26 to a Sno-Park wayside about 7 miles east of Rhododendron and 1 mile west of the entrance to SkiBowl

Yocum Falls

Resort. The cataract is immediately downstream from Mirror Lake Trailhead. The only view is from the parking area, where you can look down upon the upper portion of the falls.

Little Zigzag Falls ★★   ① 🚶

Form: fan   *Magnitude:* 45   *Watershed:* sm (g)
Elevation: 3200 feet   *USGS Map:* Government Camp (1980 ns)

The Little Zigzag River tumbles 35 to 45 feet downward. Turn off U.S. 26 onto signed Forest Road #2639, located 2.4 miles east of the turn for Devil Canyon and 3.1 miles west of Yocum Falls (described previously). Drive 2.2 miles to the road's end at Little Zigzag Falls Trail #795C. Hike 0.3 mile to a vista immediately in front of the cataract.

3. Bennett Pass

The waterfalls listed in this section are found south of Mount Hood within Mount Hood National Forest.

Sahalie Falls ★★★

Form: horsetail   *Magnitude:* 67   *Watershed:* sm (g)
Elevation: 4590 feet   *USGS Map:* Mt. Hood South (1980)

Bright water tumbles 60 to 100 feet along the East Fork Hood River within Hood River Ranger District. The cataract was named many decades ago by George Holman as part of a competition sponsored by the Portland *Telegram. Sahalie* is a Chinook word meaning "high."

From S.R. 35 turn north at the entrance to Mount Hood Meadows Ski Area, then bear right on an old paved road. Stop near the bridge crossing in 0.4 mile. The display is a short distance upstream.

Umbrella Falls ★★   ② 🚶

Form: fan   *Magnitude:* 51
Watershed: sm (g)
Elevation: 5250 feet   *USGS Map:*
Mt. Hood South (1980)

Just a bit of imagination is needed to see that this 40- to 60-foot waterfall along the East Fork Hood River in Hood River Ranger District is aptly named. Drive 0.8 mile up the access road for Mount Hood Meadows Ski Area (described previously) to a sign marking Umbrella Falls Trail #667

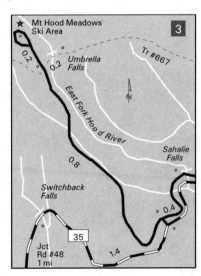

on the right (east) side of the road. Follow the trail 0.2 mile to the base of the falls.

Others: *Switchback Falls* ★ USGS Mt. Hood South (1980). North Fork Iron Creek cascades steeply 100 to 200 feet next to S.R. 35. The waterfall is aptly named for a winding turn in the highway. Located within Zigzag Ranger District. Drive to the unsigned turnout along S.R. 35, 1 mile past Road #48 and 1.4 miles from the entrance to Mount Hood Meadows Ski Area (described previously). Look for the falls immediately above the road. It can be easily missed due to the heavy foliage.

4. Northeast Mount Hood

This fourth section completes the waterfall tour around Mount Hood within Mount Hood National Forest.

Tamanawas Falls ★★★★ ③ 🚶

Form: plunge
Magnitude: 82
Watershed: med (g)
Elevation: 3440 feet
USGS Map: Dog River
(1979)

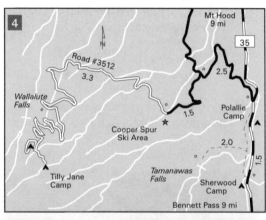

Located within Hood River Ranger District, Cold Spring Creek plunges 100 to 150 feet over a rock ledge in a deep woods setting. *Tamanawas* is a Chinook word for "friendly or guardian spirit." Drive on S.R. 35 to Sherwood Campground, 9 miles north of Bennett Pass or 10.5 miles south of the town of Mount Hood. The parking area to the trail system is 0.2 mile north of the camp. Gently sloping Trail #650 leads 2 miles to the falls.

Tamanawas Falls

Wallalute Falls ☆☆

Form: plunge   *Magnitude:* 77 (h)   *Watershed:* sm (g)
Elevation: 5000 feet   *USGS Map:* Mt. Hood North (1980)

Although the view from the road is a distant one, Eliot Branch can still be heard roaring over 100 feet downward with the specter of Mount Hood in the background. The waterfall was named in 1893 by Miss A. M. Long. She is believed to be the first white person to have seen the falls, whose name is a Wasco Indian term meaning "strong water." Eliot Branch straddles Mount Hood Wilderness within Hood River Ranger District.

Turn west off S.R. 35 onto Cooper Spur Road. After 4 miles, turn right (northwest) on Cloud Cap Road #3512. Follow this steep, winding road to an unsigned viewpoint in 3.3 miles. Look at the northeast base of the mountain (to your lower left) to locate the cataract.

5. Oregon City

Waterfalls and cities are not mutually exclusive. Indeed, it is not uncommon for cataracts along large rivers to be harnessed for industry, which in turn attracts settlement. The following entry is a classic example.

Willamette Falls ☆☆☆

Form: block   *Magnitude:* 61 (h) *Watershed:* lg
Elevation: 50 feet   *USGS Map:* Oregon City (1985 ns)

Despite its appearance being altered by the construction of a lock system for navigating the Willamette River, this 15- to 20-foot drop is

Willamette Falls

still impressive due to its several-hundred-foot breadth. Several picturesque vistas are available. One vantage is afforded by departing I-205 at Oregon City (Exit 9). Go south on S.R. 99E and drive 1.2 miles to the signed viewpoint. A perspective from the opposite side of the river can be gained by stopping at the marked scenic wayside 1 mile past Exit 6 on I-205; this is accessible only to northbounders.

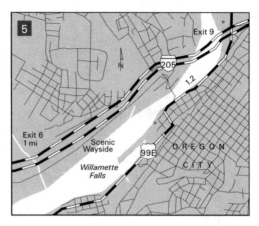

6. Eagle Creek

The following pair of small cataracts lie outside the national forests. Turn southeast off S.R. 211 onto Southeast Eagle Creek Road, which is located 0.1 mile east of the junction of S.R. 211 with S.R. 224. Proceed 1.2 miles and turn left (east) on Southeast Wildcat Road. Continue 1.8 miles, then bear right (south) on County Road #40.

Middle Falls ☆☆ ② 🚶

Form: block   *Magnitude:* 62 (h)   *Watershed:* lg
Elevation: 660 feet   *USGS Map:* Estacada (1985 nl)

Water pours 20 to 30 feet over a wide breadth of Eagle Creek. Unofficially called *Eagle Creek Falls* in previous editions of this book. Fishing is prohibited. Drive 3.5 miles along County Road #40 and park at the yellow-gated road to the right (south). Walk along the dirt road for 0.8 mile until the descent is heard. A short path leads to its base.

Others: *The Falls* ☆ USGS Estacada (1985). A modest drop of 20 to 30 feet along Eagle Creek. This generic moniker is really its official name. Drive 1.8 miles along County Road #40 to a yellow-gated turnout to the right. Take a short walk down a well-worn path from the turnout for a view.

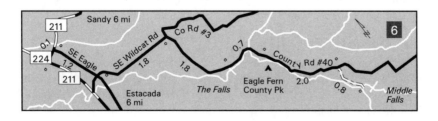

7. Bagby Hot Springs

Hikers can enjoy the therapeutic effects of Bagby Hot Springs, located deep within Estacada Ranger District, Mount Hood National Forest. Motorists cannot drive to the hot springs, but everyone can visit the following pair of modest descents.

Pegleg Falls ☆☆

Form: block   *Magnitude:* 38   *Watershed:* lg
Elevation: 2030 feet   *USGS Map:* Bagby Hot Springs (1985)

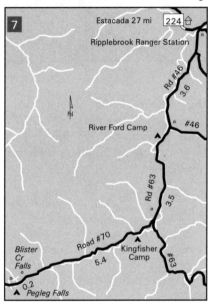

Water descends 10 to 15 feet along Hot Springs Fork, with a fish ladder bypassing the falls. Drive 27 miles southeast from Estacada on S.R. 224 to Clackamas River Road #46, which is 0.5 mile past Ripplebrook Ranger Station. Turn right (south) on Road #46, and after 3.6 miles bear right (south) on Collawash River Road #63. Turn right once more in another 3.5 miles onto Road #70, and reach Pegleg Falls Campground in 5.6 miles. Drive into the camp and stop at the first parking area. The falls is located just upstream. Bagby Hot Springs Campground is 0.4 mile farther with trail access to the springs.

Blister Creek Falls (u) ☆☆

Form: horsetail   *Magnitude:* 33   *Watershed:* sm
Elevation: 2190 feet   *USGS Map:* Bagby Hot Springs (1985 nl)

Blister Creek streams 25 to 35 feet into a small pool. The falls can be seen from a bridge 0.2 mile before Pegleg Falls Campground (described previously). Fishermen's paths offer closer views of the cataract.

8. Silver Falls State Park

This is a paradise for waterfall seekers. Silver Creek Canyon has ten major waterfalls, all of them within moderate walking distances of the main highway. S.R. 214 goes through the park 14 miles southeast of Silverton and 25 miles east of Salem.

Pegleg Falls

Upper North Falls ★★★ ① 🚶

Form: plunge   *Magnitude:* 68   *Watershed:* lg

Elevation: 1520 feet   *USGS Map:* Elk Prairie (1985)

North Silver Creek drops 65 feet in the first of a series of nice falls that get better as you progress through the park. Find the trail at the south

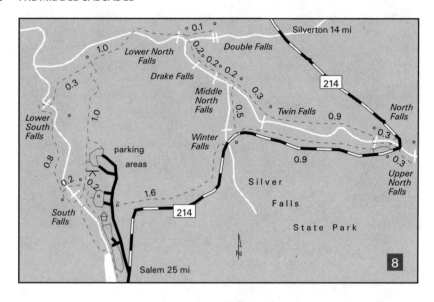

side of the parking lot at the east end of the park. Cross under the highway and walk east 0.3 mile to path's end at the falls.

North Falls ★★★★   ②
Form: plunge   *Magnitude:* 76   *Watershed:* lg
Elevation: 1400 feet   *USGS Map:* Elk Prairie (1985)

There are exciting views both beside and behind this impressive 136-foot waterfall, located along North Silver Creek. Take the trail mentioned in the previous entry 0.3 mile westward to trailside vantages.

Twin Falls ★★   ②
Form: segmented   *Magnitude:* 45   *Watershed:* lg
Elevation: 1230 feet   *USGS Map:* Drake Crossing (1985)

North Silver Creek diverges in two parts as it tumbles 31 feet over weathered bedrock. Follow the trail 0.9 mile downstream from North Falls (described previously), a total of 1.2 miles from the trailhead.

Middle North Falls ★★★   ② ⚑
Form: plunge   *Magnitude:* 42   *Watershed:* lg
Elevation: 1120 feet   *USGS Map:* Drake Crossing (1985)

This unique waterfall hurtles through the air for two-thirds of its 106-foot drop, then veils over bedrock along the final portion. A side trail goes behind and around this descent from North Silver Creek. Walk 0.5 mile downstream from Twin Falls (described previously), a total of 1.7 miles from the trailhead, or 0.7 mile past Winter Falls (described later) to view this entry.

Drake Falls ☆☆   ③

Form: horsetail   *Magnitude:* 35   *Watershed:* lg
Elevation: 1060 feet   *USGS Map:* Drake Crossing (1985)

North Silver Creek drops 27 feet in a curtain of water. Trailside views. Hike 0.2 mile downstream from Middle North Falls (described previously) to this entry.

Middle North Falls

Double Falls ★★★   ③
Form: tiered   *Magnitude:* 37 (l)   *Watershed:* sm
Elevation: 1220 feet   *USGS Map:* Drake Crossing (1985)

Water drops a total of 178 feet in tiered fashion. The lower portion descends four times as far along Hullt Creek as the upper part. Walk 0.3 mile past Drake Falls (described previously) to the signed spur trail. Walk up the side path a short distance for views.

Lower North Falls ★★   ③
Form: block   *Magnitude:* 63   *Watershed:* lg
Elevation: 1030 feet   *USGS Map:* Drake Crossing (1985)

This is the last major falls, descending 30 feet, along North Silver Creek. Walk a few yards downstream from the spur path for Double Falls (described previously) along the main trail. It is 1 mile back to Winter Falls trailhead, or 2 miles to the trailhead near North Falls.

Winter Falls ★★   ②
Form: plunge   *Magnitude:* 33 (l)   *Watershed:* vsm
Elevation: 1360 feet   *USGS Map:* Drake Crossing (1985)

Winter Creek falls 134 feet in two forms. Initially it plunges down then becomes a horsetail. Walk a short distance north from the signed turnout 0.9 mile west of the trailhead for North Falls (described previously).

South Falls ★★★★★   ②
Form: plunge   *Magnitude:* 82
Watershed: med
Elevation: 1200 feet   *USGS*
Map: Drake Crossing (1985)

This is the highlight of the park. South Silver Creek drops 177 feet over a ledge of basalt. Several vistas, including a trailside view behind the cataract, reveal the many faces of this entry. Walk about 0.4 mile west from the parking areas in the western portion of the park, as shown on the accompanying map. There is a lodge and gift shop between the main parking area and South Falls.

South Falls

Lower South Falls ★★★   ③

Form: plunge   *Magnitude:* 75   *Watershed:* med
Elevation: 980 feet   *USGS Map:* Drake Crossing (1985)

The trail passes behind this 93-foot plummet along South Silver Creek. Continue 0.8 mile downstream from South Falls (described previously), a total of 1.2 miles from the trailhead.

9. Scotts Mills

Butte Creek Falls ★★   ④

Form: block   *Magnitude:* 49   *Watershed:* med
Elevation: 1760 feet   *USGS Map:* Elk Prairie (1985)

Butte Creek plunges 15 to 25 feet into a pool. Behind this falls, located within Santiam State Forest, is a grotto, or cavern-like recess. Drive to Scotts Mills via S.R. 213 and Scotts Mills Road. Proceed to Third Street, which becomes Crooked Finger Road upon leaving town. Continue 9.6 miles to the end of the pavement, then 2 miles farther on gravel. Turn left onto another gravel road (not signed). Travel 2 miles down this route to an unmarked turn-out to the left. A moderately steep, occasionally slippery trail leads to the cataract in 0.3 mile.

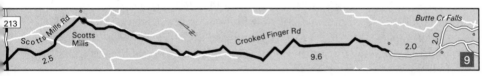

10. Mehama

Several falls occur within this locality, three of which are accessible. The first one is located on a Bureau of Land Management parcel, while the other two are both found within Santiam State Forest.

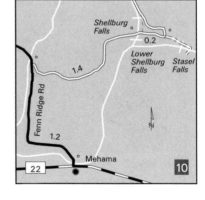

Lower Shellburg Falls ★★

Form: plunge   *Magnitude:* 46
Watershed: sm
Elevation: 1250 feet   *USGS Map:*
Lyons (1985)

Shellburg Creek tumbles 20 to 40 feet. At Mehama turn north off S.R. 22 onto Fenn Ridge Road. Drive uphill 1.2 miles, then take a sharp right (east) turn onto an unsigned gravel road and drive 1.4 miles eastward. Park at a wide spot along the road near the stream.

Shellburg Falls ★★★★   ② 🚶

Form: plunge   *Magnitude:* 61   *Watershed:* sm
Elevation: 1340 feet   *USGS Map:* Lyons (1985)
This 80- to 100-foot plume along Shellburg Creek descends over bulging basalt so you can walk behind the waterfall. From Lower Shellburg Falls (described previously), find the unmarked trail on the north side of the road. The gentle trail reaches this upper counterpart in 0.2 mile.

Others: *Stasel Falls* ★ USGS Lyons (1985). This 100- to 125-foot descent along Stout Creek would deserve a higher rating, but the side view is partly obstructed by the gorge. Drive 0.2 miles beyond Lower Shellburg Falls (described previously) and park next to a dirt road junction. Follow this unimproved route about 100 yards to paths leading to the top of abrupt and unprotected cliffs with a partial view upstream to the falls.

11. North Fork River

Access to the pleasant Elkhorn Valley and the waterfalls upstream is easiest via North Fork Road #2209, which joins S.R. 22, 1 mile east of Mehama. Alternatively, adventurous drivers with reliable brakes may wish to tackle (in low gear) Gates Hill Road. Beginning in the town of Gates, this gravel route proceeds up, up, up, then down, down, down on its route to the Elkhorn Valley.

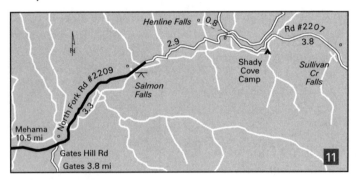

Salmon Falls ★★★

Form: segmented   *Magnitude:* 56 (h)   *Watershed:* lg
Elevation: 1120 feet   *USGS Map:* Elkhorn (1985)
Located within Salmon Falls County Park, this high-volume 25- to 35-foot waterfall drops down along the Little North Santiam River. A fish ladder bypasses the cataract. Drive 3.3 miles up the valley (east) from the

Salmon Falls

junction of Gates Hill Road and North Fork Road #2209. Turn at the sign for the county park.

Henline Falls ★★★★   ②

Form: plunge   *Magnitude:* 74   *Watershed:* sm
Elevation: 1880 feet   *USGS Map:* Elkhorn (1985)

       Henline Creek shimmers 75 to 100 feet over the mountainside. Located within the Detroit Ranger District of Willamette National Forest. The entrance to the old Silver King Mine is near the base of the falls. Look, but do not enter! A listing for *Silver King Falls*, USGS Elkhorn (1985 ns) can be found in the federal government's Geographic Names Information System. This may be another name for this entry, although it is also possible that there is an additional descent somewhere along this stream.

       Continue past Salmon Falls (described previously) for 2.9 miles, then bear left, staying on Road #2209 and go 0.1 mile. Park and walk up the tributary road to the left. After about 0.5 mile, turn left onto a dirt road, which quickly becomes a well-worn trail. The falls are reached in 0.3 mile.

Others: *Sullivan Creek Falls* (u) ★ *USGS Map:* Elkhorn (1985 ns). Located on a square-mile section of private land surrounded by Willamette National Forest, this steep 40- to 60-foot cascade deserves a higher rating, but not until the surrounding clear-cut is healed. Turn right off Road #2209 onto Road #2207 about 2.9 miles past Salmon Falls (described previously). Drive along this gravel road for 3.8 miles to a roadside view of the cataract directly above a bridge over Sullivan Creek.

12. Niagara Park

Niagara Park was the site of a small town from 1890 to 1934. A rubble masonry dam was built in the late 1890s to provide power for a paper mill, but difficulties in constructing the dam caused the mill project to be abandoned and the village faded. Historic remnants of the town can be seen at a marked turnout along S.R. 22, 4.2 miles east of Gates and 13 miles west of Detroit.

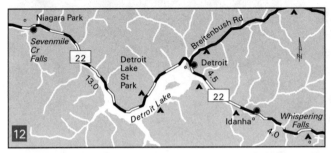

Sevenmile Creek Falls (u) ★★   ③

Form: punchbowl   *Magnitude:* 29   *Watershed:* sm
Elevation: 1050 feet   *USGS Map:* Elkhorn (1985 ns)

Look across the North Santiam River where Sevenmile Creek slides into the main river. Walk down a short pathway from Niagara Park to the river. Scramble on interesting rock formations to a vantage of the falls.

Others: *Whispering Falls* ★ USGS Idanha (1985 ns). Misery Creek tumbles 40 to 60 feet into the North Santiam River across the river from Whispering Falls Campground, which is located 4 miles east of Idanha on S.R. 22 in Detroit Ranger District, Willamette National Forest.

13. Marion Forks

As you head farther up the drainage basin of Marion Forks, located within the Detroit Ranger District of Willamette National Forest, the waterfalls become increasingly scenic.

Gooch Falls ★★★★   ③

Form: block   *Magnitude:* 85   *Watershed:* lg
Elevation: 2810 feet   *USGS Map:* Marion Forks (1988)

An absolutely beautiful 75- to 100-foot display drops from Marion Creek. The federal government's Geographic Names Information System lists *Gatch Falls*, USGS Marion Lake (1993 ns), at a location different from that of this entry, but "Gatch Falls" has also been documented elsewhere as an alternative name for this feature. So are they are the same or different?

Turn southeast off S.R. 22 at Marion Forks Camp onto Marion Creek Road #2255. Follow the gravel road for 3.5 miles, then turn right on Road #2255/850. Park where the dirt road widens in less than 0.2 mile. Walk

Gooch Falls

carefully toward the creek for a natural, unfenced view above and into the falls.

Marion Falls ☆☆☆   ④, 🚶 and 🚶
Form: tiered   *Magnitude:* 81 (h)   *Watershed:* med
Elevation: 3980 feet   *USGS Map:* Marion Lake (1993)

        The outlet of Marion Lake plunges 120 to 160 feet in the form of two powerful descents along Marion Creek. Located within Mount Jefferson Wilderness in the Detroit Ranger District, this cascade is recommended for adults only. Drive 1 mile past the turnoff for Gooch Falls (described previ-

ously) to the end of Marion Creek Road #2255. Hike 1.5 miles along Marion Trail #3493 to Lake Ann. Continue 0.3 mile farther to a trail junction; bear right on Marion Outlet Trail #3495. Proceed about 0.1 mile to an unsigned path to the right. If you encounter a rocky slope along Trail #3495, you have passed the junction by

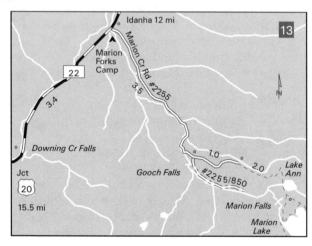

100 to 200 yards and will need to backtrack. Follow the path 0.1 mile to its end at an unguarded cliff at the top of the falls. Best views are from a faint path along the east side of the canyon.

Others: *Downing Creek Falls* (u) ☆ USGS Marion Forks (1988 nl). Downing Creek flows 20 to 30 feet down a chute. Drive 3.4 miles south from Marion Forks Camp on S.R. 22 to an unsigned turnout and camping site on the left (east) side of the highway. Bushwhack upstream until the falls come into view.

14. McKenzie River

The waterfalls along the McKenzie River descend with fury, except for Tamolitch Falls, which has been artificially turned off. They all occur within the McKenzie Ranger District, Willamette National Forest.

Sahalie Falls ☆☆☆☆

Form: segmented   *Magnitude:* 99 (h)   *Watershed:* lg (d)
Elevation: 2800 feet   *USGS Map:* Clear Lake (1988)

This roaring 140-foot torrent can be seen from several developed viewpoints. The smaller of the two segments disappears during periods of lower discharge. *Sahalie* is a Chinook word meaning "high." Depart S.R. 126 at the point-of-interest sign located 5 miles south of U.S. 20 and 6.1 miles north of Belknap Springs.

Koosah Falls ☆☆☆☆☆

Form: block   *Magnitude:* 95 (h)   *Watershed:* lg (d)
Elevation: 2680 feet   *USGS Map:* Clear Lake (1988)

The McKenzie River thunders 80 to 120 feet over a sharp escarpment. The cataract usually appears in a segmented form during late summer. Drive 0.4 mile south of Sahalie Falls (described previously) along S.R. 126 to the entrance marked Ice Cap Campground. Turn here and proceed to the parking area and developed viewpoints in 0.3 mile.

Tamolitch Falls ☆☆   ③

Form: punchbowl   *Magnitude:* 0
Watershed: none
Elevation: 2380 feet   *USGS Map:*
Tamolitch Falls (1989)

A 60-foot dry rock wall is the only thing left where water once poured from the McKenzie River. But by all means, visit this

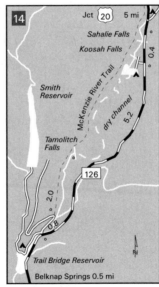

location! This circular basin inspired the name *Tamolitch,* which is Chinook for "tub" or "bucket." At this site, you will see a rare phenomenon: a full-sized river beginning at a single point. Springs feed the plunge pool at the base of the dry cataract. What happened to the falls? The river's water has been diverted 3 miles upstream at Carmen Reservoir, where a tunnel directs the water to Smith Reservoir and the power-generating facilities in the adjacent drainage.

Turn off S.R. 126 at the north end of Trail Bridge Reservoir, 0.5 mile north of Belknap Springs or 5.2 miles south of Koosah Falls (described previously). Drive about 0.8 mile to the McKenzie River Trailhead. Hike up the trail along the river for 2 miles to a crystal-clear, cyan-colored pool with the dry falls at its head (and a dry channel above it).

15. House Rock

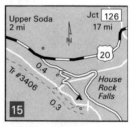

House Rock Falls (u) ☆ USGS Harter Mtn (1984 nl). This 20- to 30-foot drop along the South Santiam River would be more scenic except it is nearly covered by several large boulders that have fallen into the stream from the north slope of the gorge. Situated within Sweet Home Ranger District, Willamette National Forest. Drive to House Rock Campground, located 2 miles east of Upper Soda along U.S. 20. Proceed 0.4 mile into the camp and park just before a creek crossing at House Rock Loop Trail #3406. It is a 0.3-mile walk to the falls along a nice trail.

16. Cascadia

Lower Soda Falls ☆☆☆   ③ 🚶

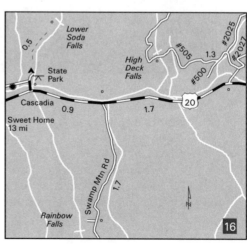

Form: tiered   *Magnitude:* 25 (l)   *Watershed:* sm   *Elevation:* 1270 feet   *USGS Map:* Cascadia (1985)

Soda Creek tumbles 150 to 180 feet in three tiers among moss-covered rocks. Located within Cascadia State Park. Start at the state park, located 13 miles east of Sweet Home along U.S. 20. Find the unmarked trail at the far north end of the campsite area and hike a moderately steep 0.5 mile to the descent.

Lower Soda Falls

Rainbow Falls ✰✰   ③ 🏃

Form: punchbowl   *Magnitude:* 40   *Watershed:* sm
Elevation: 1460 feet   *USGS Map:* Cascadia (1985)

      Dobbin Creek pours 20 to 30 feet into a pool. The waterfall lies outside national forest land, most likely on private property. Drive 0.9 mile east of the community of Cascadia, then turn right (south) off U.S. 20 onto

Swamp Mountain Road. Follow this gravel route for 1.7 miles, parking at an unsigned, old dirt road to the right. Follow the dirt road for about 100 feet, then descend along the top of a small ridge to an open view of the falls.

Others: *High Deck Falls* (u) ☆ USGS Cascadia (1985 ns). Water cascades steeply for more than 100 feet along an unnamed creek. Unofficially named after a nearby mountain. Probably located on private property. Continue east along U.S. 20 for 1.7 miles past Swamp Mountain Road (described previously) to Moose Creek Road #2027. Follow the turns as shown on the accompanying map to Road #505 and the cataract in 1.3 miles.

17. McDowell Creek Falls County Park

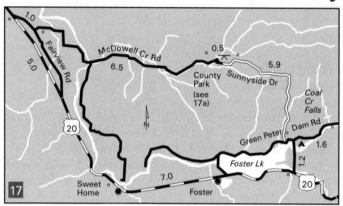

Four of the five waterfalls described in this section are within McDowell Creek Falls County Park, a pleasant and thoughtfully planned day-use recreation area. Turn off U.S. 20 at Fairview Road. Proceed east for 1 mile, then turn left onto McDowell Creek Road. The county park and first parking turnout are 6.5 miles farther east.

Lower Falls ☆☆

Form: tiered   *Magnitude:* 45   *Watershed:* med
Elevation: 800 feet   *USGS Map:* Sweet Home (1984 nl)

This minor pair of descents drops 5 to 10 feet along McDowell Creek. Park at the southern access point of the park's trail system. This entry is located a very short walk away, immediately downstream from the first footbridge.

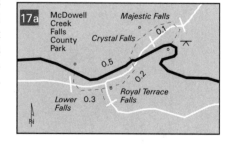

Royal Terrace Falls ★★★   ②

Form: tiered   *Magnitude:* 39 (l)   *Watershed:* vsm
Elevation: 1000 feet   *USGS Map:* Sweet Home (1984 ns)

Fall Creek sprays 119 feet down in a fountain-like tiered display. A marked spur path ascends to a viewpoint above the top of the cataract. Walk an easy 0.3 mile upstream from Lower Falls (described previously) to this waterfall.

Majestic Falls ★★★

Form: block   *Magnitude:* 58   *Watershed:* med
Elevation: 980 feet   *USGS Map:* Sweet Home (1984 nl)

A porch-like overlook allows a close-up view of this 30- to 40-foot drop tumbling from McDowell Creek. Drive to the north end of the park. A stairway leads a short distance to the vista. Hikers can also reach it by continuing northward along the main trail from Royal Terrace Falls (described previously).

Coal Creek Falls (u) ★★   ④

Form: plunge   *Magnitude:* 32 (l)   *Watershed:* sm
Elevation: 920 feet   *USGS Map:* Green Peter (1984 nl)

Coal Creek drops 40 to 60 feet in a waterfall located outside McDowell Creek Falls County Park. Most likely situated on private property. Depart U.S. 20 at the east end of Foster Lake and drive north on Sunnyside Drive to Green Peter Dam Road. You can also reach this road by following Sunnyside Drive for 6 miles southeast of McDowell Creek Falls County Park. Once you reach the Middle Santiam River, drive east 1.6 miles and park at the dirt road to the left (north). Walk to the end of the road, then scramble up the crumbly slope to a faint path. A short distance farther will be a fairly distant view of this entry.

Others: *Crystal Falls* ★ USGS Sweet Home (1984 nl). McDowell Creek skips 10 to 15 feet into punchbowl-shaped Crystal Pool. Continue on foot 0.1 mile past Majestic Falls (described previously) to a vista of this modest descent.

THE SOUTH CASCADES

South-central Oregon presents a collage of scenic outdoor settings typical of the Cascade Range. The area's major peaks include Three Sisters, Bachelor Butte, Diamond Peak, and Mount McLoughlin—all of them volcanic in origin. The region also boasts five national forests, four wilderness areas, an abundance of mountain lakes, and Crater Lake National Park. Waterfalls are well distributed throughout the South Cascades. Most of the 114 recognized falls in the region are relatively accessible; 66 of them are listed in this book.

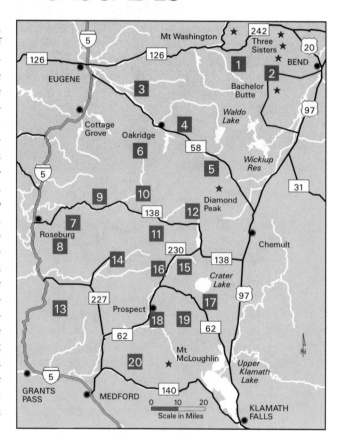

Many of this region's waterfalls are among the most majestic of the Pacific Northwest. They often occur streaming down the walls of canyons carved by alpine glaciers. During the last major Ice Age, 10,000 to 14,000 years ago, these glaciers extended their range to areas below 2,500 feet in elevation in the South Cascades. Large, U-shaped glacial troughs remain as evidence of the intense erosive powers of these glaciers. Today rivers follow the valleys abandoned by the retreating glaciers. As tributary streams flow into the troughs, they often drop sharply as waterfalls. *Rainbow Falls, Proxy Falls,* and *Vidae Falls* are examples. Many physical geographers and geologists refer to this type of descent as a *ribbon* falls.

The western portion of the South Cascades formed in the same manner as the central portion described in the preceding chapter. Where layers of resistant basalt and weak sandstone meet along a stream's course, the sandstone erodes faster than the basalt. The graceful *Toketee Falls* and *Grotto Falls* are good examples of cataracts shaped in this way.

I. Three Sisters Wilderness

The peaks of North Sister (10,085 feet), Middle Sister (10,047 feet), and South Sister (10,358 feet) dominate the Cascade scenery along S.R. 242. The following trio of waterfalls are just inside Three Sisters Wilderness, which is located within the McKenzie Ranger District of Willamette National Forest, and are readily accessible.

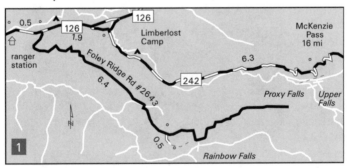

Rainbow Falls ★★★   ② 🏃

Form: horsetail   *Magnitude:* 85 (h)   *Watershed:* med
Elevation: 2960 feet   *USGS Map:* Linton Lake (1988)

The peaks of the Three Sisters provide a background to a cross-valley view of Rainbow Creek distantly descending 150 to 200 feet. About 0.5 mile east of McKenzie Bridge Ranger Station turn south off S.R. 126 onto Foley Ridge Road #2643. Follow Road #2643 for 6.4 miles, then turn right on the marked dirt road and proceed 0.5 mile to the start of Rainbow Falls Trail #3543. The moderately gentle trail ends in 0.8 mile at an unfenced vista.

Upper Falls ☆☆   ②🚶

Form: segmented   *Magnitude:* 28 (l)   *Watershed:* vsm
Elevation: 3000 feet   *USGS Map:* Linton Lake (1988 ns)

Water cascades steeply 100 to 125 feet from springs issuing from a high canyon wall. Turn southeast off S.R. 126 onto S.R. 242 and drive 6.3 miles east to the turnout for Proxy Falls Trail #3532. Hike about 0.5 mile, then take a left fork, which soon leads to this entry.

Proxy Falls ☆☆☆☆   ②🚶

Form: fan   *Magnitude:* 91   *Watershed:* med
Elevation: 3000 feet   *USGS Map:* Linton Lake (1988)

Gain a close-up view of Proxy Creek pouring 200 feet in impressive fashion. Also called *Lower Falls.* Toward the end of Trail #3532 (described previously), follow the right spur. It quickly leads to a developed viewpoint overlooking this cataract.

2. Cascade Lakes Highway

Drive west from Bend for 28 miles on the Cascade Lakes Highway, also known as Century Drive and County Road #46. Turn at the signed access for Green Lakes Trail. There are two parking areas: the one to the right (east) accesses waterfalls along Soda Creek Trail; the other leads to Green Lakes Trail and its cataract. This area is a part of Bend Ranger District, Deschutes National Forest.

Soda Creek Falls (u) ☆☆   ③🚶

Form: tiered   *Magnitude:* 39   *Watershed:* sm
Elevation: 5900 feet   *USGS Map:* Broken Top (1988 nl)

Soda Creek drops 5 to 10 feet in block form before fanning downward another 20 to 30 feet. The minor descent of *Soda Spring Falls* (u) ☆ USGS Broken Top (1988 ns), will be encountered a few hundred yards before reaching this entry.

Hike along Soda Creek Trail for 2.1 miles through a lava field, then a meadow. After the trail reaches a wooded area, it is 0.6 mile farther to both falls. The main display is situated just upstream from the point where the trail departs the stream and switchbacks uphill.

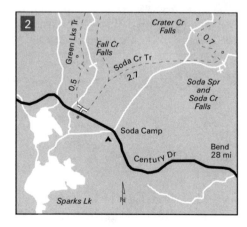

Crater Creek Falls (u) ★★   ⑤, 🏃 and 🚶

Form: fan   *Magnitude:* 41   *Watershed:* sm
Elevation: 6240 feet   *USGS Map:* Broken Top (1988 nl)

Water sprays 40 to 50 feet downward along Crater Creek. Recommended for adults only. After passing Soda Creek Falls (described previously), the trail steepens considerably. After 0.7 mile, Crater Creek will come into view. Leave the trail and proceed down the ridge top for about 100 yards. Stay off the steep slopes in the canyon!

Fall Creek Falls ★★★   ④ 🏃

Form: block   *Magnitude:* 61   *Watershed:* med
Elevation: 5500 feet   *USGS Map:* Broken Top (1988 nl)

Fall Creek explodes 25 to 35 feet over a rock escarpment. Starting at Green Lakes Trail (described previously), walk up the moderately steep path for 0.5 mile. The sound of the falls will be plainly heard. Find the short side trail, which leads above the cataract and to several paths that take you below to full views.

3. Big Fall Creek

Chichester Falls ★★★

Form: punchbowl   *Magnitude:* 34   *Watershed:* med
Elevation: 1100 feet   *USGS Map:* Saddleblanket Mtn (1986)

This idyllic 20- to 30-foot drop along Andy Creek is located within Lowell Ranger District, Willamette National Forest. The easiest way to view it is from the highway bridge. Look closely to observe an interesting grotto around the plunge pool. Moss and plants enhance the setting.

There are several interesting scenes on the way to this entry. Turn off S.R. 58 at the Lowell Exit, where an old covered bridge looks out of place above the reservoir of Lookout Point Lake. To reach the falls, follow the Lowell–Jasper Road through town and just before reaching a second covered bridge turn right (east) in 2.9 miles on Big Fall Creek Road. Take this

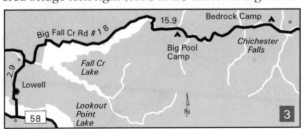

secondary road, which becomes Road #18, for 15.9 miles to an unsigned turnout at Andy Creek.

4. Salmon Creek

Reach the following pair of waterfalls by turning north off S.R. 58 at Fish Hatchery Road, which is located on the east side of Oakridge. Follow the

Chichester Falls

route 1.4 miles to its end, then proceed right (east) on Salmon Creek Road #24. Both cataracts are located within Oakridge Ranger District, Willamette National Forest.

Lithan Falls ★★

Form: cascade   *Magnitude:* 25   *Watershed:* sm
Elevation: 3980 feet   *USGS Map:* Waldo Lake (1986)

Nettie Creek steeply cascades 60 to 80 feet. Follow Salmon Creek Road #24 eastward past Salmon Creek Falls (described later). At 6.2 mile, the

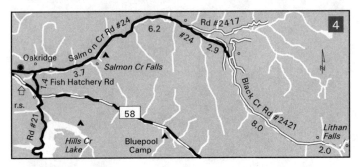

paved road crosses Salmon Creek and becomes a single lane. Continue 2.7 additional miles to a crossing at Black Creek. About 0.2 mile farther, bear right (south) on graveled Black Creek Road #2421. The road ends in 8 more miles at the start of Black Creek Trail #3551. Hike the moderately steep route to a trailside view of the falls in 2 miles. The federal government's Geographic Names Information System catalogs a *Lillian Falls*, USGS Waldo Lake (1986 ns), in the same vicinity as this falls, but it is not clear whether this is simply an alias for this falls or whether there is a second waterfall in the area.

Others: *Salmon Creek Falls* ✪ USGS Huckleberry Mtn (1986). Salmon Creek is interrupted by this 5- to 10-foot descent. Drive 3.7 miles east along Salmon Creek Road (described previously) to Salmon Creek Falls Campground.

5. Salt Creek

A concentration of six impressive cataracts occurs within an area of only 2 square miles in the Oakridge Ranger District of Willamette National Forest. Drive 21 miles east from Oakridge or 6 miles west from Willamette Pass along S.R. 58. Park at the Salt Creek Falls turnout or in Salt Creek Falls Picnic Area.

Salt Creek Falls ☆☆☆☆☆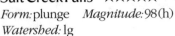

Form: plunge   *Magnitude:* 98 (h)
Watershed: lg
Elevation: 4000 feet   *USGS Map:*
Diamond Peak (1986)

This cascade is the gem of the South Cascades, as Salt Creek plummets 286 feet into a gorge. Trails and a fenced vista provide a variety of views of the cataract, which was first seen by Anglos (Frank S. Warner and Charles Tufti) in March 1887. The falls is easily accessible from the turnout or the picnic area (described previously).

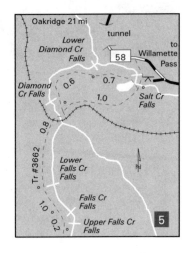

Lower Diamond Creek Falls ★★   ② 🚶

Form: tiered   *Magnitude:* 82   *Watershed:* med
Elevation: 4000 feet   *USGS Map:* Diamond Peak (1986 nl)

Although it is 200 to 250 feet high, this entry's scenic rating is diminished by obscured views. When last visited in 1988, a couple of trees prevented a clear vantage of the bottom portion of the falls. From Salt Creek Picnic Area (described previously), follow Diamond Creek Falls Trail #3598 for a gentle 0.7 mile along the rim of Salt Creek Canyon to one of several viewpoints.

Diamond Creek Falls ★★★★   ③ 🚶

Form: fan   *Magnitude:* 72   *Watershed:* med
Elevation: 4240 feet   *USGS Map:* Diamond Peak (1986 nl)

This superb cataract occurs where Diamond Creek pours 70 to 90 feet downward. Follow Trail #3598 for 0.6 mile beyond Lower Diamond Creek Falls (described previously). A trail provides a good viewpoint above

Diamond Creek Falls

the descent, plus a short spur trail quickly leads to its base. A loop route can be taken back to Salt Creek Picnic Area by continuing a short distance, bearing left onto Vivian Lake Trail #3662, and walking 1 mile.

Lower Falls Creek Falls (u) ★★   ④
Form: tiered   *Magnitude:* 45   *Watershed:* sm
Elevation: 4440 feet   *USGS Map:* Diamond Peak (1986 ns)

This double waterfall along Falls Creek totals 30 to 50 feet. At the junction of Diamond Creek Falls Trail #3598 with Vivian Lake Trail #3662 (described previously), turn right onto Trail #3662. Cross some railroad tracks and proceed 0.8 mile up the moderately steep path to views just off the trail.

Falls Creek Falls ★★   ⑤
Form: plunge   *Magnitude:* 54   *Watershed:* sm
Elevation: 4780 feet   *USGS Map:* Diamond Peak (1986)

Falls Creek plunges 40 to 60 feet. Continue climbing steeply for 1 mile past Lower Falls Creek Falls (described previously). A sign tacked to a tree points to a moderately distant view of this entry.

Upper Falls Creek Falls (u) ★★★   ⑤
Form: fan   *Magnitude:* 69   *Watershed:* sm
Elevation: 5000 feet   *USGS Map:* Diamond Peak (1986 ns)

This is the best of the cataracts along Falls Creek, descending 50 to 80 feet. Hike 0.2 mile past Falls Creek Falls (described previously) to a trailside vantage. From here, it is 3 miles back to Salt Creek Picnic Area.

6. Row River

Several waterfalls are to be found within the Row River drainage basin. Access the area by departing I-5 at Cottage Grove (Exit 174) and driving east on Cottage Grove–Dorena Road for 17 miles to the community of Culp Creek. All but Wildwood Falls are situated within Cottage Grove Ranger District, Umpqua National Forest.

Upper Falls Creek Falls

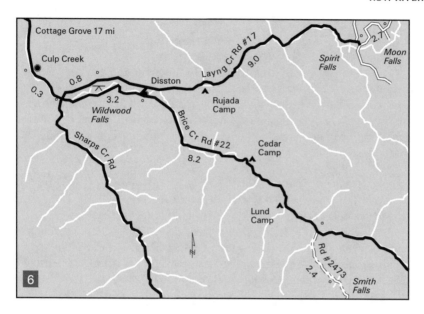

Wildwood Falls ★★

Form: punchbowl   *Magnitude:* 34   *Watershed:* lg
Elevation: 1000 feet   *USGS Map:* Culp Creek (1986)

The Row River is interrupted by this 10- to 15-foot drop. Drive to the east side of Culp Creek townsite, then bear left in 0.3 mile onto an unsigned road, remaining on the north side of the Row River. Views of the descent are available at the Wildwood Falls Picnic Area in 0.8 mile, and at a developed roadside vista just before.

Smith Falls ★★

Form: segmented   *Magnitude:* 42   *Watershed:* med
Elevation: 2640 feet   *USGS Map:* Fairview Peak (1986)

Champion Creek tumbles 15 to 25 feet along a route dubbed the "Tour of the Golden Past," which was once a thoroughfare leading to the historic Bohemia Mining District, only remnants of which remain. A sign indicating the location of Jerome #9 Placer Claim is posted near the falls. Drive east from Culp Creek to the hamlet of Disston, bearing right (southeast) on Brice Creek Road #22. After an additional 8.2 miles, turn right (south) onto Champion Creek Road #2473. Vehicles with decent clearance can usually drive up the road during summer, though the 2.4-mile journey will be slow.

Spirit Falls ☆☆☆   ③

Form: fan   *Magnitude:* 34 (l)   *Watershed:* sm
Elevation: 1920 feet   *USGS Map:* Rose Hill (1986)

This aptly named 60-foot veil, located where Alex Creek gouges into a bulging mass of moss-covered substrate, has a surrealistic feel. From Disston (described previously), stay on the main road. After crossing the Row River, the route changes its name to Layng Creek Road #17. Proceed 9 miles to a signed trailhead and a path which leads moderately steeply 0.5 mile to a picnic table at the base of this entry.

Moon Falls ☆☆   ②

Form: fan   *Magnitude:* 24 (t)   *Watershed:* vsm
Elevation: 3000 feet   *USGS Map:* Holland Point (1986)

The upper reaches of Alex Creek drop 120 feet. The approach is an easy 0.5-mile walk, complete with a picnic table. Continue 0.2 mile past the trailhead for Spirit Falls (described previously) to Road #1702. Turn left and drive 2.7 miles; then bear right on Road #1702–728. Drive along this unimproved surface for 0.3 mile before turning left on Road #1702–203; in another 0.1 mile reach the trailhead.

7. Little River

As you progress up the Little River Valley you will pass one waterfall after another. Access the area by turning southeast off S.R. 138 at Glide onto Little River Road #27. All but the first descent described are located within North Umpqua Ranger District, Umpqua National Forest.

Wolf Creek Falls ☆☆☆   ③

Form: tiered   *Magnitude:* 26 (l)   *Watershed:* med
Elevation: 1280 feet   *USGS Map:* Red Butte (1989)

Water slides down a mountainside in two parts. The upper portion drops 75 feet and the lower 50 feet. The trail to the falls is courtesy of the Bureau of Land Management. Drive southeast 10.6 miles from S.R. 138 along Little River Road #27 and stop at the signed parking area across the road from Wolf Creek Trailhead. It is a gently sloping 2-mile trip to the falls.

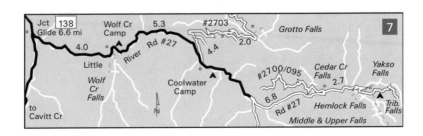

Wolf Creek Falls

Hemlock Falls ☆☆

Form: horsetail   *Magnitude:* 63   *Watershed:* med
Elevation: 2800 feet   *USGS Map:* Quartz Mtn (1989)

Water rushes 80 feet along the lower reaches of Hemlock Creek. Drive along Little River Road #27 for 14.8 miles past Wolf Creek Falls (described previously) and turn at Lake in the Woods Camp. Hemlock Falls Trail #1520 begins just before you reach the campsites. Follow this steep path for 0.5 mile down to this entry.

Tributary Falls (u) ★★   ③ 🚶

Form: horsetail   *Magnitude:* 40   *Watershed:* vsm
Elevation: 3260 feet   *USGS Map:* Quartz Mtn (1989 ns)

Dropping 20 to 30 feet along an unnamed creek, this is the first of a trio of waterfalls visible along the recently reconstructed Hemlock Trail #1505. Drive 0.1 mile eastward past Lake in the Woods Camp (described previously). Turn right (south) on a dirt road and proceed an additional 0.1 mile to the trailhead. Hike up the moderately steep route for 0.5 mile to a viewing platform.

Middle Hemlock Falls (u) ★★   ④ 🚶

Form: tiered   *Magnitude:* 41   *Watershed:* sm
Elevation: 3340 feet   *USGS Map:* Quartz Mtn (1989 nl)

From the trail only the upper portion of this descent can be seen tumbling 30 to 40 feet from Hemlock Creek. Hike the steep trail past Tributary Falls (described previously) for 0.3 mile to trailside vantages.

Upper Hemlock Falls (u) ★★★   ④ 🚶

Form: plunge   *Magnitude:* 43   *Watershed:* sm
Elevation: 3580 feet   *USGS Map:* Quartz Mtn (1989 nl)

The best of the cataracts along Trail #1505, as water hurtles 30 to 40 feet along Hemlock Creek. Follow the steep trail another 0.2 mile past Middle Hemlock Falls (described previously) to a trailside view. It is 1 mile back down the mountain to the trailhead.

Yakso Falls ★★★   ③ 🚶

Form: fan   *Magnitude:* 71   *Watershed:* sm
Elevation: 3100 feet   *USGS Map:* Quartz Mtn (1989)

This is a classic example of a fan form, as the Little River takes a 70-foot drop. Yakso Falls Trail #1519 starts across the road from the entrance to Lake in the Woods Camp (described previously). Proceed 0.7 mile down to the base of the falls.

Grotto Falls ★★★   ② 🚶

Form: segmented   *Magnitude:* 37 (l)   *Watershed:* med
Elevation: 3120 feet   *USGS Map:* Mace Mtn (1989)

The shimmering waters of this pleasant waterfall plunge 100 feet along Emile Creek. In the previous edition of this book, this waterfall was said to be also known as Emile Falls. However, *Emile Falls*, USGS Mace Mtn (1985), is actually another cataract farther downstream and was not accessible when this entry was field-truthed in 1991. The creek and its namesake falls, plus Shivigny Mountain, are named after Emile Shivigny, who homesteaded nearby in 1875.

Backtrack 9.5 miles from Lake in the Woods Camp or continue 5.3 miles past Wolf Creek Falls along Little River Road #27 (described previously). Turn north onto Road #2703, drive 4.4 miles, then turn left on Road #2703/150. Follow this gravel route up the mountain 2 miles farther to Grotto Falls Trail

Yakso Falls

#1503, located on the far side of Emile Creek bridge. The trail goes behind the descent in 0.3 mile.

Others: *Cedar Creek Falls* ☆ USGS Taft Mtn (1989 ns). Cedar Creek trickles 40 to 60 feet from the adjacent cliff. Wet your head if you dare! Continue 12.1 miles past Wolf Creek along Little River Road #27 (described previously). Turn left (north) on Road #2700/095, where a sign points toward Cedar Creek Falls. Drive 1 mile to the creek where there is a sharp switchback in the road.

8. Cavitt Creek

Shadow Falls ★★★   ③ 🚶

Form: tiered   *Magnitude:* 42   *Watershed:* med
Elevation: 2200 feet   *USGS Map:* Red Butte (1989)

       This triple waterfall totaling 80 to 100 feet along Cavitt Creek is aptly named. Over time the falls has worked its way upstream through a rock fracture, forming a narrow, natural grotto that always offers some shade. Immediately downstream from the falls, next to the trail, are interesting weathered bedrock formations.

       Turn right (south) off Little River Road (described previously) onto Cavitt Creek Road #25, which is located 6.6 miles from Glide. Drive southeast 11.3 miles and stop at the signed turnout. Follow Shadow Falls Trail #1504 to the cataract in 0.8 mile.

Others: *Cavitt Falls* ☆ USGS Lane Mtn (1987). Take a footbath in the refreshing pool at the base of this 10- to 15-foot descent. To find this waterfall drive 3.3 miles south on Cavitt Creek Road #25 (described previously) to Cavitt Falls Park, administered by the Bureau of Land Management.

9. Idleyld Park

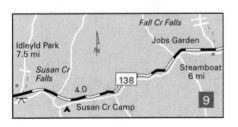

Scenic S.R. 138 serves as a convenient corridor between Glide and Crater Lake, making the following waterfalls accessible to the traveler.

Susan Creek Falls ★★★   ②

Form: fan   *Magnitude:* 50   *Watershed:* med
Elevation: 1060 feet   *USGS Map:* Old Fairview (1989)

This 30- to 40-foot cataract along Susan Creek is situated on a Bureau of Land Management parcel. Those hiking beyond the falls can see Indian mounds. Drive east from Idleyld Park along S.R. 138 for 7.5 miles to Susan Creek Picnic Area. The trailhead is across the road from the parking area. Reach the falls by hiking 1 mile along a relatively gentle path.

Fall Creek Falls ★★★   ③

Form: tiered   *Magnitude:* 57   *Watershed:* sm
Elevation: 1400 feet   *USGS Map:* Mace Mtn (1989 nl)

Fall Creek tumbles twice, with each tier dropping 35 to 50 feet. Located within the North Umpqua Ranger District of Umpqua National Forest. Reach this entry by walking around and through slabs of bedrock and past the natural, lush vegetation of Jobs Garden.

Drive 4 miles east from Susan Creek Picnic Area (described previously) on S.R. 138 to the marked turnout for Fall Creek Falls National Recreation Trail. This beautiful path leads 0.9 mile to the falls.

10. Steamboat

Fishing is prohibited in the entire basin encompassing Steamboat Creek in order to provide undisturbed spawning grounds for the salmon and steelhead of the North Umpqua River drainage. The following waterfalls are all situated within North Umpqua Ranger District, Umpqua National Forest.

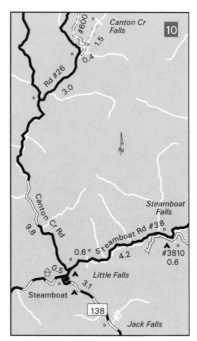

Steamboat Falls ★★★

Form: block   *Magnitude:* 47
Watershed: lg
Elevation: 1380 feet   *USGS Map:*
Steamboat (1989)

A developed viewpoint showcases this 20- to 30-foot drop along Steamboat Creek. Some fish attempt to jump the falls, while others use the adjacent ladder. Turn northeast off S.R. 138 onto Steamboat Road #38 at Steamboat Junction. Drive 5.3 miles and turn right

Steamboat Falls

(southeast) on Road #3810. Continue 0.6 mile to the entrance of Steamboat Falls Campground and the cataract.

Jack Falls ☆☆   ④
Form: tiered   *Magnitude:* 32 (l)   *Watershed:* sm
Elevation: 1460 feet   *USGS Map:* Steamboat (1989)
          This set of three falls is closely grouped along Jack Creek. The lower descent slides 20 to 30 feet in two segments. The middle and upper falls are of the horsetail type, descending 25 to 40 feet and 50 to 70 feet, respectively.
          Park at an unsigned turnout at mile marker 42, located 3.1 miles southeast of Steamboat junction along S.R. 138. Walk 100 yards farther to Jack Creek. Follow the brushy streambank to the base of the lower falls.

Canton Creek Falls ☆☆   ③ ⚡
Form: horsetail   *Magnitude:* 41   *Watershed:* sm
Elevation: 2480 feet   *USGS Map:* Fairview Peak (1986 nl)
          Walk to a gorge-rim vista of this 60- to 80-foot slide along Canton Creek. From S.R. 138, turn northeast on Steamboat Road #38, then left in 0.5 mile onto Canton Creek Road. Follow this route for 9.8 miles to Upper Canton Road #26 and turn right. Take Road #26 for 3.0 miles and turn right (east) on

Saddle Camp Road #2300-600. Reach the trailhead in 0.4 mile. Hike 1.5 miles along Canton Creek Falls Trail #1537 to your destination.

Others: *Little Falls* ☆ USGS Steamboat (1989). Watch fish negotiate this 5- to 10-foot break along the course of Steamboat Creek. Turn northeast off S.R. 138 onto Steamboat Road #38 at Steamboat junction. Drive 1.1 miles to the unsigned turnout next to the falls and the adjacent bedrock slabs.

II. Toketee

The following pair of waterfalls are among the most impressive in the South Cascades and are not very difficult to access. Both are located within Diamond Lake Ranger District, Umpqua National Forest.

Toketee Falls ☆☆☆☆

Form: tiered   *Magnitude:* 61   *Watershed:* lg (d)
Elevation: 2340 feet   *USGS Map:* Toketee Falls (1986)

These falls are an inspiring sight, as the North Umpqua River drops 30 feet before plunging 90 feet over a sheer wall of basalt. *Toketee* is a Native American word meaning "graceful." The Toketee Pipeline can be seen along the walk to the falls. Pacific Power diverts water from Toketee Lake via its 12-foot redwood-stave pipe. A portion of the North Umpqua River is bypassed for 1,663 feet via a mile-long tunnel. The water then plunges down a steel penstock pipe to the Toketee Powerhouse, where it can generate as much as 210,000 kilowatts of electricity.

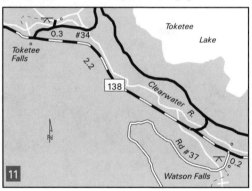

Turn north off S.R. 138 on Road #34, heading toward Toketee Lake. Drive 0.3 mile to the left (west) turn marked Toketee Falls Trail #1495. Follow the easily hiked path 0.6 mile to a viewpoint looking into the falls.

Watson Falls ☆☆☆☆☆

Form: plunge   *Magnitude:* 99 (h)   *Watershed:* med
Elevation: 3200 feet   *USGS Map:* Fish Creek Desert (1989)

Peer up at Watson Creek plummeting 272 feet from a cliff. The first good vantage is from a footbridge, with the trail continuing more steeply to the base of the waterfall. Drive east 2.2 miles past Toketee Lake along S.R. 138 to Fish Creek Road #37; turn right (south). Proceed 0.2 mile to

Watson Falls

Watson Falls Picnic Ground. Follow Watson Falls Trail #1495 to the first vista in 0.3 mile.

12. Northeast Umpqua

The cataracts never seem to cease in the North Umpqua River watershed. This section describes four more descents within Diamond Lake Ranger District, Umpqua National Forest.

Whitehorse Falls ☆☆

Form: punchbowl   *Magnitude:*
37   *Watershed:* lg
Elevation: 3660 feet   *USGS Map:*
Garwood Butte (1985)

Relax at the viewing area
overlooking this 10- to 15-foot punchbowl
along the course of the Clearwater River.
Depart S.R. 138 at the signed turn for
Whitehorse Falls Camp, which is located
4.5 miles east of Toketee. Park at the picnic area adjacent to the cataract.

Clearwater Falls ☆☆ ①🚶

Form: segmented   *Magnitude:* 48
Watershed: med
Elevation: 4200 feet   *USGS Map:*
Diamond Lake (1985)

The Clearwater River tum-

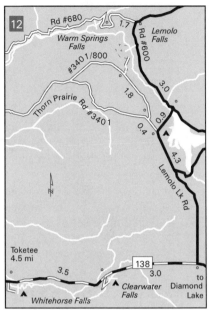

bles 30 feet. Drive 3.5 miles east from Whitehorse Falls (described previously) along S.R. 138 to the marked turn for Clearwater Falls Camp. Follow
the access road 0.2 mile to a picnic area, from which a path quickly leads to
the falls.

Lemolo Falls ☆☆☆☆   ④🚶

Form: horsetail   *Magnitude:* 75 (h)   *Watershed:* lg (d)
Elevation: 3720 feet   *USGS Map:* Lemolo Lake (1986)

While the prior pair of entries are conducive to meditation, this
75- to 100-foot monster along the North Umpqua River won't allow such tran-
quillity. *Lemolo* is a Chinook word meaning "wild" or "untamed." Depart S.R.
138 by turning north onto Lemolo Lake Road #2610, located 3 miles east of
Clearwater Falls (described previously). Proceed toward Lemolo Lake and
bear left (north) after 4.3 miles onto Thorn Prairie Road #3401. Go 0.4 mile,
then turn right on Lemolo Falls Road #3401/800. The trailhead is 1.8 miles
farther. Lemolo Falls Trail #1468 descends steeply, reaching the base of the
thunderous falls in 1 mile.

Warm Springs Falls ☆☆☆   ①🚶

Form: block   *Magnitude:* 68   *Watershed:* med
Elevation: 3580 feet   *USGS Map:* Lemolo Lake (1986 ns)

Warm Springs Creek plummets 50 to 70 feet over cliffs of basalt.
Follow the directions to Lemolo Falls (described previously), but instead of
turning at Road #3401, continue 0.9 mile on Lemolo Lake Road #2610 to the
far side of Lemolo Dam. Turn left (northwest) on Road #600, and drive 3 miles

to Road #680. Bear left here and proceed 1.7 miles to the start of Warm Springs Falls Trail #1499. At the trail's end in 0.3 mile is an unguarded vista above the cataract.

13. Azalea

Next to Devils Flat Camp are a pair of historic buildings, providing visitors the opportunity to envision how homesteaders lived. The following small descent is nearby. Access the area by departing I-5 at Azalea (Exit 88) and proceed eastward along Cow Creek Road for 17.2 miles.

Cow Creek Falls ★ USGS Cedar Springs Mtn (1986 ns). Cow Creek drops 25 to 40 feet along a series of rock steps. Across the road from the campground is a short loop trail that passes the falls.

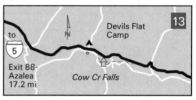

14. South Umpqua

The following trio of modest waterfalls occur within the watershed of the South Umpqua River, Tiller Ranger District, Umpqua National Forest. Access the area by driving along S.R. 227 to the hamlet of Tiller.

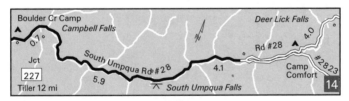

Campbell Falls ★★   ②

Form: punchbowl   *Magnitude:* 36 (h)   *Watershed:* lg
Elevation: 1430 feet   *USGS Map:* Dumont Creek (1989)

The South Umpqua River tumbles 10 to 15 feet. The name of the falls honors Robert G. Campbell, a former U.S. Forest Service employee who was killed in action during World War II. Turn off S.R. 227 onto South Umpqua Road #28, located just northwest of the ranger station at Tiller. Proceed 12.7 miles to the signed turnout, 0.7 mile past Boulder Creek Camp. A trail leads quickly to the river in 0.2 mile.

South Umpqua Falls ★★

Form: cascade   *Magnitude:* 25   *Watershed:* lg
Elevation: 1640 feet   *USGS Map:* Acker Rock (1989)

Water slides 10 to 15 feet over wide slabs of bedrock along the South Umpqua River. A fish ladder bypasses the falls. Drive southeast on

South Umpqua Road #28, 5.9 miles past Campbell Falls (described previously) to South Umpqua Falls Picnic Area and Observation Point.

Deer Lick Falls ★★

Form: tiered   *Magnitude:* 43   *Watershed:* lg
Elevation: 2280 feet   *USGS Map:* Twin Lakes Mtn (1989)

Peer from a moderate distance into a series of five blocklike descents ranging from 5 to 20 feet in height along Black Rock Fork. Drive 4.1 miles northeast past South Umpqua Falls (described previously) along South Umpqua Road #28. Do not cross the river at the junction, but bear left on Road #28 toward Camp Comfort. Four miles farther find unsigned vantages along the road.

15. Upper Rogue River

The following entries are all situated within Prospect Ranger District, Rogue River National Forest.

Upper Rogue Falls (u) ★★   ③

Form: cascade   *Magnitude:* 44   *Watershed:* med
Elevation: 4590 feet   *USGS Map:* Hamaker Butte (1985 nl)

Upper Rogue River Trail #1034 passes next to two falls along its northerly route. This entry descends steeply 30 to 50 feet along the Rogue River. The 15- to 25-foot drop of *Middle Rogue Falls* (u) ★ USGS Hamaker Butte (1985 nl), will be encountered 1.5 miles downstream. The closest trailhead to the Upper Falls is at Mazama Viewpoint, which is located 6 miles west of S.R. 138 on S.R. 230. Trail access is also possible to the south from Hamaker Campground, as shown on the accompanying map.

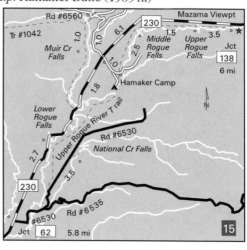

National Creek Falls ★★   ③

Form: segmented   *Magnitude:* 50   *Watershed:* med
Elevation: 3860 feet   *USGS Map:* Hamaker Butte (1985 nl)

National Creek pours 30 to 50 feet downward in three segments. From S.R. 62, turn north on S.R. 230. In 5.8 miles, turn right (east) on Road #6530. Follow this secondary route 3.5 miles to the marked parking area for

National Creek Falls Trail #1053. The path descends fairly steeply to the base of the cataract in 0.5 mile.

Others: *Muir Creek Falls* ☆ USGS Hamaker Butte (1985 nl). East Fork Muir Creek drops a total of 15 to 25 feet into Muir Creek. Trailside views are available from the opposite side of the small gorge. Leave S.R. 230 at Road #6560, which is located across from Hamaker Camp (described previously). Drive about 1 mile to a turnout signed for Buck Canyon Trail #1042 and hike 1 mile downstream.

Lower Rogue Falls (u) ☆ USGS Hamaker Butte (1985 nl). This block-type waterfall drops 10 to 15 feet where S.R. 230 follows a sweeping bend in the Rogue River. Drive to an unsigned turnout 1.8 miles south of Road #6560, or 2.7 miles north of Road #6530.

16. Natural Bridge

Two hundred feet of the Rogue River disappears underground, pro-

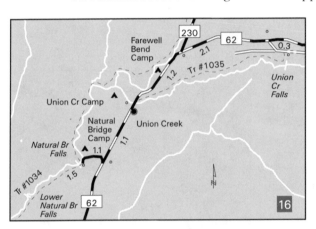

viding a "natural bridge" across the stream. Drive 1.1 miles south of the community of Union Creek along S.R. 62 to the signed turn, then another 1.1 miles to this geologic oddity and Rogue River Trail #1034. Three waterfalls occur within this portion of Prospect Ranger District, Rogue River National Forest.

Natural Bridge Falls (u) ☆☆

Form: cascade   *Magnitude:* 33   *Watershed:* lg
Elevation: 3200 feet   *USGS Map:* Union Creek (1989 ns)
     The Rogue River tumbles 20 to 30 feet near Natural Bridge. The waterfall is adjacent to a man-made footbridge that crosses Rogue River Trail #1034 (described previously).

Lower Natural Bridge Falls (u) ☆☆   ③ 🚶

Form: punchbowl   *Magnitude:* 24   *Watershed:* lg
Elevation: 3020 feet   *USGS Map:* Union Creek (1989 nl)
     Water froths 10 to 15 feet along the Rogue River. Follow Rogue River Trail #1034 (described previously) for 1.5 miles downstream from Natural Bridge. An old four-wheel-drive road serves as the trail for the last 0.3 mile.

Others: *Union Creek Falls* (u) ☆ USGS Union Creek (1989 nl). A 15- to 20-foot slide along Union Creek. At the junction of S.R. 230 and S.R. 62 bear right, drive 2.1 miles, and turn right (south) on an unsigned gravel road. Proceed 0.2 mile, then bear left on a dirt road. Park in another 0.1 mile and find the trailhead for Union Creek Trail #1035. Walk 0.4 mile to the stream and its falls.

17. Crater Lake National Park

The center of attraction in the park is the enormous depression presently occupied by Crater Lake. Known as a *caldera*, this crater formed as a result of a cataclysmic eruption of volcanic Mount Mazama 6,600 years ago. Heavy annual precipitation maintains the lake level. In addition to the lake, the following falls are readily accessible within the park.

Vidae Falls ☆☆☆

Form: tiered   *Magnitude:* 48   *Watershed:* vsm
Elevation: 6700 feet   *USGS Map:* Crater Lake East (1985 nl)

Vidae Creek sprays 70 to 90 feet from Crater Lake's south rim near Applegate Peak. From the park headquarters drive 3 miles southeast to a turnout near the falls.

Others: *Annie Falls* ☆ USGS Maklaks Crater (1985). Peer into a gorge to see water rushing 30 to 50 feet along Annie Creek, a modest distance away from this unprotected viewpoint. Drive 4.7 miles north from the

Vidae Falls

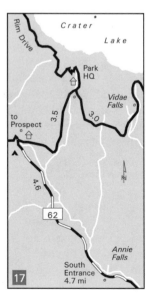

park's south entrance to an unsigned turnout off S.R. 62. Heed the warning signs at the canyon rim! The slopes are very unstable and impossible to walk on.

18. Mill Creek

Three of the following five waterfalls are part of Boise Cascade Corporation's Mill Creek Falls Scenic Area. The timber company has constructed public trails on a tract of pristine land.

Mill Creek Falls ☆☆☆☆   ①

Form: plunge   *Magnitude:* 71   *Watershed:* lg
Elevation: 2360 feet   *USGS Map:* Prospect South (1988)

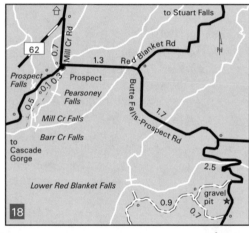

Look across the canyon cut by the Rogue River to this thundering 173-foot plunge along Mill Creek. Turn off S.R. 62 onto Mill Creek Road at either Cascade Gorge or Prospect. Park at the turnout marked by a large trail system sign 0.9 mile from Prospect. Follow the interpretive trail immediately south of the parking area and walk 0.3 mile to the viewpoint.

Barr Creek Falls ☆☆☆☆   ②

Form: fan   *Magnitude:* 94 (h)   *Watershed:* med
Elevation: 2360 feet   *USGS Map:* Prospect South (1988 nl)

This waterfall makes a beautiful display as Barr Creek shimmers 175 to 200 feet into Rogue River Canyon. In historical documents this cataract is also called *Bear Creek Falls.* Follow the trail 0.1 mile past Mill Creek Falls (described previously) to a rocky outcrop providing a superb cross-canyon vista.

Prospect Falls (u) ☆☆☆   ②

Form: cascade   *Magnitude:* 40 (h)   *Watershed:* lg
Elevation: 2500 feet   *USGS Map:* Prospect South (1988 ns)

The Rogue River rushes 50 to 100 feet, neatly framed by the bridge spanning its gorge. Unofficially named by the author after the nearby community. Drive 0.5 mile beyond the Mill Creek parking area (described previously) to an unsigned turnout on the east side of the Rogue River

Prospect Falls

bridge. A well-trodden path leads to many good, unfenced views. Worth the stop, considering it is readily accessible but not advertised.

Pearsoney Falls ★★   ① 🯄

Form: segmented   *Magnitude:* 45   *Watershed:* lg
Elevation: 2480 feet   *USGS Map:* Prospect South (1988 ns)

  Mill Creek drops 15 to 25 feet. The waterfall is named after two early pioneer families of the Prospect area: the Pearsons and the Mooneys. Continue 0.1 mile north of the Rogue River bridge (described previously) to the signed parking area off Mill Creek Road. Follow the main trail 0.2 mile to a trailside view of this entry.

Lower Red Blanket Falls (u) ★★   ⑤, 🯄 and 🚙

Form: tiered   *Magnitude:* 75   *Watershed:* lg
Elevation: 2440 feet   *USGS Map:* Prospect South (1988 nl)

  Red Blanket Creek plummets a total of 90 to 140 feet in a secluded setting. The moderately distant cross-canyon vista is recommended for experienced adventurers only. Probably located on private land. Take Red Blanket Road east from Prospect and turn right after 1.3 miles on Butte Falls–Prospect Rd. Continue another 1.7 miles, then bear right (south) toward Butte Falls. After the route switchbacks uphill, look for a jeep trail to the right (west) in another 2.5 miles. It is the first road past a short gravel road ending at a gravel pit. Follow the jeep trail for 1.6 miles as shown on the accompanying map. Park at a short, abandoned jeep trail, which leads toward the canyon rim. Follow the trail for a few hundred yards, then cut through the woods toward the roaring sound of the falls. Pick a route partway down the moderately steep slope until the falls come into view on the opposite side of the gorge. It will be 0.3 mile to get back to your vehicle.

19. Sky Lakes Wilderness

  Access to the following waterfalls is via Upper Red Blanket Trail #1090. Reach the trailhead by driving east of Prospect along Red Blanket Road for 15 miles to the road's end. All of the falls are located within Sky Lakes Wilderness, Rogue River National Forest.

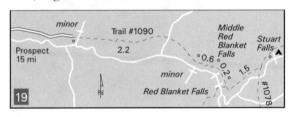

Red Blanket Falls ★★

Form: tiered   *Magnitude:* 50   *Watershed:* med
Elevation: 5060 feet   *USGS Map:* Union Peak (1985)

Red Blanket Creek takes a double-drop, the upper portion descending 50 to 70 feet. Only the top of the lower tier is visible from the trail. Begin hiking the moderately steep Upper Red Blanket Trail #1090. Just beyond the trailhead and at 2.2 miles you will pass small falls along tributaries. At 2.8 miles *Middle Red Blanket Falls*(u) ★★ USGS Union Peak (1985 ns) drops 20 to 25 feet. Proceed another 0.2 mile to trailside views of the main entry.

Stuart Falls ★★★

Form: fan   *Magnitude:* 47   *Watershed:* med
Elevation: 5460 feet   *USGS Map:* Union Peak (1985)

Refresh yourself in the cool mist of water veiling 25 to 40 feet along Red Blanket Creek. Continue 1 mile past Red Blanket Falls (described previously) to the end of Trail #1090. Follow Stuart Falls Trail #1078 to the left (north) and proceed 0.5 mile to the cataract.

Stuart Falls

20. Butte Falls

Butte Falls ★★   ② 🏃

Form: block   *Magnitude:* 54   *Watershed:* lg
Elevation: 2340 feet   *USGS Map:* Butte Falls (1988)

The nearby community is named after this 10- to 15-foot waterfall, which slices diagonally across South Fork Butte Creek. Turn off S.R. 62 at
Butte Falls junction, located 5 miles north of Eagle Point. Reach the town of

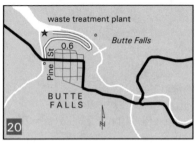

Butte Falls in 16 miles. Upon entering
the village, look for Pine Street to the
left (north). Backtrack 1 block to an
unmarked gravel road. Take this un-
paved route north past a waste treat-
ment plant to an unsigned parking
area in 0.6 mile. Well-worn paths
quickly lead to the falls.

THE COLUMBIA PLATEAU

The landscape of eastern Oregon is dominated by a broad region of generally low relief called the Columbia Plateau. This plain, which extends into southeastern Washington, northern Nevada, and southwestern Idaho, is composed of thick layers of basalt which formed from widespread lava flows 30 million years ago. Waterfalls are scarce in the Oregon portion of the plateau. Because of the consistent erosion resistance of the basaltic bedrock, cataracts are lacking along most of the region's major rivers. In addition, low annual precipitation means that few tributary streams flow over the rims of the larger river canyons. Of the region's 78 known waterfalls, 20 are listed in this chapter.

Most of the cataracts in this region are found where other geomorphic processes have contributed to waterfall formation. Recent lava flows inundated the course of the Deschutes River 5,000 to 6,000 years ago. When the lava cooled, jumbled basaltic rock was formed. The river cuts into and tumbles over these rocky obstructions.

The Strawberry Mountains near the town of John Day were shaped by the accumulation of basalt, rhyolite, and breccia due to volcanic activities 10 million to 13 million years ago. The extreme differences in the erosional resistance of these rock types produce waterfalls in places where streams flow across the contact point between two or more different varieties of rock.

The Wallowa Mountains of northeastern Oregon are one of the few non-volcanic areas of the region. Here large masses of granite and sedimentary rocks were displaced thousands of feet above the surrounding plain 100 million to 150 million years ago. The range's high relief stopped subsequent lava at its western perimeter. Since the Wallowas rise over 8,000 feet above sea level, their climate was sufficiently cold and moist for alpine glaciation to have occurred. The erosive work of these glaciers left vertical breaks for stream courses to plunge over.

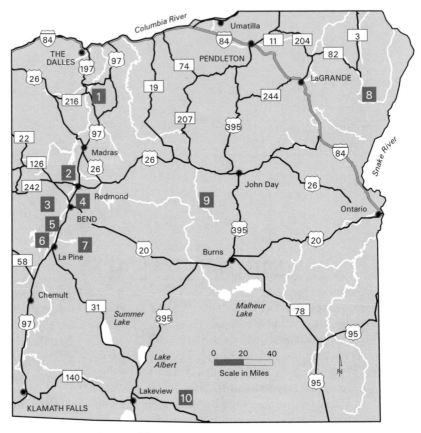

1. Tygh Valley

Both the Deschutes and White Rivers appear as oases in the dry climate of central Oregon. Scientifically, these are known as *exotic streams*, because they are fed by the waters of the cooler and moister Cascade Mountains. The following cataracts are sure to quench the thirst of any traveler.

Sherars Falls ☆☆☆

Form: block   *Magnitude:* 46 (h)   *Watershed:* lg
Elevation: 680 feet   *USGS Map:* Sherars Bridge (1962 ns)

Watch Native American fishermen net for salmon where the Deschutes River roars 15 to 20 feet in a sagebrush setting. The waterfall is owned by the Warm Springs Tribe. The State Department of Natural Resources and the tribe together regulate fishing on the river.

Drive along S.R. 216 to Sherars Bridge over the Deschutes River. The

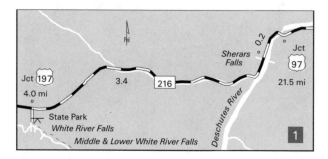

bridge is located about 7.5 miles east of U.S. 197 and 21.5 miles west of U.S. 97. Stop for views of this entry 0.2 mile south of the bridge. Supervise your children, as the tumultuous river is extremely dangerous.

White River Falls ☆☆☆

Form: segmented   *Magnitude:* 72   *Watershed:* lg
Elevation: 1000 feet   *USGS Map:* Maupin (1987 ns)

A viewing platform offers an outstanding vista of rivulets of the White River pouring 70 to 80 feet downward off a 150- to 175-foot-wide escarpment. Also known as *Tygh Valley Falls*, this waterfall is located within White River Falls State Park. Drive 3.4 miles westward past Sherars Falls (described previously) along S.R. 216 to the signed turnout for this day-use park. Proceed another 0.2 mile to the parking area and walk 150 feet to the fenced overlook.

Middle White River Falls (u) ☆☆☆☆

Form: tiered   *Magnitude:* 75   *Watershed:* lg
Elevation: 920 feet   *USGS Map:* Maupin (1987 ns)

This second of a trio of falls is actually a single 25- to 35-foot plunge. The trailside vantage, however, includes the upper falls (described previously), revealing a dramatic tiered combination. Walk down the paved trail in the downstream direction into the small canyon. The trail quickly turns to dirt, with this entry soon coming into view.

Lower White River Falls (u) ☆☆

Form: punchbowl   *Magnitude:* 50   *Watershed:* lg
Elevation: 760 feet   *USGS Map:* Maupin (1987 ns)

The last of the falls in White River State Park tumbles 25 to 35 feet into a large amphitheater. Continue past Middle White River Falls (described previously), down some wooden steps past an old powerhouse. Follow the trail through the high desert vegetation. Continue on the trail beyond the falls for the best views.

Middle White River Falls

2. Redmond

The aptly named Deschutes River (*Deschutes* is French for "of the Falls") has ten cataracts along its course from La Pine to the Columbia

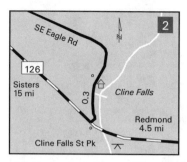

River. Of the five falls near Redmond, only the following one is accessible.

Cline Falls ☆ USGS Cline Falls (1962). The force of this cascade is reduced because a portion of the river has been diverted to a rustic powerhouse nearby. Named for Dr. C. A. Cline, who once owned it, the waterfall is now a part of Cline Falls State Park. Drive 4.5 miles west of Redmond on S.R. 126. Turn right (north) at the west side of the Deschutes River on SE Eagle Road. In 0.3 mile park at the entrance and look into the canyon at the falls and power facility.

3. Tumalo Creek

All of the following waterfalls, located within the Bend Ranger District of Deschutes National Forest, can be visited as you head toward the eastern flank of the Cascade Range. Turn off U.S. 97 in Bend onto westbound Franklin Avenue. In 1 mile, at Drake City Park, the street becomes Galveston Avenue. Proceed west 11 miles and turn left (west) on graveled Road #1828. Continue 3 miles to Tumalo Falls Picnic Area.

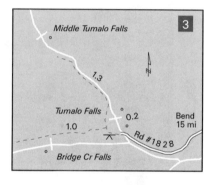

Tumalo Falls ☆☆☆
Form: plunge   *Magnitude:* 81   *Watershed:* lg
Elevation: 5080 feet   *USGS Map:* Tumalo Falls (1988)

This 97-foot plummet is framed by stark tree snags—brown remnants of a forest fire during the summer of 1979. While managed fire is an important component in modern forestry, this particular case was not planned. The Tumalo scene is a reminder of the old adage that "only you can prevent forest fires."

From the picnic area, look upstream along Tumalo Creek into the falls. Closer views are also possible from the adjacent trail.

Middle Tumalo Falls (u) ☆☆   ④, 🏃 and 🏃
Form: tiered   *Magnitude:* 52   *Watershed:* lg
Elevation: 5240 feet   *USGS Map:* Tumalo Falls (1988 nl)

Tumalo Creek tumbles a total of 46 to 65 feet in tiered fashion. Follow the trail to Tumalo Falls (described previously), continuing upstream for 1.3 miles until the way deteriorates into a well-worn path to the creek. Bushwhack streamside for the final 0.2 mile to the base of the cataract.

Tumalo Falls

Bridge Creek Falls (u) ★★ ② 🚶

Form: horsetail   *Magnitude:* 46   *Watershed:* sm
Elevation: 5270 feet   *USGS Map:* Tumalo Falls (1988 nl)

  Watch water pouring 25 to 35 feet from Bridge Creek. From Tumalo Falls Picnic Area (described previously), locate the trailhead to Bridge Creek Trail. Proceed along this moderately gentle route for 1 mile to this entry.

4. Bend

Canal Falls (u) ☆☆

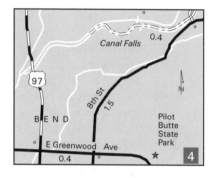

Form: segmented   *Magnitude:* 43 (h)   *Watershed:* lg (d)
Elevation: 3540 feet   *USGS Map:* Bend (1981 nl)

Fed by the irrigation system of the area, this pair of drainageways, actually part of the North Unit Main Canal, drops forcefully 10 to 15 feet over basalt. The cataract is likely located on either Bureau of Land Management land or private property.

In the city of Bend, exit U.S. 97 onto East Greenwood Avenue. Proceed east 0.4 mile and turn left (north) onto 8th Street. Go 1.5 miles to an unsigned dirt road. Follow this road 0.4 mile to the site.

Canal Falls

5. Lava Butte Geological Area

The Deschutes River drops three times along the western fringe of Lava Butte Geological Area, which is located within Fort Rock Ranger District, Deschutes National Forest. From downtown Bend drive west on Franklin Avenue toward Tumalo Falls (described previously), but turn left (south) on Cascade Lakes Highway (also known as Century Drive). Continue 6.3 miles and turn left (south) on gravel Road #41 at the sign to Dillon Falls.

Lava Island Falls ★★

Form: segmented   *Magnitude:* 24   *Watershed:* lg
Elevation: 3920 feet   *USGS Map:* Benham Falls (1981)

This entry is simply a set of small cascades, but the jumbled lava rock being split by the Deschutes River makes the site intriguing. Follow Road #41 south for 0.4 mile from Century Drive. Turn left (east) on dirt Road #620 and continue to the end of its northern extension in 0.8 mile.

Dillon Falls ★★★

Form: cascade   *Magnitude:* 37 (h)   *Watershed:* lg
Elevation: 4040 feet   *USGS Map:* Benham Falls (1981)

The Deschutes River froths 40 to 60 feet within a ¼-mile chasm cut into the basaltic bedrock. The waterfall is named for local homesteader Leander Dillon. Take Road #41 south 3 miles from Century Drive. Turn left (southeast) on dirt Road #500 and drive to its end in 0.9 mile. A trail goes from the parking area to views of the gorge and its cascade. The observation points at the rim are unprotected, so be careful.

Benham Falls ★★★

Form: cascade   *Magnitude:* 36 (h)
Watershed: lg
Elevation: 4130 feet   *USGS Map:* Benham Falls (1981)

The Deschutes River "chutes" down 40 to 60 feet through a narrow canyon. The cataract is named for J. R. Benham, who unsuccessfully filed a homesteading claim for land nearby in 1885. Bear south on Road #620 (described previously) at its four-way intersection with Road #500. Park where the road meets the river in 3.3 miles. The falls is immediately downstream. A short pathway leads to secure, but unfenced views.

6. La Pine

Fall River Falls ☆☆   ① 🚶

Form: fan   *Magnitude:* 22   *Watershed:* lg
Elevation: 4120 feet   *USGS Map:* Pistol Butte (1981)

The Fall River tumbles 10 to 15 feet next to grassy banks surrounded by pine trees. Located within La Pine State Recreation Area. Leave U.S. 97 at South Century Drive 13 miles south of Bend. Drive west 10.5 miles and turn left (south) on dirt Road #4360. Continue 0.8 mile, then park at the wide turnout preceding the Fall River bridge. Follow the jeep trail 0.2 mile to this pleasant setting.

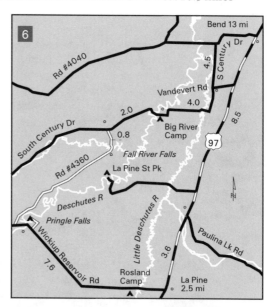

Others: *Pringle Falls* ☆ USGS La Pine (1981). Although pictured in travel guides and labeled on road maps, the main portion of this descent can no longer be seen by the public. A housing development now lines the Deschutes River in the area near the falls and its security system

Fall River Falls

makes it clear that visitors are not welcome. Only uninspiring views remain at the beginning and the end of the falls, which were named for O. M. Pringle, who bought land nearby in 1902. At the junction of U.S. 97 and Wickiup Reservoir Road 2.5 miles north of La Pine turn toward Wickiup Reservoir. The first view of the falls occurs in 7.6 miles at the bridge crossing at the headwaters of the falls. Another view is available at Pringle Falls Camp immediately downstream from the falls. From the bridge follow dirt Road #218 to the campground.

7. Newberry Crater

A dominant feature of the geology south of Bend is a large, gently sloping *shield volcano.* Atop this mound is a *caldera,* the Newberry Crater, where the central portion of the volcano collapsed about 200,000 years ago. Paulina Lake and East Lake currently fill the depression. The erosive power of Paulina Creek as it flows from Paulina Lake has cut through the volcano's layers of basalt at a greater rate than through the more resistant rhyolite

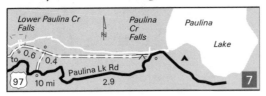

layers. Waterfalls occur where these two rock layers meet along the stream's course. This area is a part of Fort Rock Ranger District, Deschutes National Forest.

Lower Paulina Creek Falls (u) ☆☆☆   ③
Form: tiered   *Magnitude:* 51   *Watershed:* med
Elevation: 5340 feet   *USGS Map:* Paulina Peak (1981 nl)

Paulina Creek descends a total of 50 to 80 feet as the creek diverges along its upper portion before fanning out below. The scenic rating decreases during low water periods in late summer. Turn east off U.S. 97 at Paulina Lake Road, 6 miles north of La Pine. Drive 10 miles to a large, unsigned parking area to the left (north). Hike along an old jeep trail beginning at the far end of the turnout. At a junction in 0.4 mile, bear left (west) and walk 0.6 mile until the falls can be heard. Here an unsigned trail leads across a footbridge over the creek and downstream to views of the falls.

Paulina Creek Falls ☆☆☆☆☆   ①
Form: segmented   *Magnitude:* 84   *Watershed:* med
Elevation: 6200 feet   *USGS Map:* Paulina Peak (1981)

This 100-foot dual segmented cataract is best seen in early summer when Paulina Creek has substantial flow. Drive along the paved road for 2.9 miles past the turnout for Lower Paulina Creek Falls (described

Paulina Creek Falls

previously). Park at Paulina Falls Picnic Ground. A short trail leads to a developed vista offering superb vantages of the falls.

8. Wallowa Lake

Wallowa Lake is a stunningly beautiful example of a form of *paternoster lake,* in this case a body of water formed by a natural dam blocking part of a glacial valley. Drive 6 miles past the town of Joseph along S.R. 82 to Wallowa Lake State Park, which is located within Wallowa-Whitman National Forest. Turn left (south) toward the picnic area and away from the main boating and camping facilities.

Wallowa Falls ★★★   ③, 🏃 and 🏃
Form: punchbowl   *Magnitude:* 52 (h)   *Watershed:* lg
Elevation: 4660 feet   *USGS Map:* Joseph (1990 nl)

Peer down at the West Fork Wallowa River pouring over a 30- to 50-foot escarpment. Not recommended for children or skittish adults. To reach the falls, follow West Fork Trail #1820, which starts at the picnic area, toward Ice Lake. A footbridge crosses the East Fork Wallowa River, then ascends shortly to a rocky outcrop adjacent to the West Fork in 0.1 mile. From this natural vista, follow the ridge a short distance downstream to a well-worn path above the river.

Adam Creek Falls ★★★   ⑤ 🏃

Form: tiered   *Magnitude:* 66   *Watershed:* sm
Elevation: 7200 feet   *USGS Map:* Eagle Cap (1990 ns)
Accessible by aerial tram

This series of falls descends hundreds of feet along Adam Creek and can be seen collectively or individually, depending upon whether you hike to them or take the aerial tram. Hikers should proceed 3 miles along West Fork Trail #1820 (described previously), then turn right (west) on Ice Lake Trail #18. The tiers of this cataract will be encountered one at a time, as you make the 4-mile trek to its end at Ice Lake. Tourists atop Mount Howard will see this entry as silvery threads along the mountainside. For unforgettable views of Eagle Cap Wilderness, Wallowa Lake, and the Columbia Plateau take the High Wallowas gondola 3,700 feet above the valley. Look for the falls toward the southwest.

9. Ochoco

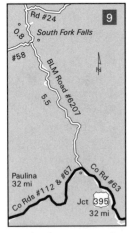

South Fork Falls ★★

Form: cascade   *Magnitude:* 28
Watershed: lg
Elevation: 3540 feet   *USGS Map:* Suplee Butte (1981)

Water tumbles 75 feet over a 200- to 300-foot reach of the South Fork John Day River. Located on Bureau of Land Management land, the cascades are locally known as *Izee Falls*. The surrounding steep canyon walls are composed of impressive columns of basalt.

Drive 32 miles west from U.S. 395 on County Road #63, or 32 miles east from Paulina along County Roads #112 and #67, to BLM Road #6207. Proceed north, following the river, for 5.5 miles to Forest Road #58. Bear right, staying on #6207, for 0.8 mile to an unsigned turnout next to the top of the cataract.

South Fork Falls

10. Adel

Deep Creek Falls ☆☆☆

Form: block   *Magnitude:* 56   *Watershed:* lg
Elevation: 4800 feet   *USGS Map:* Adel (1968)

This 30- to 50-foot drop along Deep Creek Canyon is framed by columns of basalt in a sagebrush setting. It is likely situated on either private property or Bureau of Land Management land. For a roadside view of this entry, drive 2.7 miles west from Adel or 30 miles east from Lakeview along S.R. 140.

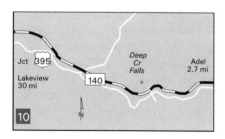

THE IDAHO PANHANDLE

The Panhandle of northern Idaho separates Washington from Montana. Stretching 170 miles southward from the Canadian border to Lewiston, its width varies from 45 to 125 miles. Although many states have unusual shapes, Idaho's is unique in its historical and political significance. No other state was shaped wholly by boundaries originally set by its neighbors. Idaho is made up of land not annexed by Montana, Wyoming, Utah, Nevada, Oregon, or Washington.

The Panhandle is a region of large lakes and rolling to rugged mountains. Lake Coeur d'Alene, Lake Pend Oreille, Priest Lake, and Dworshak Reservoir

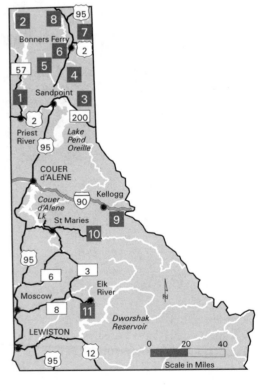

cover large areas. All but Dworshak are natural. Mountain ranges such as the Selkirks, the Purcells, the Bitterroots, and the Clearwaters are distributed through the region. The Panhandle has 36 recognized waterfalls, of which 25 are described here.

Geomorphologists, scientists who study landforms, classify waterfalls as *destructive* or *constructive*. Most cataracts, including almost all of those in the Pacific Northwest, are of the destructive variety. The force of running water slowly erodes the streambeds, usually causing the falls to recede upstream through geologic time. Constructive descents, on the other hand, mostly flow over mineral deposits and migrate downstream as the deposits accumulate. (*Fall Creek Falls,* listed in the Snake River Plain chapter, is a constructive falls.)

Destructive falls are further classified by how they developed. *Consequent* falls are located where a preexisting break occurs along the course of a stream. An example is water plunging into a glacier-carved valley, as at *Copper Falls.* When streams erode along rock materials of varying rates of erosional resistance, *subsequent* falls may form, as at *Lower Snow Creek Falls.*

The waterfalls of the Northwest can be enjoyed for their beauty alone, but they are even more interesting when one ponders the variety of ways in which they were created.

1. Priest River

Access this area from the town of Priest River by departing U.S. 2 onto S.R. 57.

Torrelle Falls ☆☆

Form: punchbowl   *Magnitude:* 32   *Watershed:* lg
Elevation: 2300 feet   *USGS Map:* Quartz Mtn (1967)
A rustic restaurant spans the West Branch Priest River at the base of this 10- to 15-foot descent. Drive 8.5 miles north from the town of Priest River along S.R. 57. Find this unique site on the left (west) side of the highway.

Others: *Mission Falls* ☆ USGS Outlet Bay (1967). Water tumbles a total of 5 to 10 feet along a breadth of the Upper West Branch Priest River in Priest Lake Ranger District, Idaho Panhandle National Forest. Continue north on S.R. 57 for 11.5 miles past Torrelle Falls (described previously). Park at the northeast side of the bridge across the river. Follow a jeep trail next to the bridge for 0.2 mile to a road junction. Take the right fork and follow the dirt route for 1.5 miles farther, bearing right at all junctions. When you near the river, a well-worn trail leads to the falls in a few hundred yards.

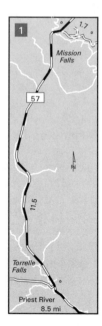

2. Priest Lake

Recreational activities occur year-round near 26,000-acre Priest Lake. The area's waterfalls are remote, however, and are easiest to visit from early summer through late autumn.

Granite Falls ✮✮✮   ② 🚶

Form: horsetail   *Magnitude:* 55 (h)
Watershed: med
Elevation: 3460 feet   *USGS Map:* Helmer Mtn
(1986)

Granite Creek slides 50 to 75 feet within Priest Lake Ranger District, Idaho Panhandle National Forest. This entry is actually located in Washington, but it is listed in this chapter because the primary access is from Idaho.

Drive 37 miles north of Priest River along S.R. 57 to Nordman. Continue 13 miles and turn onto the entrance road to Stagger Inn Camp and Granite Falls. (*Note:* S.R. 57 becomes Granite Creek Road #30 about 2 miles past Nordman.) The trailhead is at the south end of the camp. The sign to the falls is misleading. Do not cross the log over the stream to which the arrow points. Instead walk straight past the sign less than 100 yards to the cataract.

Upper Priest Falls ✮✮✮✮   ⑤, 🚶 and 🚙

Form: fan   *Magnitude:* 71 (h)   *Watershed:* lg
Elevation: 3420 feet *USGS Map:* Continental Mtn (1968)

The Upper Priest River noisily crashes 100 to 125 feet within the secluded northwest tip of Idaho. Located within Priest Lake Ranger District, Idaho Panhandle National Forest. This falls is also known as *American Falls* to distinguish it from *Canadian Falls,* located farther upstream in British Columbia.

Drive 1.7 miles north of Stagger Inn Camp (described previously) on Road #302 and turn

Granite Falls

right (northeast) on Road #1013, which eventually turns into Road #637. Proceed approximately 11.5 miles to the Upper Priest River Trailhead #308. This path follows the river for 9 miles, ending at the falls. If your vehicle has good road clearance, continue along Road #637 for another 11 miles to Continental Trail #28. Hike 0.7 mile north on Trail #28 and turn right on Trail #308 for another 1.5 miles to the descent.

3. Pend Oreille

Char Falls ☆☆☆   ④ 🏃

Form: horsetail   *Magnitude:* 61 (h)   *Watershed:* med
Elevation: 4140 feet   *USGS Map:* Trestle Peak (1989)

      Lightning Creek descends powerfully for 50 to 75 feet, with the viewpoint framed by coniferous trees. Located within Sandpoint Ranger District, Idaho Panhandle National Forest. Turn east off U.S. 2/95 onto S.R. 200 and drive 12.2 miles along S.R. 200 to Trestle Creek Road #275. Turn left (east) and proceed 13 miles to Lightning Creek Road #419. Turn right (south) and

continue 0.6 mile to a primitive road to the left. Park here and follow the rocky road 0.5 mile to a wide trail at its end. Take the trail only 20 yards, then find a faint path to the right. It leads to an unfenced overlook of the falls in less than 100 yards.

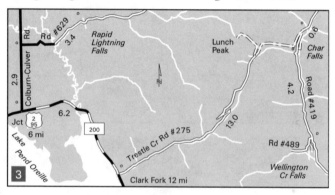

Wellington Creek Falls (u) ☆☆☆   ③, 🏃 and 🚙

Form: punchbowl   *Magnitude:* 56   *Watershed:* med
Elevation: 3120 feet   *USGS Map:* Trestle Peak (1989 ns)

      Lush vegetation surrounds this wonderful 50- to 75-foot waterfall along Wellington Creek. Be careful near the edge of the vista's unfenced precipice in this undeveloped area. Located within Sandpoint Ranger District, Idaho Panhandle National Forest.

      Continue 4.2 miles past Char Falls (described previously) along Lightning Creek Road #419 to Augor Road #489, and turn right (west). Cross Lightning Creek and either drive or hike down the primitive road to the left. Bear right at the fork in 0.4 mile and continue 0.4 mile on this bumpy road to its end. Walk toward the creek and a bit upstream, listening for the falls. Continue toward Wellington Creek for good overviews of this obscure entry.

Others: *Rapid Lightning Falls* (u) ☆ USGS Elmire (1989 ns). Water rushes 20 to 30 feet along Rapid Lightning Creek. Probably located on private property. Turn east off U.S. 2/95 onto S.R. 200 and drive 6 miles before turning left (north) on Colburn–Culver Road. In 2.9 miles, turn right (east) at the schoolhouse onto the road marked Rapid Lightning Creek (Road #629). Park at an unsigned turnout 3.4 miles farther. The cataract is accessible from short, well-trod paths.

4. Colburn

Grouse Creek Falls ☆☆   ② 🚶

Form: cascade   *Magnitude:* 18   *Watershed:* lg
Elevation: 2670 feet   *USGS Map:* Wylie Knob (1989)

Grouse Creek cuts through bedrock in a small series of descents totaling 15 to 20 feet, situated within Sandpoint Ranger District, Idaho Panhandle National Forest. Turn east off U.S. 2/95 at Colburn onto Colburn–Culver Road. Drive east 4.5 miles and turn left on the gravel Road #280. Continue 6 miles up Grouse Creek Valley to a turnout near a dirt road to the

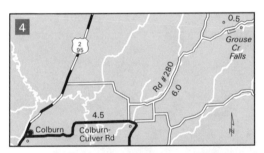

Grouse Creek Falls

right. Park and follow the road, which becomes a trail in 0.3 mile. The waterfall is 0.2 mile farther.

5. Pack River

Jeru Creek Falls (u) ★★★   ③, 🏃 and 🏃

Form: horsetail   *Magnitude:* 59   *Watershed:* sm
Elevation: 3060 feet   *USGS Map:* Dodge Peak (1967 nl)

Jeru Creek slides 100 to 150 feet. The waterfall is probably located on private property. Turn northwest off U.S. 2/95 at Samuels onto Pack River Road #231. Drive 9 miles to the unsigned turnout on the north side of Jeru Creek. The 1-mile trek from the road starts on an obsolete four-wheel-drive route and eventually turns into a seldom-used, unmaintained trail. The descent will be encountered soon after the point at which the path seems to end.

6. Bonners Ferry

The following waterfalls occur within a fairly undeveloped area of Bonners Ferry Ranger District, Idaho Panhandle National Forest.

Lower Snow Creek Falls (u) ★★   ② 🏃

Form: segmented   *Magnitude:* 64   *Watershed:* lg
Elevation: 1900 feet   *USGS Map:* Moravia (1965 ns)

Snow Creek splits as it descends 50 to 75 feet over an escarpment. Drive 2.5 miles south of Bonners Ferry on U.S. 2/95. Turn right onto Moravia Road at the golf course. Bear right in 3 miles on West Side Road #417 and drive 2 miles to a turnout and informal campsite. The unnamed trail on the north side of Snow Creek leads shortly to this entry. The named trail south of the creek goes up the ridge and does not provide any views of the falls.

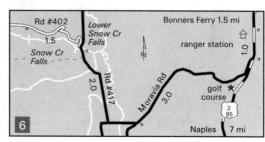

Others: *Snow Creek Falls* (u) ★ USGS Moravia (1965 nl). This 75- to 125-foot drop along Snow Creek would be impressive except there are no good views. A bird's-eye glimpse of the falls can be gained from Snow Creek Road #402. Drive about 1.5 miles west of its junction with West Side Road #417 (described previously).

7. Moyie River

Moyie Falls is purported to be one of Idaho's great scenic attractions. No argument here. But contrary to what most directions imply, you can't get good views from the main highway. The following description, however, will direct you to a picture-perfect vista.

Moyie Falls ☆☆☆☆☆

Form: tiered   *Magnitude:* 71 (h)   *Watershed:* lg
Elevation: 2020 feet   *USGS Map:* Moyie Springs (1965)

The Moyie River absolutely thunders through a small gorge in tiered form. The upper portion crashes 60 to 100 feet beneath an antiquated

Moyie Falls

span crossing the canyon. The lower portion cascades 20 to 40 feet. Probably on private property.

Turn off U.S. 2 at the Moyie Springs Exit immediately west of the Moyie River bridge. In 0.5 mile, turn left on the street adjacent to a lumber yard. Follow this residential road 0.5 mile to various turnouts offering good views into the canyon.

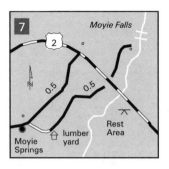

8. Boundary Line

Smith Falls ★★★

Form: plunge   *Magnitude:* 67   *Watershed:* lg
Elevation: 1800 feet   *USGS Map:* Smith Falls (1968)

A high volume of water plummets 60 feet along Smith Creek. The falls and the viewpoint are situated on private property. Please obey the posted restrictions so others can continue to enjoy this entry.

About 15 miles north of Bonners Ferry turn north onto S.R. 1 from U.S. 95. Drive 1 mile, then turn left (west) on an unsigned paved road and continue for 5 miles, crossing the Kootenai River at the halfway point. Turn right (north) onto West Side Road #417 and proceed 8 miles to a marked turnout at the falls.

Copper Falls ★★★★   ③ 🚶

Form: plunge   *Magnitude:* 77   *Watershed:* sm
Elevation: 3400 feet   *USGS Map:* Eastport (1965)

Copper Creek hurtles 160 feet from a cliff within Bonners Ferry Ranger District, Idaho Panhandle National Forest. Turn east off U.S. 95 onto Road #2517 less than 0.7 mile south of the Eastport border crossing or 14 miles northeast of the junction with S.R. 1. Follow this bumpy gravel road for

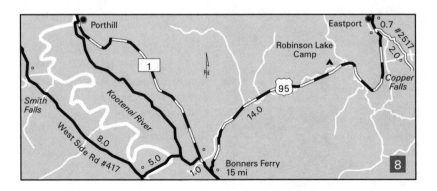

2 miles to Copper Falls Trail #20. Hike 0.3 mile along the moderately steep trail to the falls.

9. Mullan

As you travel east from Coeur d'Alene along I-90, you will pass the historic mining towns of Kellogg, Wallace, and Mullan. The following modest waterfalls, accessible from late summer to early autumn, are located near the Bitterroot Divide, which separates Idaho from Montana. Both are situated within Wallace Ranger District, St. Joe National Forest.

Stevens Lake Falls (u) ★★★   ④ 🚶

Form: tiered   *Magnitude:* 53   *Watershed:* sm
Elevation: 4420 feet   *USGS Map:* Mullan (1988 ns)

The tiers of this entry can be viewed either collectively or individually. The lower portion plunges 30 to 50 feet along Willow Creek, while the horsetail form of the upper part drops 30 to 50 feet. Leave I-90 at Mullan (Exit 68). Drive through the town and continue east. The route turns right after 1.5 miles and becomes Willow Creek Road. Continue another 1.5 miles, passing under I-90, to the road's end near an old set of railroad tracks. Follow Willow Creek Trail #8008 for 2 miles; after passing Willow Creek Falls (described below), the way steepens considerably. In 0.2 mile the lower part of the cataract will be encountered. Hike 0.2 mile farther for a close-up view of the upper tier.

Others: *Willow Creek Falls* (u) ★ USGS Mullan (1988 ns). East Fork Willow Creek cascades 10 to 20 feet downward. Reach this waterfall by following the directions for Stevens Lake Falls (described previously).

Stevens Lake Falls

10. St. Joe River

The St. Joe River is particularly known for two things: first,
it is navigable to one of the highest elevations of any river in
North America. Second, its sport
fishing is regarded as excellent,

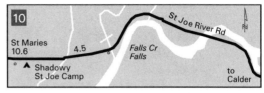

especially along the remote upper reaches where you can practically jump
across the "mighty" St. Joe.

Falls Creek Falls ✫✫

Form: block   *Magnitude:* 46 (h)   *Watershed:* med
Elevation: 1980 feet   *USGS Map:* Saint Joe (1985 ns)

Unsuspecting travelers are likely to miss this 20- to 30-foot drop
of Falls Creek into the St. Joe River. It is located on private property surrounded by St. Maries Ranger District, St. Joe National Forest. Turn east off
S.R. 3 onto the St. Joe River Road 0.5 mile northeast of St. Maries. The falls is
15 miles up the River Road, or 4.5 miles past Shadowy St. Joe Camp. Park at
the turnout closest to Falls Creek bridge.

11. Elk Creek

Many waterfalls are to be
found within this portion of
Palouse Ranger District,
Clearwater National Forest.
Drive south from Bovill toward
the Elk River on S.R. 8. After 16
miles, turn right (south) at the
signed access road. Proceed 1.6
miles to a parking area for the
Elk Creek Canyon Trailhead,
which is next to a fork in the
road. The trail system has recently been upgraded and may
vary slightly from the following

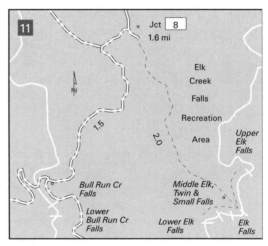

descriptions. Updated maps are available at the trailhead.

Upper Elk Falls (u) ✫✫

Form: punchbowl   *Magnitude:* 31   *Watershed:* lg
Elevation: 2660 feet   *USGS Map:* Elk Creek Falls (1969 nl)

The uppermost descent along Elk Creek drops 30 to 50 feet into a
circular basin. Hike along the left fork of the road, which soon becomes a
moderately sloped trail. Walk 2 miles to a small open area, then descend quickly

to the grassy slopes of the north rim of the canyon. Turn left, following a trail back into the woods and toward the creek for 0.3 mile to the falls.

Elk Falls ☆☆☆☆
Form: horsetail   *Magnitude:* 72   *Watershed:* lg
Elevation: 2550 feet   *USGS Map:* Elk Creek Falls (1969)

This 125- to 150-foot cataract, also called *Elk Creek Falls,* is the highest of the six waterfalls along Elk Creek. Follow the directions to Upper Elk Falls (described previously), except once at the canyon rim, follow the trail to the right among the grassy slopes. There are many views of the falls over the next 0.2 mile.

Twin Falls (u) and Small Falls (u) ☆☆
Form: tiered   *Magnitude:* 45   *Watershed:* lg
Elevation: 2400 feet   *USGS Map:* Elk Creek Falls (1969 ns)

This pair of waterfalls can be viewed in tandem from the trail. Twin Falls is a 10- to 20-foot segmented descent, while Small Falls drops 10 to 20 feet in a punchbowl form. Proceed along the trail for 0.3 mile downstream from Elk Falls (described previously).

Lower Elk Falls ☆☆☆☆
Form: plunge   *Magnitude:* 72   *Watershed:* lg
Elevation: 2350 feet   *USGS Map:* Elk Creek Falls (1969 nl)

This 75- to 100-foot plunge is the most powerful of the waterfalls along Elk Creek. It is recommended only for adults who are not deterred by some modest rock climbing. Walk to the end of the well-worn trail about 0.1 mile past Small Falls (described previously). Carefully follow the faint path to the top of the unfenced basaltic outcrop for an excellent view. It will be a 2.4-mile hike back to the trailhead.

Bull Run Creek Falls ☆☆☆ ③
Form: cascade   *Magnitude:* 60   *Watershed:* med
Elevation: 2480 feet   *USGS Map:* Elk Creek Falls (1969)

Bull Run Creek tumbles a total of 75 to 100 feet. This and the following entry straddle timber company property and an undeveloped portion of Elk Creek Falls Recreation Area. Instead of parking at the trailhead for Elk Creek Canyon (described previously), continue along the right fork of the unnamed road, turning at the junctions as shown on the accompanying map. Park in 1.5 miles. A small, faint path leads shortly to this cataract.

Lower Bull Run Creek Falls (u) ☆☆ ⑤
Form: fan   *Magnitude:* 45   *Watershed:* med
Elevation: 2420 feet   *USGS Map:* Elk Creek Falls (1969 ns)

Water pours 30 to 50 feet along Bull Run Creek. Recommended for determined bushwhackers only. Return to the road from Bull Run Creek

Lower Elk Falls

Falls (described previously) and continue walking along the ridge in the down-stream direction for 0.1 mile. After passing a small marshy area, scramble down the steep timbered slope to the creek below the base of the falls.

Others: *Middle Elk Falls* (u) ✩ USGS Elk Creek Falls (1969 ns). Water pours 20 to 30 feet from Elk Creek. Avid fishermen and other nimble individuals often bushwhack down to this reach of the stream. Proceed along the trail for 0.2 mile downstream from Elk Falls (described previously). Look down into the gorge for a path-side view of this cataract.

WILDERNESS AREAS OF CENTRAL IDAHO

The interior of Idaho is dominated by swift rivers that cut deep canyons through rugged mountains. This sparsely populated region contains the largest tracts—three million acres—of wilderness in the contiguous United States. Adventurers can explore the Selway-Bitterroot, Frank Church River of No Return, Gospel Hump, and Sawtooth Wildernesses; the Hells Canyon and Sawtooth National Recreation Areas; and the Wild and Scenic Salmon River.

The geology of this region is largely determined by the history of its igneous rocks. During the late Mesozoic era, 75 million to 100 million years ago, extensive masses of magma crystallized in the subsurface of central Idaho. Rocks ranging from igneous granite and diorite to metamorphic gneisses were formed. Over the next 50 million years, these masses, collectively called a *batholith,* were uplifted to form mountains.

The mountainous terrain of the Idaho interior has been shaped mostly by erosion. Alpine glaciers carved the batholith at least four times over the last 2 million years, sharpening peaks and widening valleys. Most waterfalls in the region were created by glaciation. *Warbonnet Falls* descends from a mountainside into a glacial valley. Other streams follow along valleys and encounter obstacles called moraines—linear rock deposits left by glacial activity. *Lady Face Falls,* for instance, breaks through and drops over a moraine.

Stream erosion also contributes to the configuration of the batholith.

The Salmon, Snake, Selway, and Lochsa Rivers have carved impressive canyons and gorges. Waterfalls tumble into these powerful waterways from tributaries that erode at a slower rate than the main rivers (*Fountain Creek Falls* and *Tumble Creek Falls* are examples). Cascades such as *Selway Falls* and *Carey Falls* are cases where heterogeneous rock material is eroded unevenly by rivers.

Because of the wild nature of central Idaho, large descents remain to be found, described, and mapped. Many of these cataracts are accessible only by plane, but a good share await discovery by hikers and backpackers. This book describes 27 of the 56 falls known to occur within the central interior.

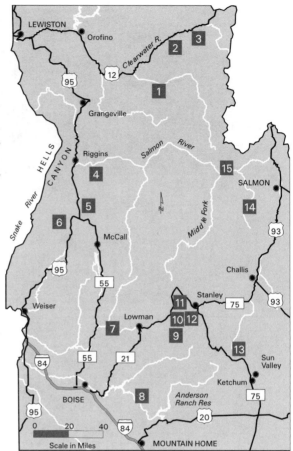

I. Selway River

The Selway River begins in the interior of the Selway-Bitterroot Wilderness. As it flows from the wilderness area, its waters become a river of substantial magnitude. Farther downstream at Lowell, the Selway meets the Lochsa River to become the Middle Fork Clearwater River.

Selway Falls ★★

Form: segmented   *Magnitude:* 39 (h)   *Watershed:* lg
Elevation: 1700 feet   *USGS Map:* Selway Falls (1987)

A long reach of the Selway River cascades a total of 50 feet within Moose Creek Ranger District, Nez Perce National Forest. Turn south-

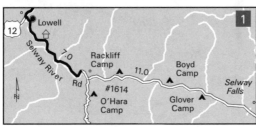

Selway Falls

east off U.S. 12 at Lowell and drive 18 miles to the end of Selway River Road #1614. The cataract can be seen beside the gravel roadway.

2. Lochsa River

U.S. 12 faithfully parallels the Lochsa River from its beginning near Lolo Pass to its confluence with the Selway River 78 miles downstream. There are plenty of campsites along this stretch of the highway, but no vehicle service is available from Lolo Hot Springs to Lowell. Be sure your automobile has a full tank of gas before you start. Several waterfalls pour from tributary streams into the Lochsa within a 2-mile stretch 16 to 18 miles northeast of Lowell. The following waterfalls occur within the Middle Fork Clearwater Wild and Scenic River area, Lochsa Ranger District, Clearwater National Forest.

Horsetail Falls ★★

Form: horsetail　*Magnitude:* 59　*Watershed:* vsm
Elevation: 2000 feet　*USGS Map:* McLendon Butte (1966 ns)

Peer across the Lochsa River to Horsetail Falls descending 60 to 100 feet from an unnamed stream. Drive to a marked turnoff along U.S. 12 between mile markers 114 and 115.

Shoestring Falls ✰✰

Form: tiered   *Magnitude:* 51   *Watershed:* vsm
Elevation: 1920 feet   *USGS Map:* McLendon Butte (1966)

Water stairsteps 150 to 200 feet in five sections where an un-named creek drops into the Lochsa River. View this waterfall from across the river at the marked turnout between mile markers 115 and 116.

Wild Horse Creek Falls (u) ✰✰   ① 🏃

Form: tiered   *Magnitude:* 48   *Watershed:* sm
Elevation: 1880 feet   *USGS Map:* McLendon Butte (1966 ns)

Wild Horse Creek descends in a double-drop totaling 40 to 60 feet. Park at the Shoestring Falls turnout (described previously) and walk 0.1 mile along U.S. 12 for a close-up view of this entry.

Wild Horse Creek Falls

Others: *Tumble Creek Falls* (u) ★ USGS McLendon Butte (1966 ns). Tumble Creek veils 20 to 30 feet before flowing beneath the highway into the Lochsa River. Look for this entry, which is not signed, along the east side of U.S. 12 between mile markers 113 and 114.

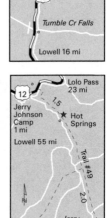

3. Warm Springs Creek

Warm Springs Creek derives its name from the thermal waters that flow into the stream from Jerry Johnson Hot Springs. Most hikers head for the rustic hot springs, often entering the waters au naturel. The area rapidly becomes secluded as you progress upstream past the springs.

Jerry Johnson Falls (u)   ★★★   ④ 🚶

Form: punchbowl   *Magnitude:* 56 (h)
Watershed: lg
Elevation: 3900 feet   *USGS Map:* Tom Beal Peak (1984 nl)

Warm Springs Creek roars 40 to 70 feet into a large basin. Located within Powell Ranger District, Clearwater National Forest. Drive to the parking area for Warm Springs Creek Trail #49, located along U.S. 12, 1 mile east of Jerry Johnson Campground. A footbridge crosses the Lochsa River before the trail reaches Warm Springs Creek and follows it upstream 1.5 miles to the hot springs. One mile beyond the springs the trail crosses a small tributary creek, then gradually climbs above Warm Springs Creek to trailside views of the falls in another mile.

4. Riggins

The town of Riggins is the western gateway to the Salmon Wild and Scenic River Area. White-water boating is extremely exciting along this "River of No Return." Riggins is downstream from most of the float "action," so jetboats carry visitors up and down the river.

Carey Falls ★ USGS Carey Dome (1989). This entry, located along the Salmon River, where it serves as a boundary between the Gospel Hump and Frank Church River of No Return Wildernesses, is more like rapids and

riffles than a waterfall. Pretty scenery, including several small cascades from tributary streams, will be experienced along the route. Less than 1 mile south of Riggins turn off U.S. 95 onto Big Salmon Road #1614. Wind along the river for 23 miles to Wind River Pack Bridge. Continue 0.4 mile beyond this point to a roadside vantage.

5. Little Salmon River

Idaho consists of two broadly settled areas—the Panhandle and the Snake River Plain—separated by the Central Wilderness. The existence of this large, mostly uninhabited area helps explain the distinctly different characters, both cultural and physical, of the two populated regions, which are connected by only one paved road, U.S. 95.

All of the cataracts described in this section occur on either private parcels or Bureau of Land Management lands bounded by New Meadows Ranger District, Payette National Forest.

Little Salmon Falls (u) ★★

Form: cascade   *Magnitude:* 35   *Watershed:* lg
Elevation: 3640 feet   *USGS Map:* Indian Mtn (1983 ns)
Several small descents occur along the Little Salmon River where it parallels U.S. 95. This 10- to 15-foot drop is the prettiest and easiest to visit. Drive 11 miles north of New Meadows to an unsigned turnout adjacent to this cataract.

Fall Creek Falls (u) ★★

Form: horsetail   *Magnitude:* 30
Watershed: sm
Elevation: 2920 feet   *USGS Map:*
Indian Mtn (1983 ns)
Fall Creek tumbles 15 to 25 feet before continuing beneath the highway and into the Little Salmon River. Drive 7 miles north of Little Salmon Falls (described previously) to an unsigned turnout along U.S. 95.

Others: *Lower Little Salmon Falls* (u) ★ USGS Bally Mtn (1983 ns). Water froths 5 to 10 feet downward along the Little Salmon River. Drive 10.3 miles north of New Meadows. Park at the unsigned turnout, located

Fall Creek Falls

immediately north of the junction signed Smoky Boulder Road. Be careful of the speeding traffic when walking along the highway.

6. Lost Valley

Lost Creek Falls ★★

Form: punchbowl   *Magnitude:* 15   *Watershed:* lg
Elevation: 4380 feet   *USGS Map:* Tamarack (1986)

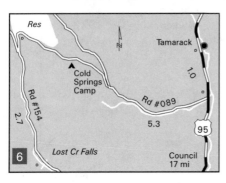

Lost Creek drops serenely 5 to 10 feet in a wooded setting. Situated within Council Ranger District, Payette National Forest. Depart U.S. 95 about 1 mile south of Tamarack, and turn right (west) onto Lost Valley Reservoir Road #089. Drive 5.3 miles to the dam, then proceed south on Road #154 for 2.7 miles to the cataract. It can be seen from the road with close-up views via fishermen's paths.

7. Garden Valley

At the town of Banks, turn off S.R. 55 onto South Fork Road, heading toward Lowman. In 11 miles you will pass the Garden Valley Ranger Station and in 16 miles the paved road will turn to gravel. Along the way you will pass many hot springs adjacent to the South Fork Payette River. The following pair of cataracts are located within Lowman Ranger District, Boise National Forest.

Little Falls ★★

Form: block   *Magnitude:* 40   *Watershed:* lg
Elevation: 3350 feet   *USGS Map:* Grimes Pass (1988)

This 5- to 10-foot drop along the breadth of South Fork Payette River is aptly named. There was once an abandoned mine shaft across the road from the falls, but it has been obliterated by highway construction. Drive 5.7 miles past the point where South Fork Road turns to gravel to a spot where this entry practically hugs the road.

Big Falls ★★

Form: punchbowl   *Magnitude:* 42   *Watershed:* lg
Elevation: 3480 feet   *USGS Map:* Pine Flat (1972)

This 25- to 40-foot waterfall is "big" only in contrast to its downstream counterpart. The best roadside views are from a moderate distance.

Continue 2.2 miles past Little Falls (described previously). Park where the road widens and look upstream;

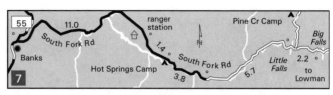

the falls is visible at the bottom of the canyon floor 100 to 150 feet below.

8. South Fork Boise River

Travel through rangeland, prairie, and wooded tracts into South Fork Canyon. The 300- to 400-foot-deep gorge is seldom visited. Leave I-84 at Mountain Home and drive 20 miles north on U.S. 20 to Road #134, signed Anderson Ranch Dam/Prairie. Proceed 5 miles to the dam. After crossing the dam, turn left (west) on Road #113 and drive 2 miles to the hamlet of Prairie. At the junction, turn left (west). The following falls are located within Mountain Home Ranger District, Boise National Forest.

Smith Creek Falls (u) ★★★

Form: plunge   *Magnitude:* 76   *Watershed:* lg
Elevation: 3700 feet   *USGS Map:* Long Gulch (1964 nl)

The waters of this 80- to 120-foot plummet roar into an impressive grotto carved by Smith Creek. Appropriate for nimble adults only. Drive westward from Prairie for 2.4 miles to the junction with Road #189. Bear left onto #189 and proceed 3.7 miles toward South Fork Canyon. About 0.1 mile before entering the canyon you will encounter a cattle guard in the road. About 200 feet or so past this guard, there is a wide spot in the road. Park here. Cross a 5- to 10-foot wide irrigation canal, in which the water may be from knee to waist deep and walk carefully through the sagebrush toward Smith Creek. In about 100 feet you will come to the canyon rim and its cliffs. Be careful!

Big Fiddler Creek Falls ★★

Form: horsetail   *Magnitude:* 35 (l)   *Watershed:* vsm
Elevation: 4000 feet   *USGS Map:* Long Gulch (1964 ns)

This 252-foot drop is the highest officially measured waterfall in Idaho. Unfortunately, the creek is seasonal and thus usually dry during summer. From the cattle guard on Road #189 (described previously), drive 2 miles into South Fork Canyon and look across the canyon to the falls. In summer

Smith Creek Falls

look for evidence of water flow along the canyon's upper tier of cliffs. Immediately upstream, on seasonal Big Fiddler Creek, another small cataract may be seen pouring 60 to 80 feet from the lower canyon tier into the South Fork Boise River.

Long Gulch Falls (u) ★★

Form: plunge   *Magnitude:* 24 (l)   *Watershed:* med
Elevation: 3600 feet   *USGS Map:* Long Gulch (1964 ns)

Long Gulch plunges 100 to 125 feet into the South Fork Boise River. The creek is seasonal, but often maintains some flow during summer. From the same location described in the Big Fiddler Creek Falls entry (see above), look toward the near side of the canyon to see this entry.

9. Sawtooths West

The rugged Sawtooth Mountains are a tribute to the strength of glacial sculpturing during the Ice Age. The following four sections all describe waterfalls within the Sawtooth Wilderness portion of Sawtooth National Recreation Area. Reach the following pair of cataracts on the western flank of the mountains by turning off S.R. 21 at the marked access road to Grandjean Camp. Drive 8 miles to the trailheads at the end of the gravel road.

Goat Creek Falls (u) ★★   ③, 🕴 and 🕴

Form: tiered   *Magnitude:* 39   *Watershed:* med
Elevation: 5260 feet   *USGS Map:* Edaho Mtn (1972 ns)

Goat Creek tumbles a total of 50 feet over a series of cascades. Start on South Fork Trail #452, which parallels the South Fork Payette River. Reach the junction of Baron Creek Trail #101 in 1.3 miles; continue on Trail #452 to Goat Creek a moderate 1.2 miles farther. Scramble a short distance upstream to a vantage of this descent.

Fern Falls ★★   ⑤ 🚶🚶

Form: tiered   *Magnitude:* 44   *Watershed:* lg
Elevation: 6380 feet   *USGS Map:* Warbonnet Peak (1972)

The South Fork Payette River tumbles twice in an attractive 30-foot display. Continue 7.5 miles past Goat Creek Falls (described previously) on South Fork Trail #452. From the falls, it is 10 miles back to the trailhead.

10. Baron Creek

Tohobit Creek Falls (u) ★★   ⑤ 🏃🏃

Form: horsetail   *Magnitude:* 42   *Watershed:* vsm
Elevation: 6960 feet   *USGS Map:* Warbonnet Peak (1972 ns)

This is the first of several ribbon falls dropping from tributaries into the glacial valley currently occupied by Baron Creek. Drive to the trailheads near Grandjean Camp as described in the Sawtooths West section. Hike 1.2 miles along South Fork Trail #452 to Baron Creek Trail #101. Turn left and follow this trail 7 miles to a cross-canyon trailside view.

Warbonnet Falls (u) ★★   ⑤ 🏃🏃

Form: horsetail   *Magnitude:* 42   *Watershed:* vsm
Elevation: 7120 feet   *USGS Map:* Warbonnet Peak (1972 ns)

An unnamed stream hurtles from the lip of a hanging valley. Continue 1 mile past Tohobit Creek Falls (described previously) along Baron Creek Trail #101. Look across the canyon to see the cataract.

Baron Creek Falls ★★★   ⑤ 🏃🏃

Form: segmented   *Magnitude:* 56   *Watershed:* sm
Elevation: 7500 feet   *USGS Map:* Warbonnet Peak (1972)

Baron Creek pours 50 feet downward as the stream breaks through a glacial moraine of rock debris. Hike along Baron Creek Trail #101 for 1 mile past the view of Warbonnet Falls (described previously) to this waterfall, located 10.2 miles from the trailhead. The route continues up to Baron Lakes.

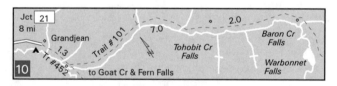

11. Stanley Lake Creek

To reach the following two waterfalls, enter the Sawtooths from the north by driving 5 miles northwest of Stanley along S.R. 21. Turn left at Stanley Lake Road #455 and drive 3.5 miles to Inlet Camp. The trailhead for Stanley Lake Creek Trail #640 is near Area B of the campground.

Lady Face Falls ★★   ③ 🏃

Form: punchbowl   *Magnitude:* 57   *Watershed:* med
Elevation: 6680 feet   *USGS Map:* Stanley Lake (1972)

Stanley Lake Creek breaks through a moraine and plunges 50 to 75 feet into a basin. Follow Stanley Lake Trail #640 for 2.6 miles. The first 2 miles are easy hiking, then the trail steepens. After another 0.5 mile look for a sign marking the falls (for some reason it faces hikers walking in the opposite direction), where a spur path leads 0.1 mile farther to a partially obscured gorge-rim view of the cataract. If you cross the creek, you've gone too far.

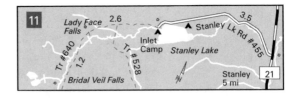

Bridal Veil Falls ★★   ④ 🏃

Form: tiered   *Magnitude:* 62   *Watershed:* sm
Elevation: 7320 feet   *USGS Map:* Stanley Lake (1972)

The outlet from Hanson Lakes cascades steeply 120 to 160 feet in two distinct drops. Hike 1.2 miles past Lady Face Falls (described previously) along Stanley Lake Trail #640 to a sign announcing the waterfall. Nearby is an open area offering a distant view up the side of the valley.

12. Sawtooths East

Grizzly bears are among the inhabitants of the Sawtooth Mountains. Don't let this fact intimidate you and prevent you from visiting this magnificent area. However do remain alert and follow the guidelines posted at the campground and various trailheads.

Goat Falls ★★★★★   ④, 🏃 or 🚗

Form: fan   *Magnitude:* 70   *Watershed:* sm
Elevation: 8100 feet   *USGS Map:* Stanley Lake (1972)

This is the best waterfall of the Sawtooths, as Goat Creek veils 250 to 300 feet down the mountainside. Distant views of this cataract are also possible from the highway. Drive 2.3 miles west of Stanley on S.R. 21 to Iron Creek Road #619. Drive 4 miles to the end of the gravel road and the beginning of Alpine Lake/Sawtooth Lake Trail #640. Hike 1 mile, then turn left (east) at the junction with Alpine Trail #528. Continue 2.5 miles to full views of the falls.

13. Ketchum

North Fork Falls (u) ★★   ④ 🏃

Form: segmented   *Magnitude:* 32   *Watershed:* med
Elevation: 7500 feet   *USGS Map:* Ryan Peak (1967 ns)

This 50- to 75-foot slide along the North Fork Big Wood River is situated inside Sawtooth National Recreation Area. Drive 8 miles north of Ketchum along S.R. 75 to the recreation area headquarters. Turn right (north)

on North Fork Road #146. The East Fork Big Wood River flows across the road after 3.5 miles; check the water level before attempting to cross the stream with your vehicle. Continue 1.5 miles to the end of the road, then begin hiking along North Fork Trail #115. Bear left (northwest) on Trail #128. After a total of 4 miles, the trail rises above the canyon floor at the falls.

14. Leesburg

The following entry is located south of the historic townsite of Leesburg. The community was born in the gold rush of 1866 and its population ballooned to 7,000 residents within twelve months. The rush soon subsided, and by 1870 only 180 people lived in Leesburg. Today the site is a mining outpost at best. Access to this area from U.S. 93 is via Williams Creek Road #021, located 5 miles south of the city of Salmon.

Napias Creek Falls ☆☆

Form: cascade   *Magnitude:* 32   *Watershed:* lg
Elevation: 5120 feet   *USGS Map:* Jureano Mtn (1989)

This series of cascades totaling 70 feet is located within the Salmon/Colbalt Ranger District of Salmon National Forest. *Napias* is Shoshoni for "money," an appropriate name considering the history of this area. Drive 20 miles on Williams Creek Road #021 to Napias Creek. Turn left (south) and continue on Road #021 as it follows the creek downstream. The cataract can be seen from the road in 1.6 miles.

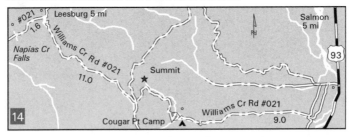

15. North Fork Salmon River

The Salmon River has carved a canyon over 1 mile deep as it flows 165 miles west through the Clearwater Mountains. There are two named falls in the eastern half of this canyon. One is accessible to motorists, while the other can only be reached by experienced rafters. Novices must not try to run the "River of No Return."

Napias Creek Falls

Fountain Creek Falls ★★

Form: tiered   *Magnitude:* 15 (l)   *Watershed:* sm
Elevation: 3200 feet *USGS Map:* Butts Creek Point (1962 ns)

Fountain Creek descends from a canyon wall in a stairstep display totaling 35 to 50 feet. Located within North Fork Ranger District, Salmon National Forest. Turn west off U.S. 93 at North Fork and follow Salmon River Road westward. Reach Shoup in 18 miles and Cache Bar Camp after another 22.2 miles. Look for the falls 0.5 mile past the campground. The road ends 4 miles beyond the falls.

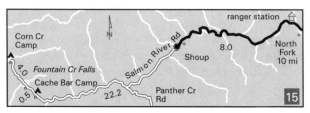

THE SNAKE RIVER PLAIN

Southern Idaho presents the traveler interested in waterfalls with a dilemma. There is no best time of the year to visit its cataracts. The prime viewing time for individual falls varies more dramatically here than in any other region of the Pacific Northwest.

The least temperamental are streams originating from springs, since they flow continuously. Jump Creek and the Thousand Springs area offer examples. Some flows fluctuate with the demand for hydroelectric power. The falls near Hagerman and Clear Lakes are altered by the amount of water being diverted to the nearby power stations. The waterfalls along the Snake River near Twin Falls actually stop flowing most summers because Milner Dam, located farther upstream, impounds water for irrigation of agricultural lands.

Some hydro projects along the Snake have destroyed waterfalls. American Falls Dam and Swan Falls Dam have replaced the original descents, and the waters of C. J. Strike Reservoir cover *Crane Falls*. The highland waterfalls northeast of Rexburg flow perennially but are easily accessible only during summer. Cross-country skis or a snowmobile are required to reach them from November to May.

The Snake River Plain has 68 recognized falls, of which 27 are described here. The majority of these were created by stream courses eroding across heterogeneous bedrock at varying rates. The falls along the Snake River formed because bedrock such as rhyolite resists stream erosion more effectively than basalt, its igneous counterpart. Most of the falls in the eastern highland areas were shaped in the same way.

Waterfalls descend from the canyon rims of the Snake River for two reasons. Runoff from irrigation finds its way into channels, which in some locales empty over solidified lava flows into the Snake. Along other reaches

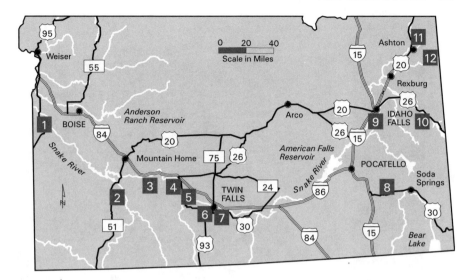

of the river, waterfalls descend from springs issuing forth from the canyon walls. Details of this latter phenomenon are provided later in the chapter.

1. Jump Creek Canyon

This small canyon is one of Idaho's hidden gems. Follow U.S. 95 to Poison Creek Road, located 2.5 miles south of the junction of 95 with S.R. 55.

In 3.5 miles, where the paved road takes a sharp right, turn left (south) on an unnamed gravel road. Follow it for 0.5 mile, then turn right (west) onto a dirt road. Do not get discouraged if you see a "No Trespassing" sign. This route is the correct public access to the canyon. In 0.4 mile, the road forks. The low road leads to a private homestead and the high road to the right ends at the mouth of the canyon in 1 additional mile. The land is administered by the Bureau of Land Management.

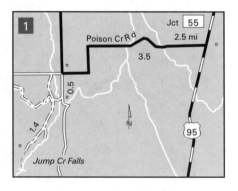

Jump Creek Falls ☆☆☆☆   ② 🚶

Form: horsetail   *Magnitude:* 55   *Watershed:* lg
Elevation: 2640 feet   *USGS Map:* Jump Creek Canyon (1989)

Water splashes 40 to 60 feet from Jump Creek into a small canyon. Interesting rock formations frame the cataract. Follow the pathway that begins at the end of the road into the canyon. Proceed along the canyon

Jump Creek Falls

floor, hopping from stone to stone across the creek and climbing over, around, and under large boulders that have fallen into the gorge. The destination is at the end of the trail in 0.2 mile.

2. Hot Springs

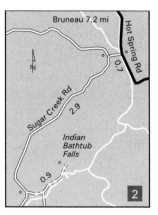

Indian Bathtub Falls (u) ☆ USGS Hot Springs (1992 nl). Although the waterfall is unimpressive, the thermal springs of this area justify a visit. Warm water trickles 7 to 12 feet from the adjacent bedrock into a small basin. This is a good place to soak, but wear something on your feet. Careless visitors have in the past left broken glass in the pool. This site is on land administered by the Bureau of Land Management. Drive along S.R. 51 to Bruneau, then continue southeast for 7.2 miles along Hot Spring Road. Turn right on the road marked Indian Bathtub, then left in 0.7 mile on the road marked Sugar Creek. After another 2.9 miles, turn left (east) on a dirt road that leads 0.9 mile to the parking area adjacent to the hot springs.

3. Deadman Canyon

Deadman Falls ☆ USGS Glenns Ferry (1992). This gaping canyon was slowly carved by the erosive powers of seasonal Deadman Creek. This entry would be a sight worth seeing if only water flowed over the 125- to 175-foot escarpment. A small Bureau of Land Management dam prevents the creek from plunging into the canyon the majority of the year. Perhaps a good show can be seen after an intense storm. Exit I-84 at Glenns Ferry. Drive

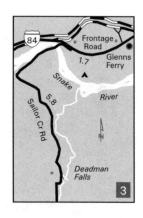

1.7 miles west of town along Frontage Road and turn left (south) onto Sailor Creek Road. Cross the bridge over the Snake River and continue 5.8 miles to the canyon rim.

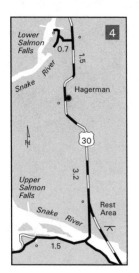

4. Hagerman

There are dams and power plants next to each of the falls along this section of the Snake River, which means that their scenic quality varies depending on the amount of water allowed to flow over their natural courses, which in turn is determined by the region's electrical demand. The area is accessible via U.S. 30, which is also called Thousand Springs Scenic Route.

Lower Salmon Falls ★★

Form: block   *Magnitude:* 50   *Watershed:* lg
Elevation: 2790 feet   *USGS Map:* Hagerman (1992)

A portion of the Snake River tumbles 10 to 15 feet downward. Turn off U.S. 30 at the marked entrance to Lower Salmon Power Plant, located 6.8 miles south of I-84 at the Gooding–Hagerman Exit 141 and 1.5 miles north of downtown Hagerman. Drive 0.7 mile to the best vantage. Look for the descent along the far side of the river below the power plant substation.

Upper Salmon Falls ★★★

Form: segmented   *Magnitude:* 70   *Watershed:* lg
Elevation: 2880 feet   *USGS Map:* Hagerman (1992)

The water in this entry diverges into four main blocks, each descending 15 to 25 feet along the Snake River. Drive 3.2 miles south of Hagerman on U.S. 30 and turn right (west) at the Upper Salmon Falls access sign. If you pass the rest area, you have missed the turnoff. Follow this secondary road 1.5 miles to the power plant. There is an obscured vista of the falls from the gravel road. For closer views, park at the east end of the road and cross an unmarked catwalk to an island halfway across the Snake, then proceed down the cement walkway to the falls. *Caution:* Periodically, the walkway area is

Upper Salmon Falls

flooded by Idaho Power, and the company is not liable if unwary visitors become trapped on the island.

5. Snake Plains Aquifer

The Snake River Plain northeast of Hagerman harbors one of the world's greatest groundwater resources. The mountain ranges in the southeastern part of central Idaho receive large amounts of precipitation, particularly during the winter. But the streams flowing south from these mountains fail to reach the Snake River because they sink into lava formations on the plain. Water collects in the pores of the subsurface bedrock, and since these rock layers gently dip southwestward, gravity pushes the groundwater toward Hagerman.

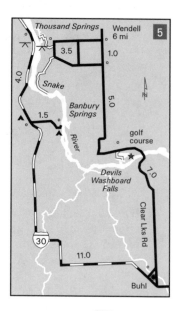

The course of the Snake River has been eroded to such an extent that it intersects with the aquifer. As a result, numerous springs gush from the river canyon's north wall. Most of these springs are high above the floor of the canyon, so are seen as waterfalls descending into the river.

Falls of Thousand Springs (u) ★★★

Form: segmented   *Magnitude:* 73   *Watershed:* lg (s)
Elevation: 3000 feet   *USGS Map:* Thousand Springs (1992 ns)

There are eight major falls and many minor falls descending 40 to 100 feet from springs along the north wall on this 1-mile stretch of the Snake River Canyon located between 15 and 16 miles northwest of Buhl. The springs increase the river's volume by up to tenfold along this reach of the river.

All the horsetail forms of these cataracts can be seen from across the Snake River along U.S. 30/Thousand Springs Scenic Route. For a close-up view of the easternmost descent, turn off Clear Lakes Road (described later) at the sign to Thousand Springs Picnic Area.

Others: *Falls of Banbury Springs* (u) ★ USGS Thousand Springs (1992 ns). Some of this 30- to 80-foot drop can be seen from across the river, but most of it is obscured by the surrounding vegetation. Turn off U.S. 30 and drive to the marked access road for Banbury Hot Springs Resort, located 4 miles south of Thousand Springs. The resort is 1.5 miles off the main highway.

Devils Washboard Falls ★ USGS Thousand Springs (1992). This is a pretty 15- to 30-foot cascade when the adjacent powerhouse isn't diverting most of the water flow from spring-fed Clear Lakes. Nearby is the Clear Lakes

Trout Company, reputed to be the largest trout farm in the world. Drive along Clear Lakes Road to the Buhl Country Club, located 7 miles north of Buhl and 12 miles south of Wendell. Find the falls by walking a short distance westward from the country club parking area.

6. Snake River Canyon West

The Snake River has carved sharply through basaltic rock layers to create a narrow, 400- to 500-foot canyon near Twin Falls. The area has several waterfalls, many of which are seasonal.

Pillar Falls ★★★   ②

Form: cascade   *Magnitude:* 53   *Watershed:* lg (d)
Elevation: 3200 feet   *USGS Map:* Twin Falls (1992)

Towers of 30- to 70-foot rhyolitic rock rise between 10- to 20-foot cascades along the Snake River. From the canyon rim, there is also a distant, but stunning view of *Shoshone Falls* (see entry below). You may wonder about the huge sand pile located along the south rim halfway between the two falls. It was the launch site for Evel Knievel's ill-fated attempt to jump the canyon on a "rocket-cycle" during the early 1970s.

From the city of Twin Falls, drive north along U.S. 93 for 1 mile to Golf Course Road and turn east. Continue along this dusty route for 0.9 mile, then stop. Walk through the old dumping grounds for about 0.3 mile to the abrupt,

Pillar Falls

unguarded canyon rim. Pillar Falls is directly below with Shoshone Falls farther upstream.

Perrine Coulee Falls ★★★★

Form: plunge   *Magnitude:* 90 (h)   *Watershed:* med
Elevation: 3500 feet   *USGS Map:* Twin Falls (1992)

Agricultural activities allow this otherwise seasonal waterfall to flow year-round. In fact, its discharge actually increases during the dry summer. This occurs because the coulee collects the water that overflows from the irrigated uplands. A natural pathway goes behind the 197-foot plunge.

Drive north from the city of Twin Falls on U.S. 93; just beyond Pole Line Road, turn west onto Canyon Springs Road. Park at the unsigned turnout in 0.7 mile. The view is inspiring.

Others: *Auger Falls* ★ USGS Jerome (1992). Water churns in strange convolutions for 25 to 50 feet over rocky obstructions along the Snake River. Public views from the north rim are rapidly dwindling as rangeland is converted into housing developments. Turn
left (west) off U.S. 93 at Golf
Course Road (described previously) and proceed 5 miles
to the subdivision area. With
luck, there will still be an undeveloped lot offering a vista.
Be careful near the rim. For
closer views, try driving about
5 miles west of U.S. 93 along
Canyon Springs Road (de-
scribed previously).

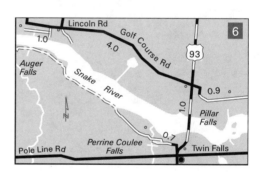

7. Snake River Canyon East

Twin Falls ★★★★

Form: segmented   *Magnitude:* 96 (h)   *Watershed:* lg (d)
Elevation: 3400 feet   *USGS Map:* Kimberly (1992)

Only one of this pair of cataracts still flows. The larger portion has been dammed. A torrent of water hurtles down 125 feet during early spring, but is reduced to a trickle in summer months as Milner Dam farther upstream draws off a large part of the Snake River for irrigation during the mid-year growing season.

From the city of Twin Falls follow Falls Avenue 5 miles east, passing the

Perrine Coulee Falls

junction to Shoshone Falls (described later). Turn left (north) at the marked road which in 1 mile leads to a picnic area adjacent to the falls.

Bridal Veil Falls ☆☆

Form: horsetail   *Magnitude:* 30   *Watershed:* sm
Elevation: 3200 feet   *USGS Map:* Twin Falls (1992 ns)

Water tumbles 25 to 40 feet from spring-fed Dierkes Lake. The stream nearly sprays onto the road before reaching a culvert which directs the water into a pond below. Backtrack from Twin Falls (described previously) for 3 miles along Falls Avenue to the marked turn for Shoshone Falls Park. This and the following entry are 2 miles from the junction.

Shoshone Falls ☆☆☆☆☆

Form: block   *Magnitude:* 120   *Watershed:* lg (d)
Elevation: 3200 feet   *USGS Map:* Twin Falls (1992)

This is the most famous waterfall in Idaho. It measures over 1,000 feet across and plunges 212 feet. The awesome display is best viewed during springtime. Later in the year, when the water is diverted upstream for agricultural uses, the river dries up and only large ledges of rhyolite can be seen. To reach the falls, located in Shoshone Falls Park, follow the directions in the previous entry.

Shoshone Falls

In pioneer days a Shoshoni Indian named Quish-in-demi told the following tale to J. S. Harrington. The story is recorded in *Idaho: A Guide*

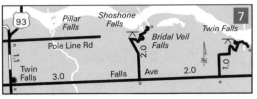

in *Words and Pictures*, published in 1937 as part of the Federal Writers' Project:

> *In the gloomy gorge above the falls there was, long ago, the trysting place of a deep-chested Shoshoni [warrior] and the slender wild girl whom he loved. Their last meeting was here on a pile of rocks which overlooked the plunging waters. He went away to scalp with deft incisions and then to lift the shaggy mane of white men with a triumphant shout; and she came daily to stand by the thundering avalanche and remember him. That he would return unharmed she did not, with the ageless resourcefulness of women, ever allow herself to doubt. But time passed, and the moons that came and ripened were many, and she still came nightly to stand on the brink and watch the changeless journeying of the water. And it was here that she stood one black night above the roar of the flood when a warrior stepped out of shadow and whispered to her and then disappeared. As quiet as the flat stone under her feet, she stood for a long while, looking down into the vault where the waters boiled up like seething white hills to fill the sky with dazzling curtains and roll away in convulsed tides. For an hour she gazed down there 200 feet to a mad pouring of motion and sound into a black graveyard of the dead. And then, slowly, she lifted her arms above her, listed her head to the fullest curve of her throat, and stood tiptoe for a moment, poised and beautiful, and then dived in a long swift arc against the falling white background . . . And the river at this point and since that hour has never been the same.*

8. Lava Hot Springs

Lower Portneuf Falls (u) ★★   ① 🚶

Form: segmented   *Magnitude:* 37   *Watershed:* lg
Elevation: 4840 feet   *USGS Map:* McCammon (1968 nl)

The Portneuf River diverges into a pair of 15- to 25-foot cataracts. One appears in the form of a plunge, the other a cascade. From the town of Lava Hot Springs drive 6 miles west along U.S. 30. Park at an old jeep trail and walk down to the stream and its modest display.

Campground Falls (u) ★★

Form: punchbowl   *Magnitude:* 37   *Watershed:* lg
Elevation: 5000 feet   *USGS Map:* Lava Hot Springs (1968 ns)

    This 10- to 15-foot drop along Portneuf River is located within a private campground, hence its unofficial name. Drive 0.3 mile past the east end of Lava Hot Springs along U.S. 30.

Others: *Falls along the Portneuf* (u) ★ USGS Haystack Mtn (1968 nl). Several small cataracts occur along a 1-mile reach of the Portneuf River north of Lava Hot Springs. The ground tends to be marshy in this area, so appropriate footwear is recommended on your cross-country trek. Drive 0.2 mile past Campground Falls (described previously) and turn off U.S. 30 onto Pebble Area Road. Proceed 2 miles north to an unsigned loop road. Bushwhack a short distance to the stream and its northernmost descent.

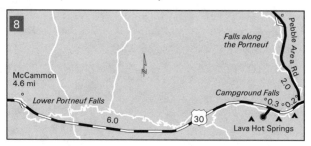

9. City of Idaho Falls

A low, turbulent descent on the Snake River shares its name with this community of 40,000. Stop and enjoy the falls from the adjacent city park.

Idaho Falls of the Snake River ★★★

Form: cascade   *Magnitude:* 71
Watershed: lg (d)
Elevation: 4670 feet   *USGS Map:*
Idaho Falls South (1979 ns)

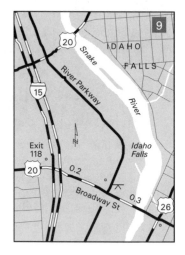

    This 15- to 25-foot falls is over 1,200 feet wide and has the distinction of being man-made. In pioneer days there were only rapids at this location. A concrete dam was first built on the river in 1909 to channel some of the water to the Eagle Rock power plant for generating electricity. By the 1970s, the dam had deteriorated severely. In order to assure reliable streamflow for newer turbines, the old dam was replaced in 1981. The artificial

Idaho Falls of the Snake River

falls was constructed as a part of the project.

Turn off I-15 at Broadway Street (Exit 118) and drive toward the city center. Immediately before the bridge crossing the Snake, turn left (north) on River Parkway and find an available parking spot.

10. Swan Valley

Fall Creek Falls ★★★★

Form: fan   *Magnitude:* 78   *Watershed:* lg
Elevation: 5280 feet   *USGS Map:* Conant Valley (1966)

Fall Creek plunges 60 feet over travertine deposits into the Snake River. On either side of the central falls the water plumes to form a natural fountain that all waterfall collectors should include on their "must-see" list. Drive 39 miles east of Idaho Falls or 3.2 miles west of Swan Valley along U.S.

Fall Creek Falls

26 to Snake River–Palisades Dam Road. Turn south and follow this gravel route 1.4 miles; park where the road widens. The best views of this cataract are a short walk farther along the roadway.

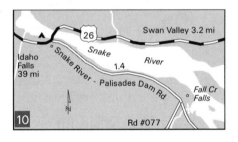

II. Henrys Fork

Henrys Fork is a wild and scenic river in all but official federal designation. It winds through the Ashton Ranger District of Targhee National Forest.

Lower Mesa Falls ☆☆☆

Form: block   *Magnitude:* 78   *Watershed:* lg
Elevation: 5420 feet   *USGS Map:* Snake River Butte (1965)

The rushing waters of Henrys Fork tumble 65 chaotic feet in this waterfall some 400 feet below an overlook. Drive 15 miles northeast of Ashton on S.R. 47 to the signed turnout, appropriately named Grandview.

Upper Mesa Falls ★★★★
Form: block   *Magnitude:* 95   *Watershed:* lg
Elevation: 5600 feet   *USGS Map:* Snake River Butte (1965)

Henrys Fork plummets 114 feet from a sheer wall of rhyolitic bed-rock. Also known as *Big Falls*. Located on private property owned by a power company which in the past has allowed access for visitors.

About 0.8 mile past Grandview (described previously) depart S.R. 47 by turning left (west) onto Upper Mesa Falls Road #295. Drive to the road's end in less than 1 mile. Side views of the falls are just a short walk away. Be careful at the canyon rim!

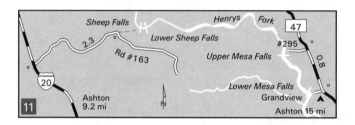

Sheep Falls ★★★   ③ 🚶
Form: block   *Magnitude:* 50   *Watershed:* lg
Elevation: 5820 feet   *USGS Map:* Lookout Butte (1965)

Henrys Fork tumbles 15 to 25 feet within Ashton Ranger District, Targhee National Forest. Drive 9.2 miles north of Ashton along U.S. 20 to signed Sheep Falls Road #163. Turn right (east) and follow the route 2.3 miles to the trailhead. Sheep Falls Trail #760, built in 1986 by Challenger Group YSC, goes down to the river and reaches the falls in 1 mile.

Lower Sheep Falls (u) ★★   ③ 🚶
Form: cascade   *Magnitude:* 47   *Watershed:* lg
Elevation: 5800 feet   *USGS Map:* Lookout Butte (1965 ns)

Water drops 15 to 25 feet along Henrys Fork within Ashton Ranger District, Targhee National Forest. Walk less than 100 yards downstream from Sheep Falls (described previously).

12. Yellowstone

Although two of the following falls are actually in Wyoming, they have been included here because they can be most easily reached from just across the border in Idaho. The Falls River, which flows out of the southwestern corner of Yellowstone National Park, is aptly named. A total of 27 cataracts are known to occur in its drainage basin. Four of these are described here.

Sheep Falls ★★★ ③

Form: segmented   *Magnitude:* 51   *Watershed:* lg
Elevation: 5890 feet   *USGS Map:* Sheep Falls (1989)

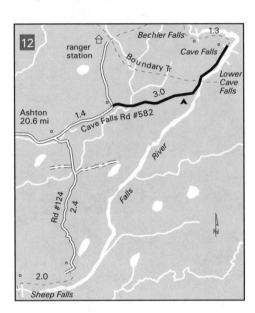

The name of this 35-foot waterfall comes from the sheep drives that once occurred in the vicinity. It is situated within Ashton Ranger District, Targhee National Forest. Drive 6 miles east from Ashton on S.R. 47 to the Cave Falls Road #582. Bear right, follow Road #582 for 14.6 miles, then turn right (south) at Wyoming Creek Road #124. Drive down this gravel road for 2.4 miles to a junction with an unsigned jeep trail on the left. (*Note:* The gravel road ends 0.3 mile farther on.) Hike down the jeep trail for 2 miles to the top of the falls. Nimble adults can follow a faint path which leads to the best views.

Cave Falls ★★★★

Form: block   *Magnitude:* 73   *Watershed:* lg
Elevation: 6260 feet   *USGS Map:* Cave Falls (1989)

This picturesque block waterfall descends 35 feet along the Falls River within Yellowstone National Park. It is named after a large recess beneath the stream's west bank. Follow the directions to Sheep Falls (described previously), but stay on Cave Falls Road #582 to its end at the falls, 25 miles from Ashton.

Lower Cave Falls (u) ★★

Form: block   *Magnitude:* 40   *Watershed:* lg
Elevation: 6220 feet   *USGS Map:* Cave Falls (1989 nl)

The Falls River descends 5 to 10 feet within Yellowstone National Park. Look for this cataract about 0.1 mile downstream from Cave Falls (described previously).

Cave Falls

Bechler Falls ☆☆

Form: block   *Magnitude:* 31   *Watershed:* lg
Elevation: 6340 feet   *USGS Map:* Bechler Falls (1989)

Water tumbles 15 to 25 feet along a wide reach of the Bechler River in Yellowstone National Park. Follow the Bechler River Trail 1.3 miles beyond Cave Falls (described previously) to this cataract.

SELECTED READINGS

Adams, Kevin. *North Carolina Waterfalls: Where to Find Them, How to Photograph Them*. Winston-Salem, N. C.: John F. Blair, 1994.

Blouin, Nicole, Steve Bordonaro, and Marylou Wier Bordonaro. *Waterfalls of the Blue Ridge*. Birmingham, Ala.: Menasha Ridge Press, 1994.

Bluestein, Sheldon. *Hiking Trails of Southern Idaho*. Caldwell, Idaho: Caxton Printers, 1981.

————. *North Idaho Hiking Trails*. Boise, Idaho: Challenge Expedition Company, 1982.

Bolnick, Bruce, and Doreen Bolnick. *Waterfalls of the White Mountains*. Woodstock, Vt.: Backcountry Publications, 1990.

Conly, Marc. *Waterfalls of Colorado*. Boulder, Colo.: Pruett Publishing, 1993.

Henderson, Bonnie. *Best Hikes with Children in Western and Central Oregon*. Seattle: The Mountaineers Books, 1992.

Idaho Atlas & Gazetteer. Freeport, Maine: DeLorme, 1992.

Maynard, Charles. *Waterfalls of Yellowstone National Park*. Seymour, Tenn.: Panther Press, 1996.

McArthur, Lewis. *Oregon Geographic Names*. Portland: Oregon Historical Society, 1991.

McKee, Bates. *Cascadia: The Geologic Evolution of the Pacific Northwest*. McGraw-Hill, 1972.

Oregon Atlas & Gazetteer. Freeport, Maine: DeLorme, 1991.

Osborne, Michael. *Granite, Water, and Light: Waterfalls of Yosemite Valley*. Yosemite Association, Yosemite National Park, California, 1983.

Ostertag, Rhonda and George Ostertag. *Day Hikes from Oregon Campgrounds*. Seattle: The Mountaineers Books, 1992.

————. *50 Hikes in Oregon's Coast Range & Siskiyous*. Seattle: The Mountaineers Books, 1989.

Penrose, Laurie, Bill Penrose, and Ruth Penrose. *A Guide to 199 Michigan Waterfalls*. Davison, Mich.: Friede Publications, 1988.

Phillips, James W. *Washington State Place Names*. Seattle: University of Washington Press, 1976.

Plumb, Gregory A. "A Scale for Comparing the Visual Magnitude of Waterfalls." *Earth-Science Reviews* 34 (1993): 261–270.

————. *Waterfalls of Tennessee*. Johnson City, Tenn.: Overmountain Press, 1996.

————. *Computer Companion to Waterfall Lover's Guide to the Pacific Northwest*. Johnson City, Tenn.: Personalized Map Company, forthcoming. (Contact: www.mymaps.com)

Spring, Ira, and Harvey Manning. *100 Hikes in the South Cascades and Olympics.* Seattle: The Mountaineers Books, 1985.

Sterling, E. M. *Trips and Trails, 2.* Seattle: The Mountaineers Books, 1983.

Sullivan, William L. *Exploring Oregon's Wild Areas.* Seattle: The Mountaineers Books, 1988.

Sullivan, William L. *100 Hikes in Northwest Oregon.* Eugene: Navillus Press, 1993.

Washington Atlas & Gazetteer. Freeport, Maine: DeLorme, 1992.

Wert, Fred. *Washington Rail-Trails.* Seattle: The Mountaineers Books, 1982.

APPENDIX

This appendix lists 724 additional waterfalls known to occur within the Pacific Northwest. It is organized into the same thirteen geographic regions used in this guidebook. The name of each waterfall is accompanied by the name of the USGS topographic map on which it can be found.

THE NORTH CASCADES

Agnes Falls, Mount Lyall (1987 ns)
Anderson Falls (u), Lawrence (1994 nl)
Angeline Falls (u), Big Snow Mtn (1965 nl)
Arbuthnet Lake Falls, Shuksan Arm (1989 nl)
Asbestos Falls, Helena Ridge (1989)
Bear Creek Falls, Monte Cristo (1982 ns)
Bessemer Mountain, Falls of (u), Mount Si (1989 ns)
Boulder Falls, Meadow Mtn (1989)
Boulder Creek Falls (u), Lewis Butte (1991 nl)
Boulder Creek Falls (u), Welker Peak (1989 nl)
Burnboot Creek Falls (u), Snoqualmie Pass (1989 nl)
Calligan Creek Falls (u), Mount Si (1989 nl)
Cherry Creek Falls, Monroe (1993 ns)
Colchuck Falls (u), Enchantment Lakes (1989 nl)
Cole Creek Falls (u), Easton (1989 nl)
Copper Creek Falls (u), Holden (1988 nl)
Crown Point Falls, Suiattle Pass (1988)
Deer Falls, Blanca Lake (1982 ns)
Dingford Creek Falls, Snoqualmie Lake (1982 ns)
East Fork Falls (u), Lester (1989 nl)
East Picket Falls (u), Mount Blum (1989 nl)
Elk Falls (u), Mount Stickney (1989 nl)
Elliott Creek Falls (u), Sloan Peak (1982 nl)
Eureka Creek Falls, McLeod Mtn (1991 ns)
Falls Creek Falls (u), Enchantment Lakes (1989 nl)
Fifteenmile Falls, Hobart (1993 ns)
Findley Creek Falls (u), Findley Lake (1989 nl)
Florence Falls, Snoqualmie Lake (1982 ns)
Fontal Falls, Monroe (1993 ns)
Friday Creek Falls (u), Lester (1989 nl)
Goat Creek Falls (u), Snoqualmie Pass (1989 nl)
Gold Creek Falls (u), Chikamin Peak (1989 nl)
Goodell Basin Falls (u), Mount Challenger (1989 nl)
Great Falls (u), Grotto (1982 ns)
Green Mountain Falls (u), Lake Philippa (1989 nl)
Greider Creek Falls (u), Mount Stickney (1989 nl)
Greider Lake Falls (u), Mount Stickney (1989 nl)
Hard Scrabble Falls, Deming (1994)
Hardscrabble Creek Falls (u), Enchantment Lakes (1989 nl)
Hart Lake Falls (u), Holden (1988 nl)
Hilt Creek Falls (u), Rockport (1982 nl)
Horseshoe Basin, Falls of (u), Cascade Pass (1963 ns)
Iceburg Lake Falls (u), Chikamin Peak (1989 nl)
Icy Peak Falls (u), Mount Shuksan (1989 nl)
Indian Valley Falls 1-2 (u), Mount Redoubt (1989 nl)
Jasper Pass Falls (u), Mount Blum (1989 nl)

Kelly Creek Falls (u), Verlot (1989 ns)
Lake Isabel Falls (u), Index (1989 nl)
Lemah Creek Falls (u), Chikamin Peak (1989 nl)
Lemah Valley Falls (u), Chikamin Peak (1989 nl)
Little Beaver Falls 1-5 (u), Mount Challenger (1989 nl)
Little Beaver Falls 6-9 (u), Mount Redoubt (1989 nl)
Lower Bald Eagle Falls (u), Mount Blum (1989 nl)
Lower Canyon Creek Falls (u), Granite Falls (1989 nl)
Lower Icy Peak Falls (u), Mount Blum (1989 nl)
Lower North Baker Falls (u), Mount Blum (1989 nl)
Lower Pass Valley Falls (u), Mount Blum (1989 nl)
Lower Wallace Falls (u), Gold Bar (1989 nl)
Lower Wells Creek Falls (u), Bearpaw Mtn (1989 ns)
Lower Whatcom Falls (u), Bellingham North (1994 ns)
Luna Basin Falls 1-2 (u), Mount Challenger (1989 nl)
Lyman Lake Falls (u), Suiattle Pass (1988 nl)
Malachite Falls, Big Snow Mtn (1965 ns)
Maple Falls, Maple Falls (1994 ns)
Marsh Creek Falls (u), Lake Chaplain (1989 nl)
Mazama Falls, Shuksan Arm (1989)
McCauley Falls, Monroe (1993)
Middle Canyon Creek Falls (u), Granite Falls (1989 nl)
Middle Lemah Creek Falls (u), Chikamin Peak (1989 nl)
Middle Pass Valley Falls (u), Mount Blum (1989 nl)
Middle Picket Falls (u), Mount Blum (1989 nl)
Middle Twin Falls (u), Chester Morse Lake (1989 ns)
Middle Wells Creek Falls 1-3 (u), Bearpaw Mtn (1989 nl)
Mineral Creek Falls (u), Mount Blum (1989 nl)
Mineral Mountain Falls (u), Mount Blum (1989 nl)
Mount Index Falls (u), Index (1989 nl)
Mount Thomson Falls (u), Chikamin Peak (1989 nl)
North Bald Eagle Falls (u), Mount Blum (1989 nl)
North Fork Cedar Falls (u), Findley Lake (1989 nl)
Olney Falls, Wallace Lake (1989)
Otter Falls, Snoqualmie Lake (1982)
Park Creek Falls (u), Shuksan Arm (1989 nl)
Perfection Lake Falls (u), Enchantment Lakes (1989 nl)
Perry Creek Falls (u), Bedal (1982 nl)
Phantom Pass Falls (u), Mount Blum (1989 nl)
Picket Basin Falls (u), Mount Challenger (1989 nl)
Pioneer Ridge Falls (u), Mount Blum (1989 nl)
Ptarmigan Basin Falls (u), Shuksan Arm (1989 nl)
Redoubt Valley Falls (u), Mount Redoubt (1989 nl)
Roaring Creek Falls (u), Stampede Pass (1989 nl)

Ruth Mountain Falls (u), Mount Shuksan (1989 nl)
Salmon Creek Falls (u), Mount Stickney (1989 nl)
San Juan Falls, Blanca Lake (1982 ns)
Scramble Creek Falls (u), Mount Blum (1989 nl)
Scramble Valley Falls (u), Mount Blum (1989 nl)
Seahpo Peak Falls (u), Mount Shuksan (1989 nl)
Seattle Creek Falls (u), Findley Lake (1989 nl)
Sholes Creek Falls (u), Mount Baker (1989 nl)
Shuksan Creek Falls (u), Shuksan Arm (1989 nl)
Shuksan Valley Falls 1-3 (u), Shuksan Arm (1989 nl)
Snow Creek Falls (u), Enchantment Lakes (1989 nl)
Snow Creek Falls (u), Leavenworth (1989 nl)
South Baker Falls (u), Mount Blum (1989 nl)
Stampede Creek Falls (u), Stampede Pass (1989 nl)
Stehekin Falls (u), McGregor Mtn (1987 nl)
Sulphide Basin Falls 1-5 (u), Mount Shuksan (1989 nl)
Sunday Falls, Monte Cristo (1982 ns)
· Swift Valley Falls 1-4 (u), Shuksan Arm (1989 nl)
Sygitowicz Creek Falls (u), Deming (1994 nl)
Teanaway Falls, Mount Stuart (1989 ns)
Tinling Creek Falls (u), Deming (1994 nl)
Twin Camp Falls (u), Lester (1989 nl)
Upper Bald Eagle Falls (u), Mount Blum (1989 nl)
Upper Canyon Creek Falls (u), Granite Falls (1989 nl)
Upper Green Mountain Falls (u), Lake Philippa
    (1989 nl)
Upper Lemah Creek Falls (u), Chikamin Peak
    (1989 nl)
Upper North Baker Falls (u), Mount Blum (1989 nl)
Upper Pass Creek Falls (u), Mount Blum (1989 nl)
Upper Pass Valley Falls (u), Mount Blum (1989 nl)
Upper Rainbow Falls (u), Shuksan Arm (1989 nl)
Upper Twin Falls (u), Chester Morse Lake (1989 ns)
Upper Twin Camp Falls (u), Lester (1989 nl)
Upper Wallace Falls (u), Wallace Lake (1989 nl)
Viola Creek Falls (u), Findley Lake (1989 nl)
West Picket Falls (u), Mount Blum (1989 nl)
Winchester Creek Falls (u), Mount Sefrit (1989 nl)

THE OLYMPICS AND VICINITY

All-in-Creek Falls (u), Hunger Mtn (1990 nl)
Bear Creek Falls, Ellis Mtn (1984 ns)
Bridge Creek Falls (u), Mount Carrie (1950 nl)
Cedar Creek Falls, Eden Valley (1993)
Dean Creek Falls (u), Dean Creek (1986 nl)
Deschutes Falls, Bald Hill (1990)
Elwha Valley Falls 1-3 (u), Mount Queets (1990 nl)
Fisk Falls, Pe Ell (1986)
Glacier Creek Falls (u), Mount Olympus (1990 nl)
Godkin Falls (u), Chimney Peak (1990 nl)
Goodman Falls (u), Toleak Point (1982 nl)
Graves Creek Falls (u), Mount Hoquiam (1990 nl)
Hamma Hamma Falls (u), Mount Skokomish (1990 nl)
Hatana Falls, Wellesley Peak (1990)
Heather Creek Falls (u), Mount Deception (1990 nl)
Herman Falls, Ellis Mtn (1984 ns)
Hoh Lake Falls (u), Bogachiel Peak (1950 nl)
Home Sweet Home Falls (u), Mount Steel (1990 nl)
Honeymoon Meadows Falls 1-3 (u), Mount Steel
    (1990 nl)

LaCrosse Falls (u), Mount Steel (1990 nl)
Lilliwaup Falls, Lilliwaup (1985)
Lower Hamma Hamma Falls (u), Mount
    Washington (1985 nl)
Martin Creek Falls (u), Mount Olympus (1990 nl)
Martins Falls (u), Mount Christie (1990 nl)
Marys Falls, Mount Angeles (1990 nl)
McKenna Falls, Wildcat Lake (1968)
Middle Martin Creek Falls (u), Mount Olympus
    (1990 nl)
Mineral Creek Falls (u), Owl Mtn (1990 nl)
Morse Creek Falls (u), Morse Creek (1985 nl)
Mount Skokomish Falls (u), Mount Skokomish
    (1990 nl)
Murphy Creek Falls (u), Quillayute Prairie (1982 nl)
Naselle Falls (u), Sweigiler Creek (1986 nl)
Pluvius Falls (u), Pluvius (1986 nl)
Rock Creek Falls, Malone (1986 ns)
Royal Creek Falls (u), Mount Deception (1990 nl)
Seattle Creek Falls (u), Mount Christie (1990 nl)
Service Falls, Mount Olympus (1990)
Skokomish Falls (u), Mount Tebo (1990 nl)
Spoon Creek Falls (u), Grisdale (1990)
Upper Martin Creek Falls (u), Mount Olympus
    (1990 nl)
Upper Service Falls (u), Mount Olympus (1990 nl)
Upper Willapa Falls (u), Pluvius (1986 nl)
Vincent Creek Falls (u), Vance Creek (1990 nl)
Warkum Creek Falls (u), Hunger Mtn (1990 nl)
Wet Weather Falls (u), Mount Townsend (1990 nl)
White Creek Falls (u), Mount Steel (1990 nl)
Whitehorse Creek Falls (u), Mount Skokomish
    (1990 nl)
Willapa Falls, Pluvius (1986)

MOUNT RAINIER REGION

Affi Falls, Sunrise (1971)
Alice Falls, Mowich Lake (1971)
American Valley Falls (u), Cougar Lake (1988 nl)
Baker Point Falls (u), Sunrise (1971 nl)
Basaltic Falls, Mt Rainier East (1971)
Boulder Creek Falls (u), Chinook Pass (1987 nl)
Bumping River Falls (u), Bumping Lake (1988 nl)
Butter Creek Falls (u), Mt Rainier West (1971 nl)
Chimneys Falls (u), Chinook Pass (1987 nl)
Clear Fork Falls (u), Old Snowy Mtn (1988 nl)
Colonnade Falls (u), Mt Rainier West (1971 nl)
Crag Lake Falls (u), Cougar Lake (1988 nl)
Crescent Creek Falls (u), Mowich Lake (1971 nl)
Cress Falls, Mowich Lake (1971)
Denman Falls, Mount Wow (1971)
Devil Creek Falls, Cliffdell (1987)
Eagle Creek Falls (u), The Rockies (1993 nl)
East Basaltic Falls (u), Mt Rainier East (1971 nl)
East Canyon Creek Falls (u), Bearhead Mtn (1986 nl)
East Nickel Creek Falls (u), Mt Rainier East (1971 nl)
East Van Trump Falls (u), Mt Rainier West (1971 nl)
Ethania Falls, Mount Wow (1971)
Falls Creek Falls (u), Bearhead Mtn (1986 nl)
Fryingpan Creek Falls (u), Chinook Pass (1987 nl)

Garda Falls, Sunrise (1971)
Giant Falls, Mowich Lake (1971)
Goat Mountain Falls (u), Sunrise (1971 nl)
Helen Falls (u), Mount Wow (1971 nl)
Huckleberry Creek Falls (u), Sunrise (1971 nl)
Jennings Falls, Packwood (1989 ns)
Jordan Basin Falls (u), Packwood Lake (1989 nl)
Kan Falls (u), Purcell Mtn (1989 nl)
Kautz Creek Falls (u), Mt Rainier West (1971 nl)
Larrupin Falls, Mount Wow (1971)
Laughingwater Creek Falls (u), Chinook Pass (1987 nl)
Lower Nickel Creek Falls (u), Mt Rainier East
    (1971 nl)
Lower Stevens Falls (u), Mt Rainier East (1971 nl)
Lower Sunbeam Falls (u), Mt Rainier East (1971 nl)
Lower Williwakas Falls (u), Mt Rainier East (1971 nl)
Margaret Falls, Mt Rainier East (1971)
Marie Falls, Mt Rainier East (1971)
Mary Belle Falls, Mt Rainier East (1971)
Middle Boulder Creek Falls (u), Chinook Pass
    (1987 nl)
Middle Fork Lake Falls (u), Packwood Lake (1989 nl)
Middle Ohanapecosh Falls (u), Chinook Pass
    (1987 nl)
Middle Ohanapecosh Falls (u), Mt Rainier East
    (1971 nl)
Needle Creek Falls (u), Chinook Pass (1987 nl)
Nisqually Valley Falls (u), Mt Rainier West (1971 nl)
Ohanapecosh Park Falls 1-6 (u), Mt Rainier East
    (1971 nl)
Pearl Falls, Mt Rainier West (1971)
Saint Johns Falls, Chinook Pass (1987)
Skate Valley Falls (u), Wahpenayo Peak (1989 nl)
South Ohanapecosh Falls (u), Chinook Pass (1987 nl)
St Andrews Falls (u), Mount Wow (1971 nl)
Stevens Valley Falls (u), Mt Rainier East (1971 nl)
Sunbeam Falls, Mt Rainier East (1971)
Sunrise Falls (u), White River Park (1971 nl)
Tilton River Falls (u), The Rockies (1993 nl)
Trixie Falls, Mt Rainier East (1971)
Twin Falls, Mt Rainier East (1971)
Upper Boulder Creek Falls (u), Chinook Pass
    (1987 nl)
Upper Chimneys Falls (u), Chinook Pass (1987 nl)
Upper Clear Creek Falls (u), Spiral Butte (1988 nl)
Upper Clear Fork Falls (u), Old Snowy Mtn (1988 nl)
Upper Davis Creek Falls (u), Purcell Mtn (1989 nl)
Upper Eagle Creek Falls (u), The Rockies (1993 nl)
Upper Falls Creek Falls (u), Bearhead Mtn (1986 nl)
Upper Mesatchee Cr Falls (u), Old Snowy Mtn
    (1988 nl)
Upper Middle Fork Falls (u), Packwood Lake (1989 nl)
Upper Ohanapecosh Falls (u), Mt Rainier East
    (1971 nl)
Upper Olallie Falls (u), Chinook Pass (1987 nl)
Upper South Fork Falls (u), Spiral Butte (1988 nl)
Upper St Andrews Falls (u), Mt Rainier West (1971 nl)
Upper Stevens Falls (u), Mt Rainier East (1971 nl)
Upper Sunbeam Falls (u), Mt Rainier East (1971 nl)
Upper Van Horn Falls (u), Sunrise (1971 nl)

Upper Voight Creek Falls (u), Wilkeson (1956 nl)
Upper Williwakas Falls (u), Mt Rainier East (1971 nl)
Vernal Park Falls (u), Sunrise (1971 nl)
Victor Falls, Sumner (1993)
Voight Creek Falls (u), Wilkeson (1956 nl)
Washington Cascades, Mt Rainier East (1971 ns)
Wauhaukaupauken Falls, Mt Rainier East (1971)
Wenas Creek Falls (u), Manastash Lake (1971 nl)
West Canyon Creek Falls (u), Bearhead Mtn (1986 nl)
West Nickel Creek Falls (u), Mt Rainier East (1971 nl)
West Ohanapecosh Falls (u), Chinook Pass (1987 nl)
West Van Trump Falls (u), Mt Rainier West (1971 nl)
Wildcat Falls, Lake Kapowsin (1987)

GIFFORD PINCHOT COUNTRY
Bear Creek Falls (u), Elk Mtn (1983 nl)
Big Rock Falls (u), Siouxon Peak (1993 nl)
Big Spring Falls (u), Steamboat Mtn (1970 nl)
Big Tree Creek Falls (u), Dole (1986 nl)
Canyon Valley Falls 1-3 (u), Siouxon Peak (1993 nl)
Cape Horn Creek Falls (u), Ariel (1971 nl)
Castile Falls, Castile Falls (1970)
Coyote Creek Falls (u), Dole (1986 nl)
Coyote Creek Falls (u), Fairview Ridge (1987 nl)
Dry Creek Falls, Camas Patch (1965)
Hellroaring Falls, Mount Adams East (1970 nl)
Husum Falls, Husum (1994 nl)
Jakes Creek Falls (u), Siouxon Peak (1993 nl)
Klickitat Falls (u), Signal Peak (1970 nl)
Little Goose Creek Falls, Sleeping Beauty (1970 ns)
Little Niagara Falls, Quartz Creek Butte (1965)
Logy Creek Falls, Logy Creek Falls (1965)
Lower Copper Creek Falls (u), Quartz Creek Butte
    (1965 ns)
Lower Klickitat Falls (u), Signal Peak (1970 nl)
Lower Rattlesnake Falls (u), Camas Prairie (1983 nl)
McCall Basin Falls (u), Old Snowy Mtn (1988 nl)
North Fork Kalama Falls (u), Elk Mtn (1983 nl)
North Huckleberry Falls (u), Walupt Lake (1970 nl)
Panther Creek Falls, Big Huckleberry Mtn (1983 ns)
Rattlesnake Falls (u), Camas Prairie (1983 nl)
Rusk Creek Falls (u), Mt Adams East 1970 nl)
Salmon Falls, Yacolt (1990)
Smith Creek Falls (u), Smith Creek Butte (1983 nl)
Snagtooth Creek Falls (u), Quartz Creek Butte
    (1965 nl)
South Huckleberry Falls (u), Walupt Lake (1970 nl)
Upper Big Tree Creek Falls (u), Yale Dam (1986 ns)
Upper Rusk Creek Falls (u), Mt Adams East 1970 nl)
Washboard Falls, Wolf Point (1984)
West Fork Falls (u), Husum (1994 nl)
West Fork Falls (u), Windy Point (1970 nl)
West Smith Creek Falls (u), Smith Creek Butte
    (1983 nl)

THE INLAND EMPIRE
Albeni Falls, Newport (1986 ns)
Buckeye Creek Falls (u), Chapman Lake (1980 nl)
Calispell Creek Falls (u), Sacheen Lake (1986 nl)
Crater Coulee Falls (u), Babcock Ridge (1966 nl)

Delzer Falls, Sullivan Lake (1968)
Flume Creek Falls (u), Boundary Dam (1986 nl)
Hompegg Falls, Eckler Mtn (1983)
Kettle Falls (historical), Marcus (1969 ns)
Little Chamokane Falls, Wellpinit (1973)
Little Nespelem Falls (u), Armstrong Creek (1989 nl)
Martin Falls, Steamboat Rock Southeast (1968)
McLoughlin Falls, Keystone (1980)
Multnomah Falls, Armstrong Creek (1989)
Nespelem Falls (u), Armstrong Creek (1989 nl)
Ninemile Falls, Ninemile Flat (1985)
Reiser Falls, Sullivan Lake (1968)
Rickey Rapids, Bangs Mtn (1982 ns)
Sheep Creek Falls (u), Stentz Spring (1983 nl)
Spray Falls, Armstrong Creek (1989)
Towell Falls, Honn Lakes (1981)
Tucannon River Falls (u), Tucannon (1967 nl)
Weimer Creek Falls (u), Falling Springs (1981 nl)
Wilson Creek Falls, Almira (1969)

THE COLUMBIA GORGE
Celilo Falls, Stacker Butte (1965 ns)
Divers Creek Falls (u), Dee (1994 nl)
Eagle Tanner Falls (u), Wahtum Lake (1979 nl)
East Fork Falls (u), Wahtum Lake (1979 nl)
Falls Creek Falls (u), Carson (1994 nl)
Falls Creek Falls (u), Tanner Butte (1994 nl)
Four Mile Falls (u), Tanner Butte (1994 nl)
Greenleaf Falls (u), Bonneville Dam (1994 nl)
Greenleaf Peak Falls (u), Bonneville Dam (1994 nl)
Lindsey Creek Falls (u), Mount Defiance (1994 nl)
Middle Four Mile Falls (u), Wahtum Lake (1979 nl)
Middle Ruckel Creek Falls (u), Bonneville Dam
    (1994 nl)
Middle Tanner Creek Falls (u), Tanner Butte (1994 nl)
Mile Five Falls (u), Dee (1994 nl)
Moffett Falls, Tanner Butte (1994 nl)
North Benson Falls (u), Wahtum Lake (1979 nl)
North Fork Falls (u), Lookout Mtn (1986 nl)
Opal Creek Falls (u), Tanner Butte (1994 nl)
Rock Falls (u), White Salmon (1978 nl)
Rock Creek Falls (u), Larch Mtn (1986 nl)
Slide Creek Falls (u), Carson (1994 nl)
Sorenson Creek Falls (u), Bonneville Dam (1994 nl)
Summit Creek Falls (u), Mount Defiance (1994 nl)
Sweeney Falls, Carson (1994 ns)
The Dalles, The Dalles South (1994 ns)
Tish Creek Falls (u), Tanner Butte (1994 nl)
Upper Bridal Veil Falls (u), Bridal Veil (1994 nl)
Upper Dog Creek Falls (u), Mount Defiance (1994 nl)
Upper Falls Creek Falls (u), Tanner Butte (1994 nl)
Upper Four Mile Falls (u), Wahtum Lake (1979 nl)
Upper Greenleaf Falls (u), Bonneville Dam (1994 nl)
Upper Moffett Creek Falls (u), Tanner Butte (1994 nl)
Upper Opal Creek Falls (u), Tanner Butte (1994 nl)
Upper Ruckel Creek Falls (u), Bonneville Dam
    (1994 nl)
Upper Tanner Creek Falls (u), Tanner Butte (1994 nl)
Upper Tenas Falls (u), Tanner Butte (1994 nl)
Upper Wauna Falls (u), Tanner Butte (1994 nl)

Upper West Branch Falls (u), Tanner Butte (1994 nl)
Wahe Falls, Tanner Butte (1994)
Waucoma North Falls (u), Wahtum Lake (1979 nl)
Waucoma South Falls (u), Wahtum Lake (1979 nl)
West Branch Falls (u), Tanner Butte (1994 nl)
Woodward Falls (u), Beacon Rock (1994 nl)

THE NORTHERN COAST RANGE
Baker Creek Falls, Fairdale (1979)
Barth Falls, Green Mtn (1977)
Berry Creek Falls, Falls City (1974)
Boulder Creek Falls (u), Warnicke Creek (1974 nl)
Burton Creek Falls (u), Springer Mtn (1979 nl)
Camp Creek Falls (u), Laurel Mtn (1974 nl)
Carcus Creek Falls (u), Baker Point (1979 nl)
Central Line Creek Falls (u), Warnicke Creek (1974 nl)
Chitwood Falls, Neskowin (1985 ns)
Clatskanie Falls (u), Delena (1985 nl)
Crowley Mine Falls (u), Warnicke Creek (1974 nl)
Cruiser Creek Falls (u), Gobblers Knob (1979 nl)
East Crowley Forks Falls (u), Warnicke Creek (1974 nl)
East Rock Valley Falls (u), Warnicke Creek (1974 nl)
Echo Falls, Devils Lake (1984)
Euchre Falls, Euchre Mtn (1984)
Far Rock Creek Falls (u), Warnicke Creek (1974 nl)
Gilbert Creek Falls (u), Springer Mtn (1979 nl)
Gnat Creek Falls, Nicolai Mtn (1985)
Haines Falls, Turner Creek (1979)
Jackson Falls, Hillsboro (1990)
Kilchis Falls, Cedar Butte (1984)
Lava Creek Falls (u), Baker Point (1979 nl)
Lee Creek Falls (u), Turner Creek (1979 nl)
Little Boulder Creek Falls (u), Warnicke Creek
    (1974 nl)
Little Luckiamute Falls (u), Fanno Ridge (1974 nl)
Lower Rock Creek Falls (u), Midway (1979 nl)
Maple Valley Falls (u), Gobblers Knob (1979 nl)
Martin Falls, Newport North (1984 ns)
Middle Rock Creek Falls (u), Warnicke Creek
    (1974 nl)
Mill Creek Falls (u), Laurel Mtn (1974 nl)
Nenamusa Falls, Springer Mtn (1979 ns)
North Fork Falls, Hamlet (1984 nl)
Rock Creek Falls (u), Midway (1979 nl)
Silver Falls, Laurel Mtn (1974)
Slide Mountain Falls (u), Fairdale (1979 nl)
Upper Lee Creek Falls (u), Turner Creek (1979 nl)
Upper Rock Creek Falls (u), Warnicke Creek (1974 nl)
Valsetz Falls, Valsetz (1974 ns)
Warnicke Creek Falls (u), Warnicke Creek (1974 nl)
Warnicke Valley Falls (u), Warnicke Creek (1974 nl)
West Crowley Forks Falls (u), Warnicke Creek
    (1974 nl)
West Rock Valley Falls (u), Warnicke Creek (1974 nl)
Wheelock Creek Falls (u), Tidewater (1984 nl)
Wilson Falls, Jordan Creek (1984 ns)

THE SOUTHERN COAST RANGE
Beulah Creek Falls (u), Ivers Peak (1990 nl)
Bone Mountain Falls (u), Rasler Creek (1990 nl)

Brewster Canyon Falls (u), Mount Gurney (1990 nl)
Briggs Creek Falls (u), Chrome Ridge (1989 nl)
Brummit Valley Falls (u), Sitkum (1990 nl)
Camas Creek Falls (u), Kenyon Mtn (1990 nl)
Camp Creek Falls (u), Old Blue (1990 nl)
Cascade Falls, Five Rivers (1984 ns)
Cedar Valley Falls (u), Callahan (1990 nl)
Coal Creek Falls (u), Eden Valley (1990 nl)
Coal Valley Falls 1-4 (u), Eden Valley (1990 nl)
Cole Creek Falls (u), Rasler Creek (1990 nl)
Coos Valley Falls (u), Coos Mtn (1990 nl)
Darius Creek Falls (u), Golden Falls (1990 nl)
East Indigo Creek Falls (u), Hobson Horn (1989 nl)
East Millcoma Falls (u), Ivers Peak (1990 nl)
Elk Creek Falls (u), Eden Valley (1990 nl)
Elk Creek Falls (u), Ivers Peak (1990 nl)
Estell Falls, Allegany (1971 ns)
Fall Creek Falls (u), Biscuit Hill (1989 nl)
Fall Creek Falls (u), Cedar Creek (1990 nl)
Fall Creek Falls (u), Rasler Creek (1990 nl)
Fish Hatchery Falls (u), Alsea (1985 nl)
Hamilton Falls (u), Sitkum (1990 nl)
Henrys Falls, Allegany (1971)
Hewett Falls, Golden Falls (1990)
Hubbard Creek Falls (u), Callahan (1990 nl)
Illinois River Falls, Pearsoll Peak (1989)
Little Dixie Creek Falls (u), Barklow Mtn (1986 nl)
Little Illinois River Falls, Cave Junction (1989)
Little Matson Falls (u), Golden Falls (1990 nl)
Lost Creek Falls, Mount Gurney (1990)
Lost Valley Falls (u), Mount Gurney (1990 nl)
Lower Elk Creek Falls (u), Ivers Peak (1990 nl)
Matson Creek Falls (u), Golden Falls (1990 nl)
Middle Creek Falls, McKinley (1971 ns)
Millicoma Falls (u), Ivers Peak (1990 nl)
Mouse Creek Falls (u), Galice (1989 nl)
Myrtle Creek Falls (u), Rasler Creek (1990 nl)
North Fork Elk Falls (u), Eden Valley (1990 nl)
North Silver Creek Falls (u), Hobson Horn (1989 nl)
Pidgeon Falls, Allegany (1971)
Rock Valley Falls (u), Rasler Creek (1990 nl)
Schoolmarm Creek Falls (u), Galice (1989 nl)
Scottsburg Falls (u), Scottsburg (1985)
Secret Creek Falls (u), Onion Mtn (1989 nl)
Silver Falls, York Butte (1989)
Stulls Falls, Elk Peak (1985)
Surprise Creek Falls (u), Loon Lake (1985 nl)
Taylor Creek Falls, Onion Mtn (1989)
The Horn, Mapleton (1984 nl)
Upper Brummit Valley Falls (u), Sitkum (1990 nl)
Upper Elk Creek Falls (u), Eden Valley (1990 nl)
Upper Fall Creek Falls (u), Cedar Creek (1990 nl)
Upper Fall Creek Falls (u), Rasler Creek (1990 nl)
Upper Little Matson Falls (u), Golden Falls (1990 nl)
Upper Matson Falls (u), Golden Falls (1990 nl)
Upper Rock Creek Falls (u), Camas Valley (1990 nl)
Upper Rock Valley Falls (u), Kenyon Mtn (1990 nl)
Upper Rock Valley Falls (u), Rasler Creek (1990 nl)
West Millicoma Falls (u), Ivers Peak (1990 nl)
Wooden Rock Creek Falls (u), Eden Valley (1990 nl)

THE MIDDLE CASCADES

Abiqua Falls, Elk Prairie (1985)
Ayers Falls, Lyons (1985)
Bald Peter Creek Falls (u), Keel Mtn (1984 nl)
Battle Ax Creek Falls (u), Battle Ax (1985 nl)
Bear Valley Falls (u), Upper Soda (1985 nl)
Bonnie Creek Falls (u), Keel Mtn (1984 nl)
Boundary Creek Falls (u), Swamp Mtn (1989 nl)
Camp Creek Falls (u), Keel Mtn (1984 nl)
Cascade Falls, Farmers Butte (1988 nl)
Cascade Falls, Yellowstone Mtn (1985)
Cedar Creek Falls (u), Sweet Home (1984 nl)
Cougar Creek Falls (u), Upper Soda (1985 nl)
Crabtree Creek Falls (u), Yellowstone Mtn (1985 nl)
Crabtree Valley Falls (u), Keel Mtn (1984 nl)
Deadman Creek Falls (u), Keel Mtn (1984 nl)
Drift Creek Falls, Drake Crossing (1985)
East Coe Branch Falls (u), Mount Hood South
   (1980 nl)
Evans Creek Falls (u), Elkhorn (1985 ns)
Fall Creek Falls, Elk Prairie (1985)
Falls Creek Falls (u), Upper Soda (1985 nl)
French Basin Falls 1-4 (u), Battle Ax (1985 nl)
Gatch Falls, Marion Lake (1993 ns)
Hall Creek Falls (u), Mill City South (1980 nl)
Hamilton Creek Falls (u), Lacomb (1984 nl)
Hideaway Falls, High Rock (1985)
Homestead Creek Falls (u), Elk Prairie (1985 nl)
Horseshoe Falls, Lyons (1985)
Husky Creek Falls (u), Upper Soda (1985 nl)
Indian Prairie Falls (u), Snow Peak (1985 nl)
Little Niagara Falls, High Rock (1985 ns)
Lower Falls Creek Falls (u), Upper Soda (1985 nl)
Lower Gooch Falls (u), Marion Forks (1988 nl)
Lower Rock Creek Falls (u), Keel Mtn (1984 nl)
McDowell Creek Falls (u), Sweet Home (1984 nl)
McNabb Falls, Chimney Peak (1984)
Middle Falls Creek Falls (u), Upper Soda (1985 nl)
Middle Moose Mtn Falls (u), Upper Soda (1985 nl)
Middle Rock Creek Falls (u), Keel Mtn (1984 nl)
Moose Creek Falls, Cascadia (1985 ns)
Moose Lake Falls (u), Upper Soda (1985 nl)
Moose Mountain Falls (u), Upper Soda (1985 nl)
Moose Valley Falls (u), Yellowstone Mtn (1985 nl)
Neal Creek Falls (u), Snow Peak (1985 nl)
Panther Creek Falls (u), Yellowstone Mtn (1985 nl)
Pencil Falls, Mount Hood South (1980 nl)
Polallie Creek Falls (u), Mount Hood South (1980 nl)
Puzzle Creek Falls (u), Marion Forks (1988 nl)
Sandy River Falls (u), Government Camp (1980 nl)
Sardine Creek Falls (u), Elkhorn (1985 nl)
Scott Creek Falls (u), Lacomb (1984 nl)
Shot Pouch Creek Falls (u), Green Peter (1984 nl)
Silver King Falls, Elkhorn (1985 ns)
Split Falls, Wolf Peak (1985)
Stein Falls, Wolf Peak (1985)
Stout Creek Falls, Lyons (1985 nl)
Tally Creek Falls (u), Upper Soda (1985 nl)
Trinity Falls, Elk Prairie (1985 ns)
Trout Creek Falls (u), Upper Soda (1985 nl)

Upper Battle Ax Creek Falls (u), Battle Ax (1985 nl)
Upper Compass Creek Falls (u), Mount Hood South (1980 nl)
Upper Downing Creek Falls (u), Marion Forks (1988 nl)
Upper Eagle Creek Falls, Cherryville (1985 ns)
Upper Falls Creek Falls (u), Upper Soda (1985 nl)
Upper Husky Creek Falls (u), Upper Soda (1985 nl)
Upper Moose Creek Falls (u), Upper Soda (1985 nl)
Upper Moose Lake Falls (u), Upper Soda (1985 nl)
Upper Moose Mtn Falls (u), Upper Soda (1985 nl)
Upper Rock Creek Falls (u), Keel Mtn (1984 nl)
Upper Soda Falls, Cascadia (1985)
Upper Tally Creek Falls (u), Upper Soda (1985 nl)
Upper West Fork Falls (u), Keel Mtn (1984 nl)
West Coe Branch Falls (u), Mount Hood South (1980 nl)
West Fork Falls (u), Keel Mtn (1984 nl)
West Fork Falls (u), Snow Peak (1985 nl)
West Fork Valley Falls (u), Yellowstone Mtn (1985 nl)
Whitcomb Creek Falls (u), Keel Mtn (1984 nl)
Wiley Creek Falls (u), Swamp Mtn (1989 nl)
Wiley Valley Falls (u), Swamp Mtn (1989 nl)
Wizard Falls, Candle Creek (1988)

THE SOUTH CASCADES

Button Creek Falls (u), Sugarpine (1989 nl)
Cascade Creek Falls (u), Hamaker Butte (1985 nl)
Chocolate Falls, Mount Ashland (1983)
Coal Valley Falls (u), Staley Ridge (1986 nl)
Dillon Falls, Gold Hill (1983)
Duwee Falls, Union Peak (1985)
Emigrant Creek Falls (u), Siskiyou Pass (1983 nl)
Emile Falls, Mace Mtn (1989)
Erma Bell Lake Falls (u), Waldo Mtn (1986 nl)
Erma Bell Outlet Falls (u), Waldo Mtn (1986 nl)
Fall Creek Falls (u), Sinker Mtn (1986 nl)
Far Upper Falls (u), Hamaker Butte (1985 nl)
Fir Creek Falls (u), Warner Mtn (1986 nl)
Flat Creek Falls (u), Sugarpine (1989 nl)
Gold Basin Falls (u), Sinker Mtn (1986 nl)
Grouse Mountain Falls, Bearbones Mtn (1986)
Honey Creek Falls, Substitute Point (1988)
Indian Holes Falls, South Sister (1988)
Lillian Falls, Waldo Lake (1986 ns)
Linton Falls, Linton Lake (1988)
Logan Creek Falls (u), Sinker Mtn (1986 nl)
Lower South Fork Falls (u), Trout Creek Butte (1988 nl)
Lower Squaw Creek Falls (u), Trout Creek Butte (1988 nl)
Mesa Creek Falls (u), South Sister (1988 nl)
Middle Fork Falls (u), Waldo Mtn (1986 nl)
Middle Red Blanket Falls (u), Union Peak (1985 ns)
Mile 44 Falls (u), Old Fairview (1989 nl)
Mosquito Valley Falls (u), French Mtn (1989 nl)
Needle Falls (u), Huckleberry Mtn (1986 nl)
Obsidian Falls, North Sister (1988)
PK Creek Falls (u), Sinker Mtn (1986 nl)
Park Creek Falls (u), Trout Creek Butte (1988 nl)

Separation Creek Falls (u), South Sister (1988 nl)
Shadow Creek Falls (u), Linton Lake (1988 nl)
Squaw Creek Falls, Trout Creek Butte (1988)
Upper Falls Creek Falls (u), Diamond Peak (1986 ns)
Upper Fir Creek Falls (u), Warner Mtn (1986 nl)
Upper Fork Falls (u), Waldo Mtn (1986 nl)
Upper Mesa Creek Falls (u), South Sister (1988 nl)
Upper Separation Creek Falls (u), South Sister (1988 nl)
Upper South Fork Falls (u), Trout Creek Butte (1988 nl)
Upper Susan Creek Falls (u), Old Fairview (1989 nl)
Verdun Fock Falls 1-3 (u), Mt David Douglas (1986 nl)
Youngs Creek Falls (u), Warner Mtn (1986 nl)
Youth Camp Falls (u), Linton Lake (1988 nl)

THE COLUMBIA PLATEAU

Awbrey Falls, Tumalo (1962)
Big Falls, Cline Falls (1962)
Bogus Creek Falls (u), Lambert Rocks (1972 nl)
Buck Falls, Chapin Creek (1983)
Chapman Hollow Falls (u), Macken Canyon (1970 nl)
Chloride Falls (u), Bourne (1984 nl)
Copper Creek Falls, Bennet Peak (1990)
Deep Creek Falls (u), Fingerboard Saddle (1990 nl)
East Fork Falls, Cornucopia (1990)
Fall Creek Falls (u), Dog Lake (1980 nl)
Fall Creek Falls (u), Mount Vernon (1983 nl)
Far Tumalo Falls (u), Tumalo Falls (1988 nl)
Glutton Falls, Hardman (1969)
Groundhog Falls, Whitehorse Butte (1980)
Horseshoe Falls, Harmony (1971)
Imnaha Falls, Deadman Point (1990)
John Henry Falls (u), North Minam Meadows (1990 nl)
Kettle Creek Falls, Krag Peak (1990 nl)
Klamath Falls, Klamath Falls (1985)
Little Willow Creek Falls (u), Ladycomb Peak (1981 nl)
Lookingglass Falls, Rondowa (1983)
Loveless Creek Falls (u), Crooked Creek Valley (1964 nl)
Lower Falls, Committee Creek (1983)
Lower Falls Little Minam River, Mount Fanny (1993 ns)
Lower Paulina Creek Falls (u), Paulina Peak (1981 nl)
Meadow Brooks Falls, Dale (1990)
Middle Sycan River Falls (u), Spodue Mtn (1988 nl)
Minam Falls, Jim White Ridge (1993 ns)
Murray Creek Falls (u), Chief Joseph Mtn (1990 nl)
North Fork Falls (u), Bourne (1984 nl)
North Fork Wolf Falls (u), Tucker Flat (1984 nl)
Odin Falls, Cline Falls (1962)
Pine Hollow Falls (u), Macken Canyon (1970 nl)
Pine Lakes Falls (u), Cornucopia (1990 nl)
Rock Creek Falls (u), Bourne (1984 nl)
Silver Creek Falls (u), Chief Joseph Mtn (1990 nl)
Squaw Falls, Elbow Creek (1983)
Steelhead Falls, Steelhead Falls (1985)
Sycan River, Falls of 1-6 (u), Spodue Mtn (1988 nl)
The Water Fall, Hoppin Springs (1982 nl)
Thompson Falls, Thompson Flat (1983)

Tumwater Falls, Quinton (1971 ns)
Upper Falls, Keys Creek (1985)
Upper Falls Deschutes River, Benham Falls (1981 ns)
Upper Rock Creek Falls (u), Bourne (1984 nl)
Upper Sycan River Falls (u), Spodue Mtn (1988 nl)
Waterfalls Hollow Falls (u), Wolf Hollow Falls
　(1970 nl)
West Fork Falls (u), Cornucopia (1990 nl)
Wolf Hollow Falls, Wolf Hollow Falls (1970)

THE IDAHO PANHANDLE

Caribou Falls, Caribou Creek (1969)
Chute Creek Falls (u), Gleason Mtn (1986 nl)
Cooper Gulch Falls (u), Thompson Pass (1988 nl)
Fern Falls, Pond Peak (1966 ns)
Hellroaring Creek Falls (u), Colburn (1968 nl)
Johnson Creek Falls (u), Clark Fork (1989 nl)
Kalispell Falls, Gleason Mtn (1986)
LaSota Falls, Helmer Mtn (1986)
Lower Bull Run Creek Falls (u), Elk Creek Falls
　(1969 ns)
McAbee Falls, Prater Mtn (1967)
Rambiker Falls, Illinois Peak (1988)
Shadow Falls, Pond Peak (1966 ns)
Snow Creek Falls, Moravia (1965 nl)
Wellington Creek Falls (u), Trestle Peak (1989 ns)

WILDERNESS AREAS OF CENTRAL IDAHO

Bear Creek Falls, Rocky Comfort Flat (1986)
Benton Creek Falls (u), Sturgill Creek (1987 nl)
Bimerick Falls, McLendon Butte (1966 nl)
Boulder Falls (u), Galena Peak (1970 nl)
Bridal Veil Falls, Stanley Lake (1972)
Dead Elk Creek Falls (u), Jeanette Mtn (1966 nl)
Devlin Falls, Leesburg (1989)
East Pass Creek Falls (u), Meridian Peak (1967 nl)
Falls Creek Falls (u), House Mtn (1973 nl)
Forge Creek Falls (u), Yellowjacket (1963 nl)
Gold Fork Falls (u), Sloans Point (1988 nl)
Hazard Falls, Indian Mtn (1963)
Hoodoo Creek Falls (u), Big Cedar (1966 nl)
Lower Little Salmon Falls (u), Bally Mtn (1983 ns)
Lower Rush Falls (u), Rush Peak (1986 nl)
Mallard Creek Falls, Whitewater Ranch (1987)
Patsy Ann Falls, Tin Cup Lake (1991)
Rush Falls, Rush Peak (1986)
Scenic Creek Falls (u), Nahneke Mtn (1972 nl)
Sixmile Creek Falls (u), Boiling Springs (1988 nl)
Slippy Creek Falls (u), McKinzie Creek (1963 nl)
Trail Creek Falls, Rock Roll Canyon (1967 nl)
Upper Goat Creek Falls (u), Warbonnet Peak
　(1972 nl)

Upper Sixmile Creek Falls (u), Sixmile Point
　(1988 nl)
Wild Horse Creek Falls (u), McLendon Butte
　(1966 ns)
Wildhorse Falls, Cuddy Mtn (1987)

THE SNAKE RIVER PLAIN

Albright Falls, Trischman Knob (1986 ns)
Austin Butte Falls (u), Austin Butte (1980 nl)
Banbury Springs, Falls of (u), Thousand Springs
　(1992 nl)
Big Drops, Shoshone (1992)
Boundary Creek Falls (u), Buffalo Lake (1986 nl)
Boundary Valley Falls (u), Buffalo Lake (1986 nl)
Camel Falls, Wagon Box Basin (1973)
Clover Creek Falls (u), King Hill (1986 nl)
Colonnade Falls, Cave Falls (1989)
Crane Falls (historical), Bruneau (1992 ns)
Dunanda Falls, Bechler Falls (1989)
Falls River Falls (u), Cave Falls (1989 nl)
Gwinna Falls, Trischman Knob (1986)
Houtz Creek Falls (u), Stump Peak (1980 nl)
Iris Falls, Cave Falls (1989)
Little Drops, Shoshone (1992)
Lower Boundary Creek Falls (u), Bechler Falls
　(1989 nl)
Lower Cave Falls (u), Cave Falls (1989 nl)
Mountain Ash Falls (u), Cave Falls (1989 nl)
Ouzel Falls, Cave Falls (1989)
Phantom Falls, Mahogany Butte (1977 nl)
Portneuf, Falls along the 1-4 (u), Haystack Mtn
　(1968 nl)
Quiver Cascade, Trischman Knob (1986)
Ragged Falls, Trischman Knob (1986)
Rainbow Falls, Cave Falls (1989)
Rainbow Falls, Palisades Peak (1966 ns)
Robinson Creek Falls, Bechler Falls (1989 nl)
Ross Falls, Pike Mtn (1978 ns)
Silver Scarf Falls, Bechler Falls (1989)
Sinking Canyon Falls (u), Balanced Rock
　(1992 nl)
Sluiceway Falls, Trischman Knob (1986)
Swan Falls, Sinker Butte (1992 ns)
Tendoy Falls, Trischman Knob (1986)
Terraced Falls, Grassy Lake Reservoir (1989)
The Falls, Auburn (1980)
The Falls, Sugarloaf (1972)
Union Falls, Grassy Lake Reservoir (1989)
Upper Mountain Ash Falls (u), Cave Falls
　(1989 nl)
Wahhi Falls, Trischman Knob (1986)
Winter Camp Falls (u), Austin Butte (1980 nl)

INDEX

Page numbers in italics indicate photographs.

Author Greg Plumb is a geographer who spent more than ten years driving and hiking many spray-soaked miles to document this collection of waterfalls. Now a Tennessee resident, he continues to vacation in the Northwest to update his data base and seek undiscovered waterfalls. He is also the author of *Waterfalls of Tennessee*.

THE MOUNTAINEERS, founded in 1906, is a nonprofit outdoor activity and conservation club, whose mission is "to explore, study, preserve, and enjoy the natural beauty of the outdoors. . . . " Based in Seattle, Washington, the club is now the third-largest such organization in the United States, with 15,000 members and five branches throughout Washington State.

The Mountaineers sponsors both classes and year-round outdoor activities in the Pacific Northwest, which include hiking, mountain climbing, ski-touring, snowshoeing, bicycling, camping, kayaking and canoeing, nature study, sailing, and adventure travel. The club's conservation division supports environmental causes through educational activities, sponsoring legislation, and presenting informational programs. All club activities are led by skilled, experienced volunteers, who are dedicated to promoting safe and responsible enjoyment and preservation of the outdoors.

If you would like to participate in these organized outdoor activities or the club's programs, consider a membership in The Mountaineers. For information and an application, write or call The Mountaineers, Club Headquarters, 300 Third Avenue West, Seattle, Washington 98119; (206) 284-6310.

The Mountaineers Books, an active, nonprofit publishing program of the club, produces guidebooks, instructional texts, historical works, natural history guides, and works on environmental conservation. All books produced by The Mountaineers are aimed at fulfilling the club's mission.

Send or call for our catalog of more than 300 outdoor titles:

The Mountaineers Books
1001 SW Klickitat Way, Suite 201
Seattle, WA 98134
1-800-553-4453
e-mail: mbooks@mountaineers.org
website: www.mountaineers.org

Other titles you may enjoy from The Mountaineers:

100 CLASSIC HIKES IN™ WASHINGTON: North Cascades, Olympics, Mount Rainier & South Cascades, Alpine Lakes, Glacier Peak, *Ira Spring & Harvey Manning*
A full-color guide to Washington's finest trails, written with a conservation ethic and a deep knowledge of the area by the authors of more than thirty hiking guides to the Pacific Northwest. Star attractions include spectacular views, flower-filled alpine meadows, lakes and streams, ancient forests, animals and birds, and solitude.

WASHINGTON'S MOUNT RAINIER NATIONAL PARK: A Centennial Celebration, *Pat O'Hara & Tim McNulty*
The official Rainier Centennial book. A percentage of sales will be donated to the Mount Rainier, North Cascades & Olympic Fund. A large-format photographic celebration of the 100th anniversary of Mount Rainier National Park, featuring brilliant color photos by one of the Northwest's preeminent photographers.

HIKING THE GREAT NORTHWEST: The 55 Greatest Trails in Washington, Oregon, Idaho, Montana, Wyoming, Northern California, British Columbia, and the Canadian Rockies, Second Ed., *Ira Spring, Harvey Manning & Vicky Spring*
A completely updated guide to *the* classic trails of the Pacific Northwest, highlighting the most spectacular hikes in six states and two provinces with all-new color photos.

100 HIKES IN™ WASHINGTON'S SOUTH CASCADES AND OLYMPICS: Chinook Pass, White Pass, Goat Rocks, Mount St. Helens, Mount Adams, Third Ed., *Ira Spring & Harvey Manning*
The best-selling hiking guide to the region, featuring a new series design and new color photos, and completely revised by the Northwest's most respected hiking gurus. With 100 daytrips and overnighters for every skill level, from the high altitude of the South Cascades to the stunning peaks and valleys of the Olympics, to the shores of the Pacific coast.

ADVENTURES IN IDAHO'S SAWTOOTH COUNTRY: 63 Trips for Hikers & Mountain Bikers, *Lynne Stone*
The complete book of where-to's and how-to's for trails near the Sun Valley, Ketchum, Hailey, and Stanley areas.